The Way Hollywood Tells It

The publisher gratefully acknowledges the generous contribution to this book provided by the Humanities Endowment Fund of the University of California Press Foundation.

The Way Hollywood Tells It

Story and Style in Modern Movies

DAVID BORDWELL

University of California Press

BERKELEY   LOS ANGELES   LONDON

University of California Press, one of the most distinguished university presses in the United States, enriches lives around the world by advancing scholarship in the humanities, social sciences, and natural sciences. Its activities are supported by the UC Press Foundation and by philanthropic contributions from individuals and institutions. For more information, visit www.ucpress.edu.

University of California Press
Berkeley and Los Angeles, California

University of California Press, Ltd.
London, England

A previous version of "A Stylish Style," entitled "Intensified Continuity: Visual Style in Contemporary American Film," appeared in *Film Quarterly* 55, no. 3 (2002).

Library of Congress Cataloging-in-Publication Data

Bordwell, David.
   The way Hollywood tells it : story and style in modern movies / David Bordwell.
       p.   cm.
   Includes bibliographical references and index.
   ISBN 13 978-0-520-24622-5 (pbk. : alk. paper)
   ISBN 10 0-520-24622-5 (pbk. : alk. paper)
   1. Motion pictures—United States—History.   2. Motion picture industry—United States—History.   3. Motion pictures—Aesthetics.   I. Title.
PN1993.5.U6B656   2006
791.430973—dc22   2005025774

Manufactured in the United States of America

15   14   13   12   11   10   09   08   07
10   9   8   7   6   5   4

The paper used in this publication meets the minimum requirements of ANSI/NISO Z39.48–1992 (R1997) (*Permanence of Paper*).

For Kristin
The road goes ever on.

Contents

Acknowledgments

The two archival linchpins of my research, the Wisconsin Center for Film and Theater Research and the Cinémathèque Royale de Belgique, were as usual magnificently cooperative over the ten years during which I gathered material for this book. So thanks to Maxine Fleckner Ducey of Madison, to Gabrielle Claes of Brussels, and to their staffs. I'd also like to thank Ted Turner and Warren Lieberfarb, two far-sighted moguls who have increased our access to the majestic range of American cinema.

Many colleagues encouraged this project, written during my last semester before retiring from the Film Studies area of our department. Joe Beres, Ben Brewster, Kelley Conway, Kevin French, Erik Gunneson, Debbie Hanson, Michele Hilmes, Lea Jacobs, the late Nietzchka Keene, Vance Kepley, Paddy Rourke, Ben Singer, and Andrew Yonda aided me in many ways. J. J. Murphy, who was writing a book on contemporary American film at the same time that I was, proved a constant source of hard questions and fruitful suggestions. Tino Balio let me draw on his vast expertise in the American film industry. He further displayed his wisdom by deciding to retire along with me.

I've also benefited from watching American movies with Noël Carroll. Our long comradeship has been a high point of my life. Paul Arthur, Doug Gomery, Jason Mittell, and Jeff Smith offered detailed and very useful criticisms of various versions of these essays. Consultant and filmmaker Tim Onosko, film editor Danny Goldberg, and screenwriter Larry Gross shared information and ideas. In Los Angeles, Cameron Crowe, Andy Fischer, and Susan Antani kindly helped in several ways. Roger Ebert and Nate Kohn expanded my access to contemporary work through their annual Overlooked and Forgotten Film Festival. Special thanks go to John Caldwell of UCLA,

Murray Smith of the University of Canterbury, and to my editor, Mary Francis; their astute criticisms have strengthened the book.

The second essay, "A Stylish Style," is based on an article originally published in *Film Quarterly*. Thanks to the editor, Ann Martin, and to the University of California Press for permission to reprint.

My students have helped too. Jake Black provided expert assistance in preparing my frame enlargements. Brad Schauer left me shrewd comments on an early draft, while helping me check facts and compile the chronology in the appendix. Jinhee Choi, Ethan de Seife, Jonathan Frome, Jane Greene, Patrick Keating, Michael Newman, and Paul Ramaeker offered several productive leads. For sharing some thoughts on puzzle films, I must thank Vincent Bohlinger, Jessica Love, Mark Minnett, and especially Barbara Klinger, who kindly gave me access to portions of her book *Beyond the Multiplex: Cinema, New Technologies, and the Home*. My last (official) seminar in the Department of Communication Arts at the University of Wisconsin at Madison was just the way you want to go out. My gratitude, then, to Masha Belodubrovskaya, Jen Chung, Eric Crosby, Stew Fyfe, Derek Johnson, Jonathan Lang, Maureen Larkin, Pearl Latteier, Charlie Michael, Jakob Nilssen, Eija Niskannen, Dave Resha, Brad Schauer, Becca Swender, and Tom Yoshikami for responding so vigorously to ideas that I floated in class, some of which drifted into these pages. Our final session, party and all, remains with me always.

The University of Wisconsin at Madison has generously supported my research for over three decades, and I thank all those faculty members who sat on committees appraising my work. Mary Anne Fitzpatrick, department colleague and dean, has been of inestimable aid as well. I particularly want to thank my former dean, Phillip Certain, who has had faith in my projects and our film program. He too has just retired (must be something in the water), but he remains a model of the thoughtful, solicitous administrator.

Then there's Kristin Thompson, for thirty years my loving companion at the movies and elsewhere. The book is dedicated to her.

Beyond the Blockbuster

Q: Do you write with specific actors in mind?
A: Always . . . but they're usually dead.

CHARLES SHYER
(Private Benjamin, Irreconcilable Differences)

This book is about the art and craft of Hollywood cinema since 1960. In two essays I trace some major ways that filmmakers have used moving images to tell stories. The narrative techniques I'll be examining are astonishingly robust. They have engaged millions of viewers for over eighty years, and they have formed a lingua franca for worldwide filmmaking.

Naturally, during the years I'm considering, American films have changed enormously. They have become sexier, more profane, and more violent; fart jokes and kung fu are everywhere. The industry has metamorphosed into a corporate behemoth, while new technologies have transformed production and exhibition. And, to come to my central concern, over the same decades some novel strategies of plot and style have risen to prominence. Behind these strategies, however, stand principles that are firmly rooted in the history of studio moviemaking. In the two essays that follow I consider how artistic change and continuity coexist in modern American film.

To track the dynamic of continuity and change since 1960, it's conventional to start by looking at the film industry. As usually recounted, the industry's fortunes over the period display a darkness-to-dawn arc that might satisfy a scriptwriter of epic inclinations. We now have several nuanced versions of this story, so I'll merely point out some major turning points.[1] The appendix provides a year-by-year chronology.

Although court decisions of 1948–1949 forced the major companies to divest themselves of their theater chains, during the 1950s Warner Bros., Disney, Paramount, Columbia, 20th Century Fox, United Artists, MGM, and Universal controlled distribution, the most lucrative area of the industry. While the studios were producing a few big-budget films themselves, they also relied on the "package-unit" system of production.[2] In some cases, in-house producers oversaw a unit that turned out a stream of releases. Alternatively, a producer, star, or agent bought a script, assembled a package of talent, and approached a studio for financing and distribution. At the start of the 1960s, the studios were providing lucrative prime-time television programming, but theatrical moviemaking was not a great business to be in. Attendance was falling sharply. Road show pictures like *The Sound of Music* (1965), playing a single screen for months on end, were for a while bright spots on the ledger, but the cycle of epic road show productions, already overstretched with the failure of *Cleopatra* (1963) and *Mutiny on the Bounty* (1965), crashed at the end of the decade. Soon studios faced huge losses and were taken over by conglomerates bearing mysterious names like Gulf + Western (which bought Paramount in 1966) and Transamerica Corp. (which bought United Artists the following year). Feature filmmaking continued to hemorrhage money—by some estimates, as much as half a billion dollars between 1969 and 1972.

Yet by 1980 the industry was earning stupendous profits. What changed? For one thing, a tax scheme sponsored by the Nixon administration allowed the producers to write off hundreds of millions of dollars in past and future investments. The studios also found ways to integrate their business more firmly with broadcast television, cable, the record industry, and home video.[3] Just as important, a new generation of filmmakers emerged. Some, modeling their work on the more personal European cinema they admired, produced Americanized art films like *Five Easy Pieces* (1970) and *Mean Streets* (1973). The young directors who found the biggest success, however, were willing to work in established genres for a broad audience. They were responsible for a burst of record-breaking hits: *The French Connection* (1971), *The Godfather* (1972), *The Exorcist* (1973), *American Graffiti* (1973), *Jaws* (1975), *Saturday Night Fever* (1977), *Star Wars* (1977), and *Close Encounters of the Third Kind* (1977). There were less innovative top-grossers as well, such as *Fiddler on the Roof* (1971) and *The Sting* (1973). In all, the 1970s lifted the ceiling on what a film could earn, and it remains the decade with the most top-grossers in adjusted dollars. On its U.S. release, *Jaws* reaped about $260 million—the equivalent of $940 million today. *Star Wars* took in over $307 million on its initial domestic release (a staggering $990 million in 2005 dollars), and after rereleases it became by far the top-earning film of the modern era.[4]

No films had ever made so much money so quickly. The studios' decision makers realized that the market for a movie was much bigger than anyone had suspected, and they settled on a business strategy to exploit the "megapicture," or blockbuster. This was a must-see movie very different from the road show attraction. Budgeted at the highest level, launched in the summer or the Christmas season, playing off a best-selling book or a pop-culture fad like disco, advertised endlessly on television, and then opening in hundreds (eventually thousands) of theaters on the same weekend, the blockbuster was calculated to sell tickets fast. By the early 1980s, merchandising was added to the mix, so tie-ins with fast-food chains, automobile companies, and lines of toys and apparel could keep selling the movie. Scripts that lent themselves to mass marketing had a better chance of being acquired, and screenwriters were encouraged to incorporate special effects. Unlike studio-era productions, the megapicture could lead a robust afterlife on a soundtrack album, on cable channels, and on videocassette. By the mid-1980s, once overseas income and ancillaries were reckoned in, few films lost money.

The new release system demanded an upgrade in exhibition as well. In the 1970s those downtown theaters or road show houses that weren't demolished had been chopped up into lopsided, sticky-floored auditoriums. But the blockbuster showed to best advantage in venues with comfortable seating, a big screen, and surround-sound systems, so in the 1980s exhibitors began building well-appointed multiplex theaters. The multiplex provided economies of scale (fewer projectionists and concession workers per screen), and it proved ideal for megapictures, which opened on several screens each weekend.[5]

The blockbuster reshaped the industry, but very few projects were conceived on that scale. In any given year, the major companies and independent distributors released between two and five hundred films. Most were genre pictures—dramas, comedies, action movies, children's fare, and other mid-range items. Cable and video had an omnivorous appetite, so independent production flourished, from the down-market Troma and its gross-out horror, to the high-end Orion, purveyor of Woody Allen dramas. A radically low-budget independent sector created its own hits, like *Stranger Than Paradise* (1984) and *She's Gotta Have It* (1986). The success of this sector in nurturing young talent and attracting upscale consumers led studios to buy the libraries of indie companies. The majors also launched specialty divisions, notably Miramax and New Line, which acquired films for niche distribution and could produce their own projects at lesser budget levels.

The industry's success nourished a new kind of acquisition mentality. Now entrepreneurs in other leisure industries saw movies as generating "content" that could be run through publishing, television, theme parks, and other platforms. The Walt Disney company had pioneered this approach, but other firms took it up, starting with Rupert Murdoch's purchase of 20th

Century Fox in 1985. By 2003, with General Electric/NBC's acquisition of Universal Pictures, no major distributor stood outside an entertainment combine. Initially, the drive was to maximize synergy. Batman could undergo a hard-edged makeover in his comic book and then become the hero of a new movie, which yielded soundtrack albums, sequels, and an animated TV series—all because Time Warner owned DC Comics, a movie distribution firm, and a music company. Synergy did not always work so smoothly, but it was clear by the mid-1980s that "intellectual property" was endlessly lucrative, and conglomerates were in the best position to nurture and market it around the world.

Consumers responded. Despite home video and other entertainment rivals, attendance at U.S. movie theaters soared to 1.5 billion viewers a year. The overseas market grew too, partly thanks to the multiplex habit. On average, U.S. films drew half their theatrical income from overseas, while worldwide home video surpassed theatrical income. The 1990s saw a boost in income for the industry generally, but the decisive development was the arrival of the DVD in 1997. Designed to be sold as well as rented, the DVD format soon pushed the videocassette into oblivion. In 2004 the studios' theatrical releases grossed $9.5 billion in North America, but DVD sales and rentals yielded over $21 billion.[6] Now DVDs were keeping virtually every movie's budget afloat. The downside was that digital reproduction made massive piracy easy. In China bootleg DVDs sold for less than a dollar. The appetite aroused by Hollywood for event pictures, the sense that you're not in touch with contemporary culture unless you've seen this weekend's hit, came back to haunt the studios when anyone with high-speed Internet access could download movies that had not yet opened. The next task for the industry would be finding a way to distribute films in digital form—to theaters, to homes via the Internet, and eventually to personal digital devices like cellular phones.

A tale of last-minute rescues—the industry saved by the blockbuster, then by home video and the multiplex, then by DVD—is always captivating, but American cinema is more than a business. Since the late 1910s, Hollywood cinema has constituted the world's primary tradition of visual storytelling, and despite the four decades of industrial upheaval just chronicled, this tradition has remained true to its fundamental premises. In an earlier book, *The Classical Hollywood Cinema* (1985), two colleagues and I sought to analyze the narrative principles governing studio-era filmmaking, from 1917 to 1960. We picked the endpoint as a matter of convenience, since we believed that the classical system was still flourishing. This book is an effort to back up that belief.

Since we made our initial foray into this terrain, the boundary lines have shifted. Some scholars have suggested that however valid our account might be for the studio era, dramatic changes have taken place since 1960, and especially since the late 1970s. There is, they claim, a "postclassical" cinema—taken either as U.S. studio filmmaking as a whole or as the dominant trend within it.[7] We can trace this line of argument through several stages, all connected in one way or another to the rise of the blockbuster.

Megapictures may have saved the major companies, but they also shrank the auteur aspirations of the early 1970s. Did Hollywood storytelling change in response to the blockbuster phenomenon, and if so, in what ways? From *American Graffiti* (1973) to *Jaws* (1975) to *Star Wars* (1977), film historian Thomas Schatz suggests, films became "increasingly plot-driven, increasingly visceral, kinetic, and fast-paced, increasingly reliant on special effects, increasingly 'fantastic' (and thus apolitical), and increasingly targeted at younger audiences."[8] Several commentators suggest that storytelling was undercut by spectacle. One scholar, denouncing the "violent spectacle" of the big-budget movie, speaks of "the collapse of narrative."[9] Others claim that stylistic unity evaporated. Contemporary Hollywood films, according to one writer, "cannot be seen as unified as was possible under the old oligopoly. Stylistic norms have changed, and perhaps no longer exist as a consistent group of norms."[10]

What made narrative cinema crumble? The causes commonly cited are industrial. Since the 1970s, companies have split and recombined, the marketplace has splintered into dozens of demographics, and merchandising has spun off ancillary products. "Equally fragmented, perhaps," writes Schatz, "are the movies themselves, especially the high-cost, high-tech, high-stakes blockbusters, those multi-purpose entertainment machines that breed music videos and soundtrack albums, TV series and videocassettes, video games and theme park rides, novelizations and comic books."[11] Contemporary cinema, claims another historian, directs its energies "more to the pursuit of synergy than to that of narrative coherence."[12] An indie producer-writer has argued that action pictures like *Volcano* (1997) and *Independence Day* (1996) don't need classical narrative construction because their narratives will be "fragmented" into CD soundtracks and T-shirt logos. "The supposed 'identity' of the filmic text comes increasingly under the dissolving pressures of its various revenue streams."[13]

Comparable arguments have been made about the "high-concept" film, typified by *Saturday Night Fever* (1976), *American Gigolo* (1980), and *Flashdance* (1983). Justin Wyatt has proposed that such films' musical interludes and stereotyped characters rendered plot and psychology secondary. Stars did not so much perform as strike magazine-ad poses, and TV-commercial imagery made style itself a major appeal; this favored the marketing of spin-off fashions, soundtracks, and videos. Wyatt argues that high concept grew out of the blockbuster syndrome and became a central development of post-classical cinema.[14]

Eventually these lines of argument encountered objections. Murray Smith proposed that claims of plot fragmentation and stylistic collapse were overstated; even blockbusters showed "careful narrative patterning."[15] Smith and Peter Krämer suggested that conceptions of "postclassical" cinema rested on intuitive comparisons rather than on thorough and systematic analyses of films.[16] When a scholar examined *Raiders of the Lost Ark* (1980), he found the film's plot and narration to be quite strongly unified.[17] Similarly, Geoff King argued that the spectacle-narrative split was not apt even for the theme-park movie: "The demands of the blockbuster may have led to an emphasis on certain genres and on more episodic forms of narrative, but this is not the same as narrative being displaced."[18]

Most comprehensively, Kristin Thompson examined several dozen post-1960s films and analyzed ten in detail in her book *Storytelling in the New Hollywood* (1999). Her studies show that even blockbusters like *Jaws* and *Terminator 2* (1990) display highly coherent storytelling. Other films she analyzes, such as *Hannah and Her Sisters* and *Desperately Seeking Susan* (both 1985), are more character centered, but these "independent" productions also remain committed to classical premises. Thompson also offered general arguments against the power of merchandising to shape storytelling. To suggest that a film's plot "fragments" into a shrapnel burst of tie-ins, she points out, is to indulge in misleading rhetoric. The film itself isn't fragmented by its publicity: "One model of car can be marketed to college kids and to young professionals using different ads, but the individual vehicles do not cease to run as a result."[19] The fact that a film will be hyped on many platforms mandates nothing about its form and style.

As for the role of high concept, it now seems clear that the term can mean at least three things. The high-concept movie, it's usually said, is one that can be encapsulated in a single sentence, usually called a *logline*.[20] Nowadays every film needs to be summed up in an enticing way on the first page of a script or during a pitch session. But any film from any period of Hollywood history can be reduced to one intriguing sentence, as TV listings in newspapers show. Although the logline is important as a production practice, by itself it doesn't seem to distinguish "high-concept" projects from others. A more specific sense of the term denotes a movie sold on the strength of an unusual plot idea that will work without stars. "High concept is story as star," notes one screenplay manual.[21] *The Exorcist, Jaws,* and *Star Wars* lured in audiences with bold premises, not stellar casts. Yet stars have embraced high-concept projects, from *Tootsie* (1982) to *What Women Want* (2000). A 2002 *Variety* report on recent concept-driven properties suggested that those without stars had trouble getting attention or getting released.[22] Wyatt's most vivid specimens of high concept illustrate a third sense of the term, one associated with a particular 1980s production cycle. *American Gigolo* and *Flashdance* do display bold music and slick visuals, but they were rarities in a field dominated by films as stylistically unprepossessing as *9 to 5* (1980), *Stir Crazy* (1980), *Any Which Way You Can* (1980), *Terms of Endearment* (1983), and *WarGames* (1983)—all of which did much better at the box office.[23] Wyatt's research skillfully captures a distinct trend in early 1980s cinema, but the films' fashion-layout gloss remains a fairly isolated phenomenon.

Given the evidence that even blockbusters can be quite narratively coherent and that the high-concept style covers only a fraction of Hollywood's output, the postclassical position has become less plausible.[24] Today, the argument revolves largely around one aspect of modern movies: their frequent allusions to other movies. Noël Carroll was one of the first scholars to write about this tendency, and his approach to the problem in an essay from 1982 is instructively concrete. After mapping out varieties of allusionism, he ascribes the impulse to a new generation of filmmakers who, brought up on TV and trained in film schools, addressed each other and a newly hip audience by citing classic films. A film could gain emotional or thematic resonance by making references to *Psycho* (1960) or *The Searchers* (1956). Seeking to add expressive dimensions to their work, filmmakers turned from "organic expression" to "an iconographic code" based on their devotion to auteurs.[25]

Since his essay, allusionism has proliferated in movies, and what Carroll took as a single trend other scholars have held to be a core feature of postclassical Hollywood. One version of this view has been broached by film critics Thomas Elsaesser and Warren Buckland. Acknowledging the arguments of Smith, Thompson, and others, they argue that postclassical cinema is at once classical and "classical-plus." It displays traditional patterns of narrative and style, but it adds a playful knowingness. The film asks viewers to appreciate its masterful use of traditional "codes." At the same time, the postclassical film's playfulness is "excessive" in that it anticipates with startling literalness how it may be read by academics. The latter conditions occur in "all those moments . . . when our own theory or methodology suddenly turns up in the film itself, looking us in the face; either gravely nodding assent, or winking." *Back to the Future* (1985) has fun with an obvious Oedipal scenario, and the web of references to racial bonding in *Die Hard* (1988) "has ensured that the interpretive community of 'race-class-gender' studies can have a field day. . . . *Die Hard* looks as if its makers had read all the relevant cultural studies literature, so as to provide 'something for everybody.'"[26]

Surely some recent films are self-conscious, but playful knowingness isn't new to Hollywood cinema. The Marx Brothers films, Bugs Bunny cartoons, *Hellzapoppin'* (1941), and the Bob Hope/Bing Crosby road pictures are shot through with references to other movies (and to themselves *as* movies). What seems new are the extensions of allusionism to noncomic genres and the tactic of addressing some allusions to only part of the audience. Carroll calls the latter a two-tiered system of communication—a straight story for everybody and allusions for the movie buffs—and suggests that these tactics can be explained by the efforts of New Hollywood directors to establish a "common cultural heritage" to replace the Bible and European canons of art.[27] My first essay pursues a complementary line of explanation by appeal to the "belatedness" confronting directors starting their careers after the decline of the studio system.

As for the postclassical film's also "knowing" about academic trends, this is a rather curious claim, and Elsaesser and Buckland don't really account for how such a state of affairs might occur. Surely some filmmakers have read film theory, but most practicing screenwriters and directors couldn't care less about postmodern subjectivity, the crisis of masculinity, or other seminar gambits. In raising this possibility, moreover, the two writers shift from claims about *how films tell their stories* to claims about *what the stories might mean.* Once we move to the realm of interpretation, there are few—some would say no—constraints on what counts as a plausible reading.

A functional analysis of *Die Hard*'s plot can point out that the broken-glass motif is part of a concrete causal logic, fulfilling the demand to make things as hard on your hero as possible. Get McClane to take his shoes off as a way of resting up after a long plane flight. To keep those shoes off, force him to flee the room. Make it impossible for him to find another pair of shoes that fits. Then during a firefight, surround him with a field of glass shards so that his bare feet make him more vulnerable. You can also expand the glass motif to include the skyscraper (a glass tower) and the windshield-shattering fall of a gunman. Such linkages are part of the economy of the classical tradition, in which a setting is milked for as many well-motivated purposes as the production team can imagine. All this is straightforward. But when Elsaesser and Buckland go on to interpret the glass motif as symbolizing the "surface texture" of the film itself, they make a claim of a more debatable order. Similar is the claim that "a piece of advice McClane receives on the plane: 'Curl your toes into a fist.' . . . functions figuratively in a wider context, that of the central contradiction of the film between male and female. . . . 'Fist,' it is easy to see, suggests masculinity and violence, but what about 'toes'? 'Curl your toes' alludes to bound feet, with distinct female connotations." This is pretty tenuous as is, but it becomes implausible when we recall that the line in the film is actually "Make fists with your toes," which smacks more of kung fu than of foot binding.[28]

Even if such interpretive claims are persuasive, they won't on their own distinguish a "postclassical" film from a studio-era one. *Kings Row* (1942) features two heroes without dads and several women with punitive fathers, one of whom amputates the legs of a man who gets too close to his daughter. Not least, the protagonist goes to Vienna to study psychiatry. Doesn't this morbid tale's "excess" anticipate academic interpretation? There is even a moment when the secondary hero, hearing his girlfriend protest that she's from the wrong side of the tracks, replies: "If you're gonna start that bunk about class again!" *Kings Row*'s blatant knowingness makes *Die Hard* seem fairly reticent. More broadly, the sorts of punning and "sliding signifiers" highlighted by Elsaesser and Buckland have been found by other critics in *The Most Dangerous Game* (1932), films noirs, and the Andy Hardy series.[29] I've argued elsewhere that interpretation is a process of elaborating semantic fields according to rules of thumb developed within a critical institution.[30] The academic institution's current heuristics encourage highly novel, if strained, interpretations. To create fresh readings, critics are encouraged to forge slender chains of associations, including those that would make any work of fiction, drama, or cinema seem to anticipate its own interpretation. For a hundred years, readers of *Hamlet* have marveled that Shakespeare laid bare the Oedipus complex as cogently as if he had studied with Freud.

The debate about postclassical Hollywood raises the question of how to gauge change over history. On the whole, I think, critics have exaggerated the novelty of current developments. This isn't surprising, since our perceptual and cognitive systems are geared to take a great deal for granted and to monitor the world for change. We are sensitive to the slightest break in our habits. More prosaically, many humanities professors are by temperament keen to spot the next big thing. But if we want to capture the nuances of historical continuity, we don't want every wrinkle to be a sea change. Did the "classical cinema" end with the playfully knowing *Singin' in the Rain* (1952), or with the playfully knowing *Citizen Kane* (1941), or with the playfully knowing *Sherlock, Jr.* (1924)? In *Boy Meets Girl* (1938), a pair of screenwriters comments on the action unfolding before them by hollering out plot points ("Boy Loses Girl!"). In *Page Miss Glory* (1935), a wisecracking flapper hears men critically appraising Garbo, Dietrich, and Harlow and remarks, "You'd have a tough time getting a date with Minnie Mouse." The studio tradition has room for citation, reflexivity, pastiche, parody, and all those tactics that have been considered recent inventions. We can't wholly trust our sense of what's brand-new; our intuitions have to be tested against a wide array of evidence.

How wide? Very wide. One drawback of the blockbuster and the high-concept positions is that they take a handful of films to represent a vast output. Hollywood has given us baseball movies, football movies, basketball movies, hockey movies, soccer movies, golf movies, surfing movies, bowling movies, fly-fishing movies, skydiving movies, poker movies, prizefighting movies, bike-racing movies, chess movies, roller-skating movies, middle-class-family movies, upper-class-family movies, working-class-family movies, coal-mining movies, cowboy movies, doctor movies, knights-of-old movies, grifter movies, adultery movies, gangster movies, transvestite movies, discreet decline-of-Empire movies, war movies, adult-lust movies, teenage-lust movies, teenage-prank movies, colorful-geezer movies, prison movies, survival movies, dog movies, cat movies, tiger-cub movies, whale movies, dolphin movies, sensitive coming-of-age movies, lovers-on-the-run movies, single-parent movies, disco movies, Thanksgiving movies, Christmas movies, stalker movies, robot movies, firefighting movies, ghost movies, vampire movies, Sherlock Holmes movies, male-bonding movies, female-bonding movies, frat movies, sorority movies, spring-break movies, summer-vacation movies, road movies, road-trip movies, time-machine movies, Civil War movies, rise-of-Nazism movies, World War II movies, Broadway-play movies, TV-spin-off movies, dance movies, motorcycle-trash movies, and movies showing fops and their ladies curt-seying in powdered wigs; and none of these is necessarily a blockbuster.

Too often, writers discussing postclassical cinema concentrate on the tent-pole films—typically action pictures and heroic fantasy—or on the acknowl-edged classics *(Chinatown, The Godfather)*. These are peaks, no doubt. But Hollywood also dwells in the valleys. Perhaps our orthodox account of the industry's recent history, focusing on the rise of the megapicture, lets all the other films slip too far to the periphery. Beyond a few blockbusters or high-concept breakouts, there are hundreds of other types of films. There are the A-pictures in well-established genres like horror, suspense, comedy, historical drama, and romantic drama. There is Oscar bait, the prestige pic-ture adapted from a tony literary source and displaying virtuosic acting aided by plenty of makeup *(The English Patient, 1996; The Hours, 2002)*. There is edgy fare from Spike Lee, Oliver Stone, or Paul Thomas Anderson. There is the indie drama (*In the Bedroom*, 2001) or comedy (*The Tao of Steve*, 2000). There are children's movies. There is today's equivalent of drive-in fare—the teen comedies, horror tales, or B-actioners. Each year, a few of these less-trumpeted efforts will find financial success, while many would-be blockbusters will have crashed on their second weekend.

Every year's most successful releases include some outliers. The eleven top-grossing films in 1984's North American market were *Ghostbusters, Indiana Jones and the Temple of Doom, Beverly Hills Cop, Gremlins, The Karate Kid, Police Academy, Footloose, Romancing the Stone, Star Trek III: The Wrath of Khan, Splash,* and *Purple Rain.* In the same year, *Rhinestone,* boasting the supposedly infallible teaming of Sylvester Stallone and Dolly Parton, wound up at number fifty, grossing about a third of what *Splash* took in. In 1993 *Jurassic Park* was far in the front, but *Mrs. Doubtfire* came in at number two, *Sleepless in Seattle* at number five, *Indecent Proposal* at number six, and *Schindler's List* at number nine. *Free Willy* (eleven), *Philadelphia* (twelve), *Groundhog Day* (thirteen), and *Grumpy Old Men* (fourteen) did much better than the Stallone vehicle *Demolition Man* (eighteen), Schwarzenegger's *Last Action Hero* (twenty-six), and Sharon Stone's erotic thriller *Sliver* (forty-five). Or note the top-fifteen worldwide grossers for 2000, dominated by *Mission: Impossible 2* and *Gladiator,* but also including *Cast Away, What Women Want, Dinosaur, Meet the Parents, What Lies Beneath, Scary Movie, Erin Brockovich,* and *Unbreakable.* Wannabe 2000 blockbusters like *The Beach, The Cell, Rules of Engagement,* and *Proof of Life* did not make the top twenty, and the deeply peculiar *Battlefield Earth,* with an estimated budget of over $100 million, came in one hundred and second, garnering a paltry $30 million worldwide.[31] Such train wrecks are a fact of modern Hollywood history, from *Cleopatra* (1963) and *Dr. Dolittle* (1967) through *Heaven's Gate* (1980) and *Ishtar* (1987) to *The Adventures of Pluto Nash* (2002) and *The Alamo* (2004). Many blockbusters just go bust.

True, a successful megapicture generates a huge payout for the distribution company (at a minimum, about 30 percent of box-office returns). Cultural buzz pays off too; every studio likes to be at the center of a phenomenon like *Spider-Man* or *The Lord of the Rings.* But the A-pictures, the children's films, the low-budget action and horror titles, and all the rest enable the companies to fill screens day in and day out. "The studio emphasis has shifted to event films to be released around the world, but they need more titles to run through the system," notes one agent. "Those additional films, which are largely dramas, genre films, or foreign content stories are an opportunity for the talent as well as the independent producer."[32] They're also an opportunity for steady money. While locomotives might earn the topline grosses, they carry the greatest risks. They have the highest budgets, the longest shooting schedules, the biggest costs for prints and advertising, and the most debt service.[33] Nearly all the top tentpole films don't recoup their costs until after they're released on home video. So studios also need to hit doubles and triples, successful movies brought to them by independent producers, shot on mid-range budgets but carrying a large profit margin. In 2003 *Love Actually*, with a budget estimated at $45 million, grossed only about $60 million in North America. But it earned much more overseas, ending with a worldwide gross of about $246 million—almost exactly the international take of *Hulk* (estimated budget $172 million), and much ahead of *The Italian Job, Anger Management, Kill Bill vol. 1, The Cat in the Hat,* and *Master and Commander: The Far Side of the World.* On DVD *Love Actually* competes briskly with 2003's aspiring blockbusters.[34]

The talent, like the output, is far more diverse than the blockbuster aesthetic would suggest. For every producer like Jerry Bruckheimer (*Pearl Harbor,* 2001) and Joel Silver (*Lethal Weapon,* 1987), there is a James L. Brooks (*As Good As It Gets,* 1997), a Mark Johnson (*Donnie Brasco,* 1997), and a Scott Rudin (*Wonder Boys,* 2000). For every director as bodacious as Tony Scott or Antoine Fuqua, there are calmer hands like Clint Eastwood and Phil Alden Robinson. And nearly everyone crosses over. Bruckheimer produced *Dangerous Minds* (1995), Silver produced *The Hudsucker Proxy* (1994), Johnson produced *Galaxy Quest* (1999), and Rudin produced *Shaft* (2000), while Scott directed the indie-inflected *True Romance* (1993). If we're to capture the dynamic of stability and change that characterizes contemporary American moviemaking, we need to recognize that it is a fluid system.

It remains, however, a system. Classical filmmaking constitutes not just one stylistic school, on the same footing as Soviet montage or Italian neorealism. The classical tradition has become a default framework for international cinematic expression, a point of departure for nearly every filmmaker. The premises of classical storytelling have played a role similar to that played by the principles of perspective in visual art. Many different schools of painting, from Renaissance classicism to surrealism and modern figural art, work with the assumptions of perspective projection. Likewise, most traditions of commercial moviemaking adopt or recast classical premises of narrative and style.

Historically, these premises sprang mostly out of other media. From popular literature and drama came principles of plotting: psychological causality, planting and payoff, rising action, and recurrent motifs. From theater, painting, photography, and the graphic arts came ideas about spatial vantage points and pictorial composition. Other premises derived from cinema's particular resources, such as the possibility of breaking a scene into closer views of the characters, or joining disparate spaces through alternating editing. Soon after movies became a public entertainment, filmmakers tested all these principles in haphazard fashion. By 1917 American filmmakers had synthesized them into a unified style, and it was this style, within the next decade, that was taken up and developed around the world.[35]

What role did this style play in the international advance of the Hollywood movie? I remember attending a silent film festival spotlighting Russian czarist dramas, all admirably mounted and acted but solemn and introspective. The programmers broke the mood by inserting Raoul Walsh's *Regeneration* (1915). A mother dies, a boy is beaten by a drunken foster father, the boy grows to be a tough gangster, he plunges into a barroom quarrel, slumming rich folks visit a bawdy nightclub, the gangster is transfixed by the sight of a beautiful debutante: more happened in the first twenty minutes of *Regeneration* than in the entirety of any of the Russian films. And the film's brief scenes, rapid cutting, and constant changes of angle probably seemed as frenetic in 1915 as any action movie looks to us today. My friend leaned over and whispered, "Now we know how America won."

Critics were as captivated as the audiences. Denouncing continental films as too theatrical, a German critic wrote in 1920: "America's healthy will has created true film. . . . What is happening or rather racing by on the screen can no longer be called plot. It is a new dynamic, a breathless rhythm, action in an unliterary sense."[36] Of course, the style didn't propel the films into foreign markets on its own. Hollywood studios have been shrewdly entrepreneurial, and the United States, home to a large and affluent moviegoing population, has given domestic films an enormous base from which to expand.[37] Still, since the late 1910s American narrative norms have been very export friendly. The plots rely on physical movement, vigorous conflicts, escalating dramatic stakes, and a climax driven by time pressure. The visual style, contoured to maximize dramatic impact, is likewise easily understood.[38] Just as Webern will never become elevator music, a highly experimental approach to cinematic storytelling is unlikely to attract a large international audience.

In a passage that has become famous, André Bazin pointed out that this tradition is at once solid and flexible: "The American cinema is a classical art, but why not then admire in it what is most admirable, i.e., not only the talent of this or that film-maker, but the genius of the system, the richness of its ever-vigorous tradition, and its fertility when it comes into contact

with new elements." The system that Bazin praised wasn't the film industry but rather a coherent approach to genre, plot, and style that can assimilate a great range of thematic material. He believed that *Picnic* (1955) and
Bus Stop (1956), underrated by his younger critical colleagues, were valu-
able partly because of their presentation of "social truth, which of course is
not offered as a goal that suffices in itself but is integrated into a style of
cinematic narration."[39]

In the essays that follow I try to show that the richness of classical American filmmaking, as an artistic system, depends on just this capacity for flexible but bounded variation. The premises of Hollywood filmmaking host an
indefinitely large number of artistic strategies. Some of those strategies have
become the most common options; others are imaginative ways of working
within the tradition. Some resources have been heavily exploited, others
have not. Some narrative strategies, such as the multiple-protagonist film,
were rarely pursued in the studio era but are being ingeniously developed
today. The situation is summed up by musicologist Leonard Meyer, who con-
siders style in any art as a hierarchical system of constraints and opportunities: "For any specific style there is a finite number of rules, but there is
an infinite number of possible strategies for realizing or instantiating such
rules. And for any set of rules there are probably innumerable strategies
that have never been instantiated."[40] The norms of any tradition are regu-
lative principles, not laws. The classical system is less like the Ten Commandments and more like a restaurant menu.

Flexibility within limits is most evident at the level of visual style. According to one convention of classical filmmaking, extensive passages of time
can be condensed through a "montage sequence," a series of images that
stands for a whole process—crossing the Atlantic, making a suit of armor,
spending wonderful days with a lover. The montage sequence originated at
the end of the silent era, and it typically linked its brief, typical images with
dissolves. The technique was elaborated more fully in the sound era; not only
was music added, but the invention of the optical printer allowed fancier
transitions, such as elaborate wipes. So important did the montage sequence
become that the studios employed montage specialists, the most famous of
whom, Slavko Vorkapich, brought an avant-garde sensibility to portraying
stock market crashes, the arrival of world war, or a hero's public humilia-
tion. By the 1960s most filmmakers had dropped the fancy transitions in
favor of simple cuts, but because the montage sequence was easily understood as a narrative summary, it could also anchor high-tech innovations,
as in recent computer-generated imagery (CGI) montages.

It's not surprising that narrative functions tend to tame visual devices.

An early montage summarizing a frenzied nightclub party in *So This Is Paris* (1926).

Thanks to the optical printer, elaborate wipe effects could present a couple separated by a rival (*Maytime*, 1937).

A CGI version of conventional montage design (*Spider-Man*, 2002).

One of Slavko Vorkapich's elaborate montages for *Meet John Doe* (1941); here the hero is spurned by the citizenry.

We grasp the flashy wipe as an ellipsis because we already understand that a montage sequence summarizes a stretch of time. Stylistic devices of all sorts depend on our following this or that bit of story. We know that characters in conversation tend to look at each other, so we construe cuts from one face to another as reaffirming that situation. We recognize flashback sequences because we know that stories, in film or literature or on stage or on a comic book page, can shuffle events out of order. And we understand stories in general because they are a heightening and focusing of skills we bring to understanding everyday social life—connecting means to ends, ascribing intentions and emotions to others, seeing the present as stemming from the past.[41] To study classical narrative forms is to examine how we make sense of story information. So when I talk of structure or style,

I'm also talking of how viewers turn dramatic and visual patterns into an intelligible story.

A complete account of Hollywood's creative options, then, should recognize both novel storytelling devices and the well-proven narrative purposes they serve. To those who think that the blockbuster era introduced a mindless uniformity, I want to suggest that American cinema continues to host innovative narrative strategies. To those who think that the tradition has collapsed, I'll try to show that the principles of that system remain firmly in force—sometimes refined and reweighted, but not rejected.

Allusionism and knowingness take on a new significance from this angle, and to see why, let us consider a historical parallel. Early-sixteenth-century Italian painters faced a problem. All believed that art progressed, but the titanic "classical" artists, Raphael, Leonardo, and Michelangelo, seemed to have conquered most realms of expression. What was left for a young artist to do? "Art had been developed to such a point," writes art historian E. H. Gombrich, "that artists were inevitably conscious of the choice of methods before them."[42] They accordingly sought out new niches. A painter might present esoteric images, or express movement in a virtuosic way, or contrive unexpected visual effects as the mannerists did, or create a tactile naturalism akin to that seen in Dutch still lifes.[43] The strivings of post-Renaissance painters help us to understand changes in American film craft. Assuming that artists compete not only with their contemporaries but also with their predecessors, we can see many developments in post-1960 Hollywood as efforts to respond to the powerful legacy of studio-era cinema. Aware of the tradition, filmmakers could extend it, refine its premises, explore its underutilized resources, apply it to new subjects and themes, even pay homage to its outstanding achievements—all without abandoning its fundamental commitments. This hypothesis explains why Hollywood storytelling ranges from relatively conservative efforts to quite bold experiments.[44] In both the following essays I examine this as a likely explanation for many artistic impulses at work in the period. What some call "postclassical" filmmaking need not be anticlassical filmmaking.

In the first essay I try to tease out these concerns by showing how time-honored principles of plot construction and narration have been actualized in a range of ways. Neither tentpoles nor programmers nor prestige items are exempt from classical storytelling strategies. Outstanding successes like *The Godfather, Jaws, The Lion King,* and *Spider-Man* are profoundly "classical," and both the action extravaganza and the throwaway comedy will rely on genre traditions. Some films revitalize classical principles in imaginative ways; my chief example of this is *Jerry Maguire*. Further along the spectrum are edgier experiments, but these demand that the filmmaker judiciously balance novelty with familiarity. If your story will be recounted backward, as in *Memento,* how do you keep the audience from getting confused? If you want to take your audience into the world of a schizophrenic, as in *A Beautiful Mind,* how do you distinguish between hallucination and reality? The traditions of Hollywood storytelling, particularly the redundancy built into the system, can make innovation accessible to audiences.

In the second essay I examine visual style, a realm of cinematic expression with its own aims and resources. As in the "baroque" 1940s and the early wide-screen-and-color era, the extremes of today's style are resolutely showy. Many movies flaunt fast cutting, hyperkinetic camerawork, and swaths of details and "atmosphere." Despite this swaggering technique, I argue that the palette is not quite as rich as it once was. Although the last forty years have opened up fresh possibilities for narrative construction, they've also made certain stylistic options quite unfashionable. This trend suggests that stylistic change in film, as in other arts, is not a simple accumulation of options, an expanding range of choice.

Most books analyzing contemporary Hollywood focus on changing subjects and themes, such as the representation of gender, ethnic groups, or cultural attitudes. The results are typically exercises in interpretation, taking films as "texts" to be deciphered. By contrast, this book emphasizes the craft of storytelling. In the spirit of reverse engineering, I want to tease apart the finished films and see what strategies of plot and visual style govern their design. We still lack knowledge of how Hollywood's "ever-vigorous tradition" tells stories in a distinctive way, so my main goal is to expose some central constructional principles of contemporary moviemaking. When we've grasped those principles, we will be in a better position to track both local and long-term changes in the ways movies work.

A secondary aim of these essays, needless to say, is to shift the burden of proof to those who believe that the megapicture ushered in a new narrative regimen. I argue that crucial practices of storytelling persisted, despite the demise of the studio system, the emergence of conglomerate control, and new methods of marketing and distribution. Whether music videos and Happy Meals have banished coherent storytelling is not a foregone conclusion but an empirical question. We have to look and see.

Two final points. First, my Hollywood covers a lot of ground. I discuss many independent films, principally because most of them are scripted, shot, and cut according to classical principles. Nowadays many off-Hollywood titles are distributed by the major companies through their boutique divisions or larger-scale subsidiaries like New Line. By seeking unusual movies with profit potential, these Indiewood companies cultivate niche audiences and scout talent for studio projects.[45] For similar reasons I include British and Canadian films that subscribe to classical premises, that find U.S. theatrical distribution, and whose directors are apt to be snapped up for the next comic-book franchise or Oscar contender.

Finally, there's the matter of quality. Although I spend some time on outstanding accomplishments, on the whole I draw my examples from movies that exemplify common strategies of plotting, narration, and visual style. I don't mean to suggest that these films are all excellent, or even good. Most are just ordinary. Too many times, after setting down words in defense of this tradition, I would immediately see a movie that left me feeling dumber than when I had started. Then I had to remind myself that we judge any tradition by its best achievements. Norms help unambitious filmmakers attain competence, but they challenge gifted ones to excel. By understanding these norms we can better appreciate skill, daring, and emotional power on those rare occasions when we meet them.

PART I

A Real Story

Out in Hollywood all they talk about is *story*—
secretaries, everybody—*story.*

JAMES M. CAIN

. . . . .

In the mid-1990s, Cameron Crowe decided to write "a movie with a real story, the kind that shows up on TV late at night, usually in black and white. For months after *Singles* [1992] I had gorged on the great storytellers and character geniuses of cinema, stalking the video shelves." He studied Ernst Lubitsch, Howard Hawks, Preston Sturges, and "the incomparable Billy Wilder." *The Apartment* (1960) was Crowe's favorite film, and it inspired him "to begin writing [his] own portrait of the contemporary man, that faceless guy who puts on a suit and tie every day, Jerry Maguire." He even tried to persuade Wilder to play the part of Dickie Fox, Jerry's mentor.[1] Eventually he would record a suite of conversations with the master, but all he got at first meeting was Wilder's autograph on an *Apartment* poster.[2] Crowe fantasized about a scene in the distant future: "Just for a moment I could glimpse my wildest dream: I'm 89, and some young schnook comes up to me with a poster from *Jerry Maguire.*"[3]

This story about stories isn't what we should expect if contemporary cinema had indeed discarded the canons of the studio era. Crowe admires Hollywood movies as triumphs of craftsmanship. They are great yarns boasting compelling situations and characters. So the problem he faces is investing a contemporary film with the vivacity of 1930s and 1940s classics. He is not out to overturn the system; he wants to sustain it, if possible, at an equal level of achievement. He would be happy if *Jerry Maguire* inspired others as *The Apartment* has inspired him.

Crowe's lesson for us is twofold. I'll argue that despite the diversity that American movies have displayed since 1960, nearly all of them depend on storytelling principles established in the studio era. Some filmmakers have reiterated received strategies, creating the run-of-the-mill movie most often neglected by theorists of "postclassical" cinema. Other filmmakers have extended or amplified traditional principles, often so subtly that viewers are hardly aware of the innovations. Still others have probed possibilities merely touched on in earlier years, enriching them in the process. A few filmmakers have recast familiar forms in more experimental shapes, but even here the tradition isn't rejected in toto. A filmmaker who innovates in one respect tends to hold other elements constant; the novelty stands out, but the film doesn't become incomprehensible. In all, Hollywood storytelling is a very supple tradition, sustaining a great deal of variety. Day by day, creative minds find fresh ways to actualize premises that have proven their effectiveness for nearly a hundred years of moviemaking.

Still—and this is the second lesson—Crowe's confession indicates that something crucial has changed. John Ford and Cecil B. De Mille suffered, it seems, no anxiety about surpassing Edwin Porter and D. W. Griffith. By 1930 they could also ignore their contemporaries overseas. And although Ford, De Mille, and their studio-era peers competed with each other, they did not meditate much on the history they had made.[4] But if you started to make films in the 1960s, you faced different circumstances. As the studios declined, a new U.S. film culture emerged. The college-age audience developed a taste for foreign cinema, for the auteur theory, even for "underground" movies. Film courses sprang up in universities, repertory houses revealed the riches of earlier decades, critics celebrated directors' "personal visions." By 1970 aspiring filmmakers knew about Jean Renoir and Akira Kurosawa and Ingmar Bergman, as well as the classic American directors. This knowledge, exhilarating though it was, posed a difficulty.

Starting out, the young director naturally asks: What is there for me to do? During the studio era, he could tackle this problem by finding out, through routine assignments, what genres he had a flair for. But in 1970 the young filmmaker faced a much keener sense that certain niches had already been occupied. Could any novice make Westerns as powerful as *Stagecoach* (1939), *High Noon* (1952), *Shane* (1953), or *Rio Bravo* (1959)? Musicals as delightful as *42nd Street* (1933), *Meet Me in St. Louis* (1944), or *Singin' in the Rain* (1952)? Comedies with the brio of *Bringing Up Baby* (1938), *The Shop Around the Corner* (1940), or *The Lady Eve* (1941)? Melodramas as piercing as *Alice Adams* (1935), *Stella Dallas* (1937), or *I Remember Mama* (1948)? Could a beginner create thrillers as audacious as those by Alfred Hitchcock and Lang? By the 1960s the Hollywood studio tradition was acknowledged as such, and it presented an awesome challenge to any beginner. Not only had everything apparently been done, but it had been done superbly. If one moved away from Hollywood—well, then there were other rivals, François Truffaut and Federico Fellini and Jean-Luc Godard and the young German directors.

Worse, the newcomer had little chance of starting as an apprentice. In the studios' production system, directors could master their craft in B-features or editing rooms and then churn out enough pictures to become skillful. Writers, cinematographers, and other creative personnel were hired on contract, often for a seven-year stretch. But now, perhaps after a stint at USC or UCLA, one had to find one's own way film by film. Hence the magnetism of producer Roger Corman, whose American International Pictures offered young people a chance to get on the set fast. "When I looked at the filmographies of the directors I admired," remarked Corman alumnus Jonathan Kaplan, "I noticed that they made a hell of a lot of movies before they made a good one. And I made the decision, consciously, to make as many movies as I could in as short a period of time as I could."[5]

With your career wholly in your own hands, facing the competition of past and present, how could you achieve something distinctive? Call this the problem of *belatedness*.[6] Belatedness is both stimulating and intimidating. Seeing great films from the studio era can spur you to become a director; how many filmmakers were inspired by *King Kong* (1933) or *Citizen Kane* (1941)? Yet classics can also be intimidating. "The big problem for a director today," remarked Peter Bogdanovich in the early 1970s, "is to get back to that spirit of innocence, directness, and simplicity."[7] The more you know, the more you understand the gap that separates you from the great tradition, and the more you fret about what you can contribute.

Your options are several. You might content yourself with recycling, via updating, the conventions of the classic era. You make your romantic comedy or melodrama. This is the default option. More boldly, you might take on the masters. You might try to match Hitchcock, as Brian De Palma did by updating and extending his narrative strategies. You might try to debunk Ford, as Sam Peckinpah did by almost blasphemously putting "Shall We Gather at the River?" in the mouths of pious townsfolk marching into a free-fire zone (*The Wild Bunch*, 1969). Or you might search out niches that the masters never cared to occupy. It's commonly said that the rise of horror, fantasy, and science fiction reflects the tastes of a generation raised on comic books and television. Surely these media did influence Steven Spielberg, George Lucas, John Carpenter, and others. But looked at from the viewpoint of the hungry creator, certain genres gave the young filmmaker a chance to excel on his or her own terms. Since Raoul Walsh filmed *White Heat* (1948), no director had made a great gangster film. Nobody as good as Ford or Hitchcock had tackled horror or science fiction. And arguably only Howard Hawks (*Hatari!* 1962) had made a "personal" action-adventure movie. By promoting genres that had been at the bottom of the 1950s hierarchy, a new generation could display its talents. That the young directors happened to enjoy these genres was an added incentive.

There were other unsettled matters. Hawks, Samuel Fuller, Fritz Lang, and Anthony Mann had occasionally explored the visceral effects of violence, but with the shower scene in *Psycho* (1960) as a benchmark, and with the loosening of the production code in the late 1960s, young filmmakers could take gore much farther. In this sense, De Palma made R-rated Hitchcock films. Likewise, no major filmmaker had mastered an impressive illusionism of special effects. My high school friends made fun of the rear projection and matte paintings that hung on throughout the sixties, and it's not surprising that our contemporary, Spielberg, insisted that his telefilm *Duel* (1971) not use these phony effects. The engineering-minded filmmaker could confront the challenge of upgrading mechanical monsters (from *Jaws*, 1975, to *Jurassic Park*, 1993) or creating truly plausible impressions of flight (*2001: A Space Odyssey*, 1968; *Star Wars*, 1977). Although critics tend to dismiss special effects, the best are triumphs of human ingenuity, and post-1970 filmmakers made them powerful additions to the tool kit of representational art.

The condition of belatedness is probably most visible in our movies' constant allusionism. Noël Carroll has suggested that from the late 1960s onward, directors began to evoke themes by shorthand reference to genres and auteurs. He points out that *Hardcore* (1978) builds its plot on that of *The Searchers* (1956), enabling director Paul Schrader to "shoplift" the theme of sexual repression and its relation to "dark doubles" (Indians in Ford, porn merchants in Schrader).[8] By the 1990s allusionism had expanded into a general recognition that popular media constituted the shared culture of movie consumers. This process isn't utterly new; studio-era films referred to current taglines from radio, vaudeville, and advertising, and a movie score might quote a hit tune. But probably the youthfulness of the audience after 1970 made movies, along with comic books, television, and pop music, a pool of media knowledge. Carroll presciently suggested that in the new democratic culture envisioned by 1960s Movie Brats, cinema would replace the Bible and literature as a cultural reference point.[9] The tradition is now freestanding, and allusions to old movies are expected in virtually every project. It's surprising when *Heat* (1995) includes no citations of the classics; Michael Mann acts as if no other crime movie had ever been made. At the other end of the spectrum stands Quentin Tarantino, whose citations overturn the canon established by the Movie Brats—replacing the Western with blaxploitation and kung fu, Ford and Hawks with Dario Argento and Chang Cheh. Today, the plethora of fan magazines and Internet cultures has bred a pop connoisseurship that demands film references as part of the pleasures of moviegoing.

Even the filmmaker who inserts these references mechanically cannot but be conscious of coming after imposing predecessors, some of whom might be fairly recent. To make films in the 1980s one had to confront the triumphs of the 1970s, overwhelmingly apparent through cable and video-cassette. Now your detective movie competed not only with *The Big Sleep* (1946) but with *Chinatown* (1974). Don Vito Corleone loomed over every later gangster film. Thus the access to video in the 1980s, like the programs of repertory cinemas of the movie-crazy 1960s and '70s, proved to be double-edged. Home video allowed filmmakers to pore over classics, but it also sharpened their need to pursue alternatives to rivals. Newcomers competed not only with Old Hollywood but with New Hollywood and with New New Hollywood, so fresh ecological niches were constantly being sniffed out. After Michael Corleone's slide into melancholic corruption, a gangster would have to be more flamboyantly aggressive (*Scarface*, 1983). After *Star Wars*, science fiction could be deheroicized, portraying a dilapidated corporate future haunted by monsters (*Alien*, 1979) or sunk in high-tech gloom (*Blade Runner*, 1982). Directors born in the 1960s would consider Lucas and Spielberg, Ridley Scott and James Cameron the oldish masters to beat; the tastes of Alex Proyas, Michael Bay, David Koepp, Antoine Fuqua, Robert Rodriguez, and the Wachowski brothers and their peers were partially formed by the new behemoth films of the 1970s and '80s.[10] Still, it's unlikely that the touchstones of the studio tradition would be wholly forgotten. Peter Jackson may have sought to turn *The Lord of the Rings* into the *Star Wars* of Generation Y, but *King Kong* remains his favorite movie. (So, naturally, he remade it.)

Of course, awareness of what came before can curdle into resentment. "Hooray for Hollywood" burbles the soundtrack at the close of Altman's *The Long Goodbye* (1973), as Philip Marlowe tap-dances homeward after killing his treacherous pal. This film, *M*A*S*H* (1970), and *Buffalo Bill and the Indians* (1976) are pitiless travesties of tradition. It's as if Altman seeks to so discredit each genre that no one will ever be able to make a war film, a whodunit, or a cowboy movie again. But such spoilsport exercises remain rare. Instead, directors have produced an endless stream of parodies, sequels, and remakes paying affectionate tribute to what came before, along with the occasional heady celebrations of Gollywood like *Movie Movie* (1978) and *Down with Love* (2003).

Cameron Crowe's hope to find a place in history isn't unique. Belatedness is a pervasive feature of modern Hollywood, creating a new self-consciousness about the act of making a film. If the critic needs to invoke the "postclassical" label, it might be most useful in reminding us that European painters had to respond to the supreme, apparently exhaustive achievements of Michelangelo, Raphael, and Leonardo. Like Mannerism in the sixteenth century, the New Hollywood testifies to a change in artists' self-understanding. After the early 1960s, most filmmakers became painfully aware of working in the shadow of enduring monuments. But this awareness didn't lead most of them to reject tradition. Instead, they sought to sustain it in fresh ways.

1. CONTINUING TRADITION,
BY ANY MEANS NECESSARY

We can see Hollywood's judicious balance of continuity and innovation in the emergence of contemporary screenwriting rules. Contrary to those who would argue that today's movies are mere agglomerations of star power, special effects, raucous comedy, and shattering violence, the dozens of screenplay manuals pouring from the presses have demanded tight plot construction and a careful coordination of emotional appeals. We can't take these manuals wholly on faith—we'll need to test them against finished films—but their consolidation of studio-era principles nicely exemplifies how modern American moviemaking pays its tribute to tradition.

Acts, Arcs, and Archetypes

Few screenplay manuals inspire confidence. If you want proof that contemporary Hollywood is formula-ridden, look no further than Syd Field's "Paradigm," with turning points absolutely required on script pages 25–27 and 85–90. One author explains that in action movies "the Sidekick's main jobs are to help the hero, provide comic relief, and be murdered by the henchman at the end of Act 1 or the end of Act 2."[11] The jacket blurbs compete in zany hyperbole. Lew Hunter dubs William Froug "THE premiere screenwriting teacher in the history of motion pictures," while Hunter's own book is praised as "the final word on screenwriting." Apparently not, though, since Hunter says of another manual, "This is the best book on screenwriting today—even better than my own!" Long on anecdotes and famous names, the books have a confessional charm. Field says that years after attending UCLA and working in the film industry, he suddenly realized that act 1 had to set up the story and introduce the main characters. Later, when teaching a course on screenwriting, a student asked him, "What is a screenplay?" "The question took me by surprise. I had no answer, so I just kept talking."[12]

Screenwriting manuals have been published for nearly a century, proliferating at moments when the industry welcomed outsiders.[13] As the studios downsized in the 1960s, writers were no longer on contract, and story departments shrank. Each film was a one-off production, and the screenplay formed the core of a package that might attract a director and a star.[14] The aspiring writer submitted an original screenplay (a "spec script") to an agent, who shepherded it to a studio or an independent producer. The odds were overwhelmingly against that script's being bought or filmed. With luck, it would serve as an intriguing writing sample for other assignments.

The flood of manuals that broke forth in the late 1970s responded to this new process of story development. Thousands of aspiring screenwriters faced a decentralized market and lacked common training. They needed advice on format, plotting, and what producers wanted. Above all, the script had to win the support of gatekeepers, the development staff known as readers or "story analysts." Dutifully plowing through spec scripts at piecework rates, the readers churned out "coverage"—a plot synopsis and an appraisal of each project's strengths and weaknesses. In effect, the screenplay manuals were guiding hopefuls to write scripts that would galvanize the frontline reader. Syd Field, Robert McKee, Christopher Vogler, and other script gurus all started their careers as story analysts.[15]

All art forms have certain structural templates. Although screenplay conventions aren't as stringent as the rules governing the Petrarchan sonnet and the twelve-bar blues, the manuals' advice points to fairly firm standards of plot construction and characterization. A film's main characters, all agree, should pursue important goals and face forbidding obstacles. Conflict should be constant, across the whole film and within each scene. Actions should be bound into a tight chain of cause and effect. Major events should be foreshadowed ("planted"), but not so obviously that the viewer can predict them. Tension should rise in the course of the film until a climax resolves all the issues.

These principles have been reiterated in screenplay handbooks since the 1910s, but the new script gurus extended them in three major ways. First, they mandated that the plot be divided into large-scale parts, like the acts in a play. Extrapolating from Aristotle's suggestion that a story should have a beginning, middle, and end, both Constance Nash and Virginia Oakley's *Screenwriter's Handbook* (1978) and Syd Field's *Screenplay* (1979) propose a three-act structure. Act 1 introduces the problems faced by the hero, ending with a crisis and the promise of major conflict. Act 2 consists of an extended struggle between the protagonist and his or her problem, and it ends at a point of even more severe testing for the hero. Act 3 shows the protagonist solving the problem. Taking a two-hour film as the norm and assuming that one script page equals a minute of screen time, the authors recommend that act 1 run about thirty pages, act 2 about sixty pages, and act 3 another thirty pages.[16] This ratio of 1:2:1 has become the standard, although some advisors object to strict page counts.[17]

Later script gurus have tweaked this structure. Several characterize the triggering event of act 1 as the "inciting event." One recommends placing a firm point of change seventeen pages into the script; another suggests splitting act 1 in half.[18] One proposes that act 1 display distinct stages: establishing the story universe, introducing the protagonist through a characteristic action, creating an auspicious occasion (such as a party or wedding), displaying the inciting event, and ending the act with the protagonist undertaking an "irrevocable act," a point of no return.[19] Act 2 is to be plotted as a string of complications, crises, and reversals along a rising action. Some guidebooks note that the second act often pivots around a midpoint, the halfway mark in the script, "a moment when the protagonist tries something new, takes control of his or her own destiny in a way that has not been done before."[20] Most agree that act 2 should culminate in what has come to be called the "dark moment" or "darkest moment."[21] It could constitute a decision or a "deliberately static moment" in which the protagonist finds the means to defeat the antagonist.[22] Act 3 should consist of a continuous climax, often a race against time (a "ticking clock"), capped by a resolution signaling a new harmony and balance.[23] Different genres fill in this scheme with characteristic incidents. In romantic comedy, the inciting event is the "cute meet" between the couple-to-be, while the third act is the "joyous defeat" of the obstacles to their union.[24]

Where did the three-act template come from? Nash and Oakley do not claim any source, while Field says he discovered it on his own.[25] Although older manuals don't mention a three-act structure, in contemporary interviews veteran screenwriters occasionally invoke it.[26] If it was once a trade secret, as Dan O'Bannon suggests, after 1980 it wasn't one any longer.[27] It was blared out in books, courses, and one-off seminars. Software programs were written to make sure every beat was present and accounted for. A few exemplars—*Casablanca* (1942), *Breaking Away* (1979), *Romancing the Stone* (1984), *Witness* (1985), and the inescapable *Chinatown*—were dissected for their adroit setups, rising second acts, and well-placed turning points. Once the three-act template became public knowledge, development executives embraced it as a way to make script acquisition routine. The page-count formulas became yardsticks for story analysts and studio staff.[28] Today most screenwriters acknowledge the three-act structure, and around the world it is taught as the optimal design for a mass-market movie.[29]

A second set of innovations bears on characterization. The authors of studio-era manuals often worried about character consistency, urging writers to blend varying traits into a plausible personality.[30] Today's manuals demand more: "Every major character should have a flaw."[31] Vulnerable, driven by demons, drawn to the dark side—all these clichés of story pitches are invoked to give the protagonist a compelling fault. The crucial flaw may be a "ghost," something from the past that must be exorcised if the lead character is to act decisively.[32] Ghosts provide inner conflicts that counterpoint the hero's struggle with the adversary. Screenplay manuals occasionally distinguish between what the character *wants* (the external goal) and what he or she *needs* (the underlying motivation, driven by flaws and ghosts). When hinted at in behavior, props, or dialogue, the fault forms part of the "subtext." "The subtext arises out of the interplay of the emotion-laden background story with the motion-laden foreground story."[33] However assured on the outside, the hero lacks self-knowledge, and this is revealed via subtext.

Given a flaw, the character must conquer it. Hence the *character arc.* "In the most simplistic terms," says screenwriter Nicholas Kazan, "you want every character to learn something. . . . Hollywood is sustained on the illusion that human beings are capable of change."[34] Through the plot's act structure, the internal and external conflicts must be reconciled.[35] At the end of the second act, the darkest moment yields to enlightenment as the hero prepares to attain the external goal. Act 3 then shows the firmness of the character's change. She has merged her wants and her needs. Such signs of personal growth are said to gratify the audience. "When the characters are forced to deal with their inner conflicts in order to solve their outer problems, our relationship with them grows and strengthens."[36]

Character development wasn't unknown in classical Hollywood, of course. Screenplay manuals occasionally recommended a change of heart.[37] Harold Lloyd made a career out of playing youths torn by paralyzing anxieties, and the heroes of films noirs and many World War II pictures are troubled souls.[38] By the 1960s, a movie was even more likely to highlight the protagonists' flaws. Consider as an example *Kramer vs. Kramer* (1979). Made in a period supposedly in the grip of blockbusters, this domestic drama became the year's top-grossing film and won five Academy Awards, including one for best screenplay.

The film opens with Joanna Kramer saying a morose good-bye to her sleeping son, Billy, while her husband, Ted, lingers at his ad agency. As Joanna packs to leave, Ted goes for drinks with his boss, who promises him a promotion if he keeps up the pace. When Ted finally comes home, he finds Joanna neurotically distraught. She declares that Billy is better off without her and leaves. After this inciting event, the rest of the first act establishes Ted's efforts to juggle his workaholic commitments with child care. His efforts to nurture Billy are perfunctory, and Billy becomes angry and distant. By the first turning point, thirty minutes into the film, father and son show no love for one another. Ted has given up trying to cook Billy's French toast, and they sit glumly at the breakfast table chewing doughnuts.

The problems intensify in act 2. Ted's job performance is slipping, and his boss threatens action. After a major quarrel with Ted, Billy feels that he's the cause of his parents' breakup. Ted starts to devote more time to his son. But just when their bonds tighten, we find that Joanna has quietly returned, spying on Billy as he enters school. Billy is hurt in a playground accident, and Ted races the boy in his arms to the emergency room. Later Joanna meets Ted and announces that thanks to a job and a therapist, she's healed: "I want my son." Ted replies, "You can't have him."

Ted now faces enormous obstacles. A mother is likely to win any custody battle, and Ted's chances dwindle further when he's fired. Now he must find a job fast. Casting off his professional ambitions, he interviews for a post below his qualifications and insists that the employer decide immediately. After waiting stubbornly during a staff Christmas party, he gets the job. But this triumph is offset by Joanna's demand to see Billy, and at a park she goes off with him, leaving Ted forlorn. Billy's joy at seeing his mommy again closes the act (at 70 minutes) and provides Ted's darkest moment. Alone, he realizes that the odds are overwhelmingly against him.

The last thirty minutes of the film, starting with the court proceedings, bristle with reversals. Direct examination by Joanna's lawyer brings out the "backstory" the audience hadn't known, building up sympathy for Joanna. She reiterates that her husband "wasn't there" for her and that she was Billy's mother for five and a half years, while Ted has been raising him for only eighteen months. The brutal cross-examination by Ted's lawyer drives Joanna to tears; in an exchange of glances, Ted conveys his compassion. Later, Ted testifies that he didn't understand Joanna's needs, but now he and Billy are a family. Just as Ted expressed concern for Joanna's treatment on the stand, she now realizes that he has sacrificed his all-important job for Billy. He withstands grilling about his low earnings, but he is thrown for a loss when Joanna's lawyer accuses him of neglect during Billy's playground accident. The attorney is exploiting Ted's guilt about the incident, which he had confided to Joanna. Deeply shaken, he watches her tilt her head in shame. Again, the exchange of looks carries the subtext (Figs. 1.1–1.2).

One other central character, Margaret, serves as a measure of Ted's arc. Before the plot started, she was Joanna's friend and advised her to leave Ted. Gradually she comes to recognize Ted's love for Billy, and at the trial Margaret serves as Ted's ally. Yet even her testimony doesn't sway the judge. Ted loses custody, and the last six minutes of the film show Billy's distraught reaction and Ted's preparation of a farewell breakfast. As they now make French toast expertly, father and son work side by side in silence—not the silence of the earlier, enervated breakfast but one that radiates affection. They have Billy's things packed, but when Joanna arrives she asks to talk to Ted alone. She tells him that she realizes that Billy has a home here and that she won't take him. Ted waits, kind and caring, while she goes in to tell Billy.

1.1. *Kramer vs. Kramer:* As Joanna's attorney attacks Ted's credibility, she averts her eyes from her husband.

1.2. On the witness stand, Ted looks at Joanna with both anger and compassion; this shot ends the scene.

The three central adults in *Kramer vs. Kramer* are flawed, and as they change they develop greater self-knowledge. Robert Benton, screenwriter and director, orchestrates the arcs carefully. Ted's adversary, Joanna, is a loving mother but fragile and lacking in confidence. The divorcée, Margaret, could have been made a snide feminist, but she forms a growing friendship with Ted. She supplies a dramatic counterpoint as well when she talks about the possibility of reuniting with her husband. Joanna's climactic change of heart is carefully prepared: she understands that she is still emotionally shaky, and she is genuinely moved by Ted's commitment to their son. Ted has won the external fight, thanks to a change in what the 1980s would have called his priorities: even if he earns less money in a more modest job, he has come to love Billy more fully. In scriptwriter's terms, he has adjusted his wants to his needs. The film's title neatly encapsulates both conflicts— not only Mr. Kramer vs. Mrs. Kramer, but also the struggle within Ted between professional ambition and fatherly duty.

Why did Hollywood screenwriters dwell on flawed characters? Probably Broadway dramas by William Inge, Paddy Chayefsky, and Tennessee Williams, along with middlebrow fiction and European art movies, led Hollywood along this path. Guidance was also supplied by two European theorists of drama. Lajos Egri's *The Art of Dramatic Writing* (1946) became a bible for many screenwriters during the 1950s and is still praised as indispensable. Egri demands that characters grow in the course of a play, and he shows how to build a plot around the process. How, he asks, can a devoted, conventional wife like Nora in *A Doll's House* become an independent woman ready to abandon her husband and children? The change is plausible only in gradual stages, so Ibsen takes Nora through phases of irresponsibility, anxiety, fear, and desperation, before she recognizes that her marriage is based on deceit.[39] Egri's recipe of modulated psychological growth helps the writer plan conflicts that will challenge the character to develop step by step, just as Ted Kramer changes from workaholic professional to sensitive father.

No less significant than Egri's emphasis on character change was Constantin Stanislavsky's theory of acting. Brought to the United States in the 1920s and revised by the Actors Studio in the 1950s, the Stanislavsky Method offered firm assistance with characterization. By proposing that characters solve both external and internal problems in the course of the play's "through-line" (character arc), the method harmonized with the goal-driven bent of Hollywood cinema. Characters' inner life was all "subtext," a cluster of unarticulated motives driving external action. Such ideas migrated to Hollywood, in all likelihood, with the popularity of Method acting and the success of director Elia Kazan. Even some of Stanislavsky's terms, like *inciting event* and *beat* found their way into screen parlance.[40]

Broader cultural factors may also have favored heroes' new vulnerability. The belief that characters must heal psychic wounds may bear traces of the West Coast self-actualization fads of the 1970s, evidenced in therapeutic movements like transcendental meditation, yoga, and Primal Scream therapy. Syd Field dedicates *Screenplay* to Werner Erhard and the people of est, "who gave me the space, the opportunity, and the support to grow and expand enough to write this book."[41] In *Kramer vs. Kramer* Joanna finds new strength by moving to California and finding a therapist who teaches her "to like herself."

Along with the three-act structure and flawed heroes came a third screenwriting innovation. In 1985 mythologist Joseph Campbell was given an award by the New York Arts Club. At the ceremony was George Lucas, who said that he had once been struggling with a script for a "children's film." He made no progress until he discovered Campbell's book *The Hero with a Thousand Faces*, which focused his energies: "It's possible that if I had not run across him I would still be writing *Star Wars* today."[42] Lucas seems not to have announced this inspiration before, but the idea that *Star Wars* was modeled on Campbell's über-myth passed into legend.[43] After the first trilogy was finished, Lucas invited the scholar to watch it and lecture at Skywalker Ranch. Campbell, Lucas claimed proudly, was "my Yoda."[44]

Campbell's synthesis of mythic traditions presents a hero called from the ordinary world to embark on adventure. The hero enters a "special world" of trials, allies, and enemies. Eventually the hero approaches the "inmost cave," the arena of a supreme ordeal. After winning, the hero returns to everyday life transformed. Stated so schematically, the mythic journey seems an unpromising model for screenwriting, but by the early 1980s some acolytes of Campbell were teaching screenplay courses based on the idea, and in 1987 one manual urged screenwriters to lead their protagonists on a "mythic journey."[45] The most successful promoter of the template was Christopher Vogler, who remembered Campbell's book when *Star Wars* and *Close Encounters of the Third Kind* (1977) found success. Working at Disney, Vogler wrote a seven-page memo applying the mythic journey to "classic and current movies" and tried out the idea in seminars. When Campbell became the subject of a highly rated PBS series, development offices all over Hollywood were asking for Vogler's memo, and his career as a story consultant took off.[46] In 1992 Vogler published *The Writer's Journey: Mythic Structure for Storytellers and Screenwriters*, which turned the Campbell synthesis into a plot outline, illustrated by films like *Rocky* (1976), *Star Wars*, and *An Officer and a Gentleman* (1982). To fill out the structure, Vogler devised several character archetypes (Mentor, Herald, Shape-shifter, Shadow) derived from Campbell, Jung, and his own imagination.

While the mythic-journey template has not been as widely influential as the three-act pattern or the concept of the character arc, it has won converts. Vogler's book was translated into several languages and became a new vade mecum for screenwriters, spawning further publications (including *The Heroine's Journey*). Vogler and others integrated the journey trajectory into three-part plot architecture.[47] Now the customary demand for inner conflict gained a mythic resonance. As Hollywood action pictures swept the world, producers were receptive to suggestions that the quest myth had cross-cultural reach. The journey idea lent a universal resonance to ordinary adventure plotlines. It also meshed with New Age spirituality, so now one finds manuals declaring that the character arc "dramatizes the writer's thematic attitudes about life's journey."[48] The embrace of the mythic journey also harmonized with the industry's growing dependence on the fantasy genre during the 1990s.

The new screenplay manuals' reliance on act structure, page counts, character arcs, and the mythic journey did not overturn classical Hollywood dramaturgy. Rather, these procedures filled it in, fine-tuned it, left less to trial and error. In the 1970s screenwriting became an academic enterprise—not only because it was studied in colleges, but also because, like nineteenth-century salon painting, it was characterized by rigid rules and a widely accepted canon. This is another sign of belatedness. The post-1960 screenwriter had to study the classics and discern in recent hits fundamental principles explaining their popularity.

It seems likely that the manuals have reshaped literary culture as well. Fiction writers unabashedly borrow these principles; one handbook advises structuring a novel by acts, rising action, and plot points at intervals of certain pages.[49] Sensing crossover potential, Vogler subtitled the second edition of *The Writer's Journey* "Mythic Structure for Writers." As movies were thrusting to the center of popular culture, Michael Crichton and John Grisham delivered not so much novels as fleshy treatments waiting to be rendered into screenplays.

If we want to grasp contemporary cinematic storytelling, the how-to books remain a fruitful point of departure. Just as we would expect a treatise on poetic forms to reveal the constraints of the sonnet or the haiku, the best manuals offer useful insights into the mechanics of movies. And they remind us that at least one sector of modern Hollywood doesn't subscribe to an aesthetic of episodic structure and wayward moments.

Storytelling by Design

In formal design, today's Hollywood cinema is largely continuous with yesterday's. There's no doubt that some changes are worth highlighting, and I'll try to do that throughout this essay. But those changes stand out against a backdrop of conventions that are as powerful today as they were in 1960, or 1940, or 1920. Once we get past generalizations about blockbusters and postmodern fragmentation, we find a lot that adheres to very old canons. Again, my aim is to shift the burden of proof, to suggest that considering a wider body of evidence in depth leads us to doubt the most sweeping claims about "postclassical" Hollywood. The best way to discover the continuing stability of the tradition is to scrutinize a range of films, guided by the discourse of the industry, notably the screenplay manuals, but also by the most nuanced theories of narrative practices we can build.

The theory that rests most firmly on close analysis is put forth in Kristin Thompson's *Storytelling in the New Hollywood*. In discussing structure, Thompson argues that most mainstream narrative features from both the studio era and recent years consist of four large parts, plus an epilogue. These parts are articulated through the central feature of classical storytelling: one or more protagonists seeking to achieve clearly defined goals. From this primary condition spring screenwriters' maxims about delineating character and building conflict. Thompson shows that Hollywood films tend to structure their large-scale parts around the ways in which goals are defined, redefined, thwarted, and then decisively achieved or not. Turning points are created by reversals of intention, points of no return, and new circumstances demanding that goals be recast.[50]

According to Thompson, the Setup (typically running 25 to 30 minutes in a 100-to-120-minute film) is congruent with the screenplay manuals' first act. It establishes the characters' world, defines the main characters' purposes, and culminates in a turning point near the half-hour mark. Twenty-eight minutes into *The Tailor of Panama* (2001), the diplomat Osnard explains to the tailor Harry the conditions for working as an informant for the embassy. *Who's Afraid of Virginia Woolf?* (1966) opens by presenting the quarrelsome central couple, George and Martha, and introduces the younger couple as their guests. About 30 minutes in, Martha's goal of tormenting George crystallizes, and she changes into a sexy outfit in order to seduce the young husband. This Setup portion may fall into two phases, with the manuals' "catalyst" or "inciting incident" coming at the 12-to-15-minute mark. Thus in *Tailor of Panama* Osnard offers Harry a job 15 minutes into the film, and at the same point in *Virginia Woolf* the young couple arrives at George and Martha's home.

In proposing two more large-scale parts, Thompson in effect splits up the canonical "second act," the better to track character aims. What she calls the "Complicating Action," typically another 20 to 30 minutes in an average-length movie, focuses or recasts the film's central goals. Either the protagonist changes tactics for achieving her goal, or she faces an entirely new situation—a sort of "countersetup." At the first turning point in *Witness* (1985), the boy Samuel identifies the killer, but this action precipitates the ambush of detective John Book. In the Complicating Action, Book flees to the Amish farm, where he must adjust to very different circumstances.[51] The second part of *Gremlins* (1984) is launched at around 25 minutes when Gizmo clones himself; the ensuing complications create a new "normality" for the characters, culminating in the next turning point (at 60 minutes, the explosive breeding of predatory gremlins in the swimming pool). *Cast Away* (2000) is committed to the same pattern. After the plane crash, at the 30-minute mark Chuck Nolan wakes up on the island's shore, facing a brand-new set of circumstances. During this second part Chuck struggles for survival, nearly expiring until, at around 60 minutes into the film, he finally decides to open the salvaged Federal Express parcels.

Very frequently, as here, the major event ending the Complicating Action arrives about halfway through the film's running time. Midway through *Telefon* (1977), we are given the crucial information that the spy center in Moscow will kill the protagonist when his mission is finished. Thompson would find the Complicating Action of *Kramer vs. Kramer* to consist of Ted and Billy's accommodation to each other in the film's second section. This countersetup, the formation of a new family, is then disturbed by Joanna's demand to take Billy back, which does occur at the 50-minute midpoint.

Any break between large-scale parts can trigger a switch in viewpoint or the introduction of new characters. In *Sisters* (1972), the turning point of the Setup shows Dominique stabbing her lover (at about 26 minutes), but then the countersetup shows Grace Collier investigating the crime. *Quills* (2000) concentrates its opening half hour on de Sade and his relation with the asylum's maids, but the Complicating Action is centered on the asylum's new supervisor and his young wife. In *Mystic River* (2003), the first 33 minutes concentrate on Jimmy's missing daughter, culminating in the discovery of her body. The Complicating Action, running about another 33 minutes, shifts among various points of view in tracing the aftermath of the death and the beginnings of the investigation. *Mystic River*'s next turning point arrives when the cops start to suspect Dave and Jimmy vows to find the killer.

Thompson calls the third stretch of the film (the second portion of the traditional act 2) the Development: "By now an extensive set of premises, goals, and obstacles has been introduced. This is where the protagonist's struggle toward his or her goals typically occurs, often involving many incidents that create action, suspense, and delay."[52] In *Drumline* (2002), the Setup shows college freshman Devon trying to make the top tier of the marching band's drum section. He achieves this, but his situation is complicated by his refusal to accept discipline. Devon's temper provokes a shameful fight between his squad and their rivals, and at the midway turning point he is kicked out of the band. The Development section consists of subsidiary characters solving their problems while Devon explores his options. He's ready to join a less disciplined rival band, until he learns that the new coach wants him to divulge his squad's march routines. Then a parcel from his estranged father includes some funk music, and this inspires Devon to write his own cadences. He offers them to his band, and his antagonistic supervisor warms to him, helping him improve his score. At the end of the Development, Devon has started to become a team player. It remains for the Climax to bring him back into the band for a showdown with the rival drumline.

Somewhat surprisingly, as Thompson points out, many Development sections show the protagonist making little progress toward the main goals. In these cases the Development serves to postpone the main action and to present delays or dwell on subplots. Montage sequences, comedy interludes, and other detours fill out this portion. (If you must fast-forward the movie, now is the time.) Thompson's point is reinforced by one script adviser who speaks of the "second-act stretch": "You can go to the bathroom and come back and Rick is still trying to figure out what to do with the letters of transit, E. T. is still trying to get home."[53] *Flashdance* (1983) offers a straightforward example. In the Setup, Alex longs to attend ballet school, but she can't face the challenge, content instead to work as a welder and to dance in a bar. The Complicating Action revolves around her blossoming affair with her boss, Nick, reinforced by the subplot of her friend Jeannie, who tries to become a professional figure skater. The Development then marks time for 26 minutes. The plot concentrates on Jeannie and the aspiring comedian Rickie, and it makes a diversionary move when Alex mistakenly thinks that Nick is two-timing her.

"Now welcome to the final act," says the mysterious killer about 90 minutes into *Scream 3* (2000). What screenplay manuals pick out as act 3 is part four for Thompson, but all agree that this constitutes the Climax. Often following the "darkest moment," the scene in which a crisis forces the protagonist to take action, this section revolves around the question of whether or not the goals can be achieved. Typically they will be. In *Flashdance,* Alex must reevaluate her life after her mentor, Hanna, dies and after Jeannie becomes a stripper. Nick has pulled strings to get Alex an audition for ballet school, and now she must definitively choose one path or another. She decides to use her acrobatic show-dancing skills to wow the judges, and she wins admission. Sometimes, however, the Climax shows the protagonist failing to achieve her goals. In *Sisters,* the investigator Grace is mistaken for Dominique and imprisoned in the asylum. In *Quills,* the Marquis's fateful decision to write "one last story" triggers a riot and a fire, allowing Dr. Royer-Collard to regain control of the madhouse. An ambivalent Climax can be found in *Mystic River,* when Jimmy's questioning and killing of Dave is followed by the revelation that Dave wasn't guilty. Jimmy's goal is achieved, but at the cost of taking another life and betraying his childhood friends.

Setup, Complicating Action, Development, and Climax are usually followed, Thompson points out, by an epilogue that confirms the stability of the situation, while settling subplots and tying up motifs. The epilogue can be very brief, as with the last 50 seconds of *Flashdance,* which show Alex running out of her audition to meet Nick, waiting at curbside with her dog. By contrast, the epilogue of *Mystic River* takes about 6 minutes, tracing out the impact of Jimmy's vendetta on the neighborhood. *The Lord of the Rings: The Return of the King* (2003) must wrap up three feature-length installments, so it's not surprising that it jams ten epilogues into about 11 minutes. *Master and Commander: The Other Side of the World* (2003) protracts its epilogue in order to introduce a new line of action in the final scene, perhaps to prime the audience for a sequel.

More daring is the epilogue to *Cast Away.* During the Development section, a hairier but brawnier Chuck Nolan masters life on his island. Yet he yearns to return to his wife, and a stiff burst of wind allows him to launch his raft out to open sea. But the toiling through storms forms only half the

Climax. Once Chuck returns, he finds he cannot pick up where he left off; his wife has remarried and borne a child. After a passionate embrace in the rain, Chuck and his wife part, some 30 minutes after the Climax started. The film could end here, but *Cast Away* provides an epilogue that resolves several motifs and symmetrically frames the opening sequence. The film starts with a FedEx carrier picking up the package emblazoned with angel wings. Now, after leaving Kelly, Chuck confides in his friend that he considered suicide before he found his raft's sail in a parcel. So now he has to survive once more. Chuck, who lived by the clock before the plane crash, has become more laid back and is willing to wait: "Who knows what the tide could bring?" Seeking the person who sent the hopeful package, he meets a woman on the road and recognizes the angel-wings insignia on her truck. He stares meditatively after her, presumably thinking about following her home. The entire epilogue runs nearly nine minutes, and by bringing the wing motif to fulfillment it hints at the protagonist's entry into a new, more unhurried life.

Some films contain two or more protagonists, but their progress toward their goals tends to follow the four-part pattern Thompson traces. The simplest instances occur when several characters share the same goal, as in dangerous-mission movies like *The Guns of Navarone* (1961). In other cases, the protagonists' plotlines don't much influence one another. Take four college women, each hoping to find romance, and you have *Where the Boys Are* (1960). By the 25-minute mark, the protagonists have hit the beach for spring break, and the three most important ones have met prospective partners. During the Complicating Action, each of the four will become attached to one boy, except for Melanie, who is being callously passed around among Ivy League buddies. At the same time, each young woman defines her sexual morality. Mel's naive search for love makes her an easy target; the intellectual Merritt passes off intercourse as "like shaking hands"; Tuggles refuses to have sex until she's married; and Angie, played by Connie Francis, expresses her sexual energy by injecting some rock and roll into her boyfriend's eccentric jazz combo. The Development is largely delay, presenting three of the couples going out for dinner and dancing, while Mel is dumped by another cad. The film's Climax, starting about 20 minutes from the end, brings the principal trio to a moment of crisis. Mel is date-raped and, staggering into traffic, is struck down. Tuggles is enraged by her boyfriend's attention to a drunken stripper. Merritt, about to succumb to her beau, Rider, finds that he wants to refrain because he feels an "old-fangled thing called love."

In a grimly square resolution, the virginal Tuggles is rewarded with her laid-back boyfriend, Angie pairs up with her befuddled jazzman, and Merritt will stay in Florida with the hospitalized Melanie. Again, the epilogue not only ties up the main plot but brings back a motif. Merritt wanders out to the deserted beach. When she and Rider had first met, he had drawn a question mark in the sand, an invitation to an affair. Now, alone, Merritt traces another question mark, echoing her memory of Rider and indicating that her earlier certainties about casual sex have become cloudier. Rider joins her, and they talk about falling in love slowly.

Multiple-protagonist plots may bend their storylines to fit the four-part structure, but the fate of one or two characters is likely to dominate. In *Where the Boys Are*, it is Merritt's goals that change the most, offer the most complex set of choices, and carry the most weight at the close. Similarly, *Glengarry Glen Ross* (1992) shows four real estate hucksters clinging to their jobs, but two men become central to the structure. Shelley Levene is given pride of place at the start of the Setup, and Ricky Roma is spotlighted at the start of the Development. They occupy the most screen time, they share the strongest bond (gradually revealed), and the Climax turns on the failure of both to consummate the hot deals they made in earlier sections. When one or two protagonists are highlighted out of several, the four-part structure tends to be calibrated around their goals.

What variants are possible? In short features, the four sections may be significantly briefer. *Cotton Comes to Harlem* (1970), with its 94-minute running time, boasts parts running 21 to 23 minutes. In addition, as Thompson acknowledges, some features may contain only three large-scale sections.[54] If the parts are of typical 25-to-30-minute length, these films, such as *The Brood* (1983), *Pee-Wee's Big Adventure* (1985), and *Phone Booth* (2003), will have fairly short running times.

Longer films may have four longer-than-average parts (like *Mystic River* and *Airport*, 1970), or they may iterate a standard-sized part.[55] *Topaz* (1969) launches one Complicating Action set largely in New York and a second one in Cuba, before shifting the Development to Washington, D.C., and setting the Climax primarily in Paris. *In Cold Blood* (1967) seems to have two Climaxes. The Setup portion crosscuts the drifters Dick and Perry as they make their way to the Clutter home, and it ends with them pausing outside (at 29 minutes). The Complicating Action skips to the next morning, with the neighbors discovering the murders. This countersetup establishes the police investigation, intercut with Dick and Perry on their way to Mexico. The section ends (at about 53 minutes) with the main investigator Dewey worrying that he may not be able to prove the boys guilty. The Development deals with the boys' lounging around Mexico and deciding to return to the States; the turning point comes when they're picked up in Las Vegas (at about 80 minutes). What I take to be the first Climax consists of the police interrogation and the flashbacks to the fateful night when Dick and Perry slaughtered the Clutters (ending around 111 minutes). This settles the duo's fate. The film's second Climax lasts about 20 minutes and shows how the boys prepare themselves for trial and execution.[56]

Although Climax sections tend to run somewhat shorter than the others, Thompson emphasizes the rough equality among most large-scale parts. She suggests that writers and directors have intuitively sought to balance the sections.[57] Akiva Goldsman seems to agree, saying that the body of a screenplay consists of "four acts, or really three acts, but the second act is really two acts, so we might as well call it four acts, and they're generally 30 pages long and they generally have cycles of rising and falling action."[58] Thompson doesn't squeeze all films to fit the typical proportions, though, and she concedes that some movies may fail to shape their parts in felicitous ways. I'd pick *Big Trouble* (2002), a fairly short feature, as one instance. The Setup functions adequately at 26 minutes, initiating farcical story lines involving teenagers, parents, and hit men. But the Complicating Action, occupying only 17 minutes, is undernourished, chiefly because the protagonist's attraction to the boss's wife is consummated immediately. Similarly, the bomb that is put aboard the plane is activated at about 62 minutes, leaving only 12 minutes for the Climax. *Big Trouble* just lacks plot material in the middle and final stretches (perhaps because the makers deleted bomb-related scenes judged disturbing to post–9/11 America). Similarly, the likable *Office Space* (1999) offers an underwhelming Development. The three cubicle drones' hacking heist, the culmination of the Complicating Action, undergoes too few twists and is abruptly curtailed after only 15 minutes. Again, additional plot material would have fleshed out the portions to better-balanced lengths.

Marking out these large-scale parts isn't merely an academic exercise. Thompson's plot anatomy has implications for the shape of the viewer's experience. The Setup acts as exposition, laying out what we need in order to follow the story and to invest some feeling in the characters' problems. The Complicating Action sharpens interest by changing the terms of the Setup in ways that raise the emotional stakes and refine the assumptions about goals and character psychology we're building up. The Development, if handled adroitly, focuses our attention on the steps the characters must take to resolve their problems or broadens the film's range to include parallel story lines that shade the main one. The Climax seeks to present the resolution in a satisfying but not wholly predictable fashion, while the epilogue asks us to recall the path the protagonists have taken and measure their success or failure. Form, as Kenneth Burke once remarked, can be thought of as the psychology of the audience, and Hollywood plot structure engages the spectator in a carefully articulated mental and emotional experience.[59]

Tightening the Plot: Narrational Tactics

Thompson shows how to derive a plot's parts from a single principle—the ups and downs of character goals—rather than vague turning points that "spin the action in a new direction" (Field's description).[60] By examining a wide range of films closely, we can capture other important regularities in Hollywood storytelling, some of them not broached in the screenplay manuals. For instance, manuals haven't noted that most Hollywood films have always had two plotlines, at least one involving heterosexual romance. The love plot can be dominant or subordinate, and the goals and obstacles in each plotline can be coordinated in a variety of ways.[61] More small-scale is the device of the "dangling cause": making sure that each scene leaves some issues unresolved, to be picked up later. Similar to this is the "dialogue hook," the line at the end of a scene that links directly to the next action we see or hear.[62]

Although some manuals emphasize a "ticking clock" in the last act, appointments and deadlines have long served to organize a film's overall time scheme.[63] Instead of having characters assemble by lucky accident, an upcoming date or deal motivates a future scene and builds up our expectations as well. Take, for example, *Diner* (1982), which also illustrates how a slice-of-life plot is handled in Hollywood. The film follows five somewhat aimless young men during Christmas in 1959 Baltimore. The plot could have become as episodic as that of Fellini's layabout comedy-drama *I Vitelloni* (1953), but *Diner* has more long-range storylines. Several of the young men face crises in their relations with women, and these build to distinct, if sometimes muffled, Climaxes. College-boy Bill learns that his pregnant girlfriend wants neither to marry him nor to abort their baby. Shrevie finds married life dull, and his wife, Beth, is almost lured into a cruel affair with the reckless Boogie. In addition, Boogie is desperate to pay his gambling debts, and at the end he is obliged to take a tiresome job to cover them. At the end, these problems are resolved, albeit mostly in undramatic fashion, as when Shrevie quietly tells Beth he's bought a vacation trip to the Poconos.

Appointments and deadlines give *Diner*'s plot a finer-grained impetus. Hovering over the entire film is Eddie's upcoming marriage to Elise, but their union is threatened by his demand that Elise pass a tough football quiz. Throughout the film, Eddie's pals comment on the impending exam, and when Elise fails it, Eddie at first calls the wedding off. The film ends, however, with the wedding and the party afterward. Running alongside this line of action are Boogie's bets that he can seduce a blond beauty, causing his friends to spy on his dates for "verification." Most scenes hook smoothly to the next, and a great many point ahead to more distant conflicts. At intervals the pals meet at Falls Point Diner to rehash what's happened, update us on the passage of time, and schedule future meetings.

Appointments are a form of foreshadowing, a strategy that has been a stock-in-trade of Hollywood dramaturgy. One screenwriter recalls that George Cukor and producer Hal Wallis "really knew their craft. 'If we are going to do this here, we had better plant it there.'"[64] In *Grosse Point Blank* (1997), our hero, a contract killer, is given a souvenir pen, which he will use to stab another hit man. In *And Justice for All* (1979), lawyer Arthur Kirkland is forced to defend the odious Judge Fleming against a rape charge. Threaded through Arthur's frantic workday is a lowlife thug whom he is helping with a paternity suit. At the start of the Climax, as payback to Arthur, the thug digs up photographs showing Fleming with a hooker. When confronted with the pictures, Fleming admits he's guilty, which forces Arthur into a crisis of conscience and precipitates his decision to denounce his own client during the trial. The thug, at first just another defendant on Arthur's crowded schedule, becomes a key causal agent, but his obligation to Arthur is foreshadowed twice before the major revelation.

Like foreshadowing, the repeated object or line of dialogue serves as a standard cohesion device and can produce a tingle of pleasure if the audience doesn't see it coming. Rick's "Here's looking at you" from *Casablanca* would count as a classic example, but the practice is a constant of Hollywood moviemaking. The patch designed by each woman in *How to Make an American Quilt* (1995) presents imagery associated with her flashback story. Food is always a reliable motif. In *Two Weeks Notice* (2002), the lonely Lucy orders Chinese take-out, while her millionaire boss George scarfs down hotdogs on the street. During their courtship, she drunkenly boasts that during sex she can contort like a pretzel, a topic George raises when they embrace at the Climax. In the epilogue, she is phoning for Chinese food again, this time ordering for two.

The very saturation of motifs can become a movie's thematic core. Throughout *Serendipity* (2001), the relentlessly reappearing gloves, ice rink, five-dollar bill, García Márquez novel, and mentions of *Cool Hand Luke* are interpreted by the separated lovers as messages announcing that destiny intends them for one another. The aptly named *Signs* (2002) creates motifs whose propitious payoffs eventually restore the hero's religious faith. Here the tidiness of the classical plot becomes, cheekily enough, identified with the hand of God.

Today's screenwriting manuals sometimes acknowledge the importance of the motif. It has been called an "echo" (aiming to illustrate character change or the film's basic theme), or more ambitiously an "image system" operating through "subliminal communication."[65] One manual distinguishes between Touchstones (recurring objects that remind us of the story world before it was plunged into disorder) and Twitches (objects that symbolize the character's internal conflict).[66] In *Die Hard*, the photograph of the McClane family on Holly's desk counts as a Touchstone, while Holly's Rolex watch becomes a Twitch. Perhaps the angel-wing fabric in *Cast Away* serves Chuck Nolan as a Touchstone, while the Wilson soccer ball is more of a Twitch.

Motifs are woven into individual scenes, which have their own tightness of texture. As in the studio era, a scene tends to start with a brief expository portion establishing the time, place, relevant characters, and relation to the previous sequence. Then the scene advances the action by (a) picking up at least one dangling causal line from some earlier scene and (b) initiating a fresh causal line, all the while sprinkling motifs through.[67] This sounds rather abstract, so I'll draw an example from *Mystic Pizza* (1988). The scene is particularly instructive because it isn't a Climax, just a quick linking portion setting up more dramatic confrontations to come.

The setting is Leona's pizza parlor, and the scene quickly establishes that our three protagonists, Jojo, Kat, and Daisy are all at work. A customer routs Jojo and Bill in the middle of a passionate session in the women's restroom. The fact that they must steal moments whenever they can foreshadows the upcoming turning point in their romance, when Jojo's parents catch them making love in the kitchen and Bill insists that they get married. Now Jojo exuberantly boxes up a couple's leftover pizza, explaining that Leona won't reveal the secret of her delicious sauce. This is a major motif of the film and the source of the title's pun: the pizza in Mystic, Connecticut, is imbued with the mysterious flavor of young love.

The scene's initiating portion starts when Kat asks Jojo to switch workdays with her because Tim, the young husband for whom she's babysitting, "needs me on Friday." This sets up a new appointment and fosters expectations about the developing Tim-Kat romance. Daisy overhears and warns Jojo that she'll be contributing to the "downfall of a saint." The line picks up the sisters' conversation from the previous scene, in which Daisy teased the virginal Kat about her crush on Tim and tossed her a box of prophylactics. In the pizza-parlor banter, Kat replies to Daisy, "Let's talk about the preppy with the Porsche." Alluding to Daisy's romance with Charles, the line becomes a dialogue hook to the next shot: Charles driving Daisy up to his mansion. In addition, the Porsche is highlighted not only to stress class differences but also because later Daisy will vengefully destroy it. In eighty-eight seconds the pizza-parlor scene reminds us that Jojo and Bill must sneak furtive moments of lovemaking, it highlights two key motifs (the secret ingredient, the sports car), and it leads us smoothly toward the next phases of two romantic lines of action. This compact narration suits that blend of causally driven action and varied repetition of motif characteristic of classical storytelling.

Our scene gathers all three young women in one spot, but most of the film follows each one's pursuit of romance. In this way *Mystic Pizza* employs Hollywood's default approach to narration. We are given a wide range of knowledge but with strategic limitations. Throughout any film, we're typically not restricted to what only one character knows. Instead we're shuttled from character to character, knowing more than any one of them does, but still not knowing everything. So within the two major plotlines of *Mystic Pizza* we see each male figure more or less as the woman does; we don't observe Tim or Charles when the women aren't present. This local restriction of knowledge to the women can trigger surprises, as when Charles reveals his wealth or when Tim's wife arrives suddenly. Throughout the film, though, we compare the fates of Kat, Daisy, and Jojo with a breadth of awareness that adds emotional weight to their encounters. For instance, we see Tim the husband give Kat his sweater to wear home. As she arrives, seeing Daisy kiss Charles (rendered as Kat's optical point of view), Kat squeezes Tim's sweater. This gesture lends poignancy to the next few moments, when the jaundiced Daisy taunts Kat about the sweater ("Looks to me like he's putting the moves on you") and offers prophylactics for her next visit. Our intimate view of Kat's naive yearning here prepares us to recognize the depths of her sadness later when her dreams are dashed.

Detective stories often restrict us largely to what the investigator knows, but in most genres the narration shuttles among a few main characters, allowing us to enjoy a wide but not absolute range of knowledge.[68] More specifically, the narration often achieves its wider compass by crosscutting two or more lines of action. This was a common tactic of the silent cinema, and it has been developed to a high pitch since the 1960s. One tactic involves pitting the protagonist against a robust antagonist, both of whom are played by top-marquee stars. The film can then build its plot around a cat-and-mouse game leading to one or two moments of confrontation: Nazi-hunter Olivier versus Nazi Peck in *The Boys from Brazil* (1978), detective Pacino versus robber De Niro in *Heat* (1995), attorney Hoffman versus jury consultant Hackman in *Runaway Jury* (2003). Such films, however, typically mix in still more lines of action. *Runaway Jury* centers on a mysterious couple who infiltrate the jury, and the "limited omniscience" typical of the Hollywood plot saves for the Climax the revelation of their true purposes.

Within this pattern of omniscience, the narration can create vivid scene-to-scene cohesion. For example, instead of simply cutting from the end of one scene to the beginning of the next, shots from Scene A may alternate rapidly with shots from Scene B, often linked by sound bridges. An early example occurs in *The Godfather* (1972), when the discussion among Don Corleone and his sons about the upcoming meeting with Sollozzo is intercut with the start of the meeting itself. Francis Ford Coppola reprises this device in *The Rainmaker* (1997), and other directors have picked it up. In *Hannibal* (2001), shots of Clarice Starling briefing the FBI officials are intercut with shots of her driving to the Verger estate. This is a revision of the device of the dialogue hook, but here it's extended across several shots. Far from fragmenting the story, the rapid cuts weld adjacent scenes together tightly.

This example also illustrates how classical narration often addresses the audience quite self-consciously. Since the 1920s, this overtness follows remarkably strict patterns, reserved for certain types of scenes and certain stretches of the movie. For example, beginnings of films tend to talk to the viewer explicitly. As in the silent era, written titles may open the movie to supply the locale, the date, and anything else deemed relevant. They can sharpen suspense too. *The Hunt for Red October* (1990) begins with digital readouts over a map of the North Atlantic. These texts sketch the story context and anticipate the Climax, while summoning up an air of mystery:

> In November of 1984, shortly before Gorbachev came to power,
> a Typhoon-class Soviet sub surfaced just south of the Grand Banks.
> It then sank in deep water, apparently suffering a radiation problem.
> Unconfirmed reports indicated some of the crew were rescued.
>   But according to repeated statements by both Soviet and American
> governments, nothing of what you are about to see
>   . . . *ever happened.*

Such overtness reappears at the end of a film, today usually not via written title but through other conventional marks of closure. *Red October*'s epilogue shows Jack Ryan asleep on the plane home, beside the stuffed bear he had promised to bring his daughter. As the music rises and the credits roll, the stewardess at the end of the aisle draws the curtain shut. A closing book or door, characters turning from the camera and retreating as the camera pulls back, or even characters looking at the camera (Fig. 1.3)—these long-lived signs of direct address are still used to announce that the narration has ended.

1.3. *Family Plot:* Once we realize where
the diamond is hidden, the heroine shares
her (telepathic?) awareness with the audience.

Such opening and closing scenes are framed by credit sequences, another zone of overt narration. The initial credit sequence became more pliable in the 1950s, sometimes appearing after a curtain-raising scene or well into the first reel. In later decades, initial credits might come before the action proper, or after a teaser scene, as in the James Bond films, or as neutral titles laid over developing plot action (e.g., *The China Syndrome*, 1979; *Groundhog Day*, 1993). During the 1990s, films began to launch the story action on the soundtrack while the credits appeared on a blank background. By the turn of the century, some films were omitting title and credits altogether, providing only the logos of the production and distribution companies.

When credits do appear, their narrational functions have remained largely the same as they were in the studio era. Credits are either discreetly informative or overt and appealing in their own right, setting a tone and sowing motifs to sprout in the story. A new convention of dramas centering on personal relationships is to show snapshots of the principals growing from childhood to adulthood under the titles (*Mystic Pizza*, 1988; *Tully*, 2000). The now-celebrated credits of *Se7en* (1995) and *Fight Club* (1999) hint at a diabolical darkness driving the plot.[69] The credits can tantalize us with hints about how the action will develop, as when *The Thomas Crown Affair* (1999) anticipates the hero's robbery scheme by shuffling letters among actors' names.

In the studio era, closing credits were perfunctory "The End" titles, since most workers were under contract and never received billing. With the development of the package-unit system of independent production, every worker was a freelancer and needed public mention. During the 1970s closing credits swelled to several minutes, and filmmakers tried to energize them with a prolonged musical score and, occasionally, a continuing stream of footage. Shots would be rerun (*M*A*S*H*, 1970), or entirely new scenes, typically an extended epilogue, might appear (as in the CB wedding ceremony under the final credits of *Citizens Band,* 1977). *Cannonball Run* (1981) accompanied the credits with bloopers culled from NG ("No Good") takes, a practice picked up in the *Rush Hour* series and parodied at the end of *A Bug's Life* (1998). Such innovations reinforce the tone of playful allusion we find throughout the period, while maintaining the tradition of presenting highly overt narration at the film's conclusion.

Further bits of story action may even be scattered among the final credits. The "credit cookies" of *Airplane!* (1980) bring back several running gags. *Wild Things* (1998) intercuts its credits with new scenes of backstory and offscreen chicanery, with the final insertion providing the plot's true epilogue. *Two Weeks Notice* plugs a crucial story hole in its very last image. Lucy has taken a job as a corporate attorney for George Wade, in exchange for his promise not to destroy her neighborhood's Community Center. The Climax starts when George's brother orders him to level the center for a condominium project. Confined to Lucy's point of view, we learn that George has found a compromise. Their romance is resolved in a tidy epilogue, but the end credits start without telling us how George saved the center. Only after the credits have rolled does a final shot present a postcard picture of the center, with the condo complex built on top of it.

Classical narration tends to be overt early on—in opening titles, at the start of the film's action—before gliding into a less explicit mode. Likewise, in any scene, the narration tends to be more noticeable at the expositional phase than it is in the development. A distant view of the setting or a shot of a sign is addressed to us, helping to establish the locale before we are plunged into an ongoing stream of action. Junctures between scenes, such as shifts in time, tend to be signaled sharply and may set up key motifs. At the end of the opening scene of *Funny Girl* (1968), Fanny relaxes in a seat of the empty theater, murmuring, "Ziegfeld is waiting for me. For me," and tipping her head back. "See, you were wrong, Mrs. Strakosh." Dissolve to young Fanny before a mirror as the offscreen Mrs. Strakosh tells her a showgirl has to be pretty. Similarly, in the prologue of *Terms of Endearment* (1983), after the death of her father, Emma watches her mother, Aurora, return from the funeral (Fig. 1.4). Later Emma cuddles with Aurora, who asks, "What are you going to do with this hair?" (Fig. 1.5). Dissolve to several years later, with a similar shot of Emma watching the movers and nervously twisting her hair as Aurora had done (Fig. 1.6). The action settles down into a less self-consciously presented conversation between Emma and her friend, but the influence of Aurora's fussiness on her daughter has been established through a motif of behavior.

1.4. *Terms of Endearment:* Emma after the funeral.

1.5. Emma and Aurora, initiating the crucial gesture . . .

1.6. . . . that Emma will carry into adulthood.

One type of scene, no matter where it occurs in the film, is a highly overt mark of narration: the montage sequence.[70] Its main purpose was to condense a large-scale process or an extensive passage of time, so that a trip could be shown through a montage of travel stickers pasted onto a suitcase, or a trial rendered by a cascade of newspaper headlines. Nothing indicates more clearly the persistence of classical construction than this summary device. We get montage sequences when *Valley of the Dolls* (1967) follows a young actress's grueling training, when *Jaws* (1975) presents the arrival of tourists at Amity Island, when *Tootsie* (1982) shows its hero-in-drag becoming a TV star, and when *Bram Stoker's Dracula* (1992) conveys the count's frenzied attack on the crew of the ship bearing him to England. The montages in *Drumline* summarize drills, performances, Devon's coursework, and most crucially his collaboration with the percussion leader in writing a snappy cadence. Montage sequences can work on a broad canvas too; in the studio era, the flamboyant montages in *The Roaring Twenties* (1939) encapsulated entire eras. The wide-ranging summary has remained an important resource, as when the opening of *The Front* (1976) uses newsreel footage to sketch the red-baiting atmosphere at the start of the Cold War. Just as improved optical-printing technology facilitated the flashy wipes and superimpositions of 1930s montages, today's computer-generated imagery has encouraged dynamic graphics (see page 15). Today's montage usually links shots by cuts rather than by dissolves or wipes, and the music is likely to be a pop song, but we accept the sequence's direct address as unquestioningly as audiences did seventy years ago.

Appointments, deadlines, causally dense scene construction, a balance of narrow and wider ranges of knowledge, passages of overtness balanced with less self-conscious ones—these narrational techniques work together to create the distinctive texture of the Hollywood film. Any scene will tend to link not only to what came before and what will follow but also, thanks to long-range goals and recurrent motifs, to sequences at a greater remove. Given the sturdy framework of character aims and psychological change (often no more than learning to be a nicer person), the classical film seeks to give each scene a propulsive interest. The result is a stable, powerful body of conventions shaping virtually every film.

Those conventions have remained in force throughout the poststudio era, constantly and sometimes ingeniously applied to fresh material. Hollywood has always updated its stories by building on current interests and emerging social trends. Just as the growth of suburbia gave Hollywood ideas for *No Down Payment* (1957) and *Bachelor in Paradise* (1961), the arrival of Generation X as a pop-sociology tag yielded romantic comedies like *Singles* (1992) and *Reality Bites* (1994). In *Norma Rae* (1979), *Boyz N the Hood* (1991), *Philadelphia* (1993), and *Boys Don't Cry* (2002) classical narrative structure and narration dramatize social critiques and present visions of equality, tolerance, and justice.[71] Religious doctrines can be squeezed into the format too; witness the evangelical movies *The Omega Code* (1999) and *Left Behind* (2000). Such changing subjects and themes are worth studying in their own right, but a complete account of Hollywood storytelling needs to recognize how the dominant tradition assimilates them to its formal demands. Bazin was right: the "classical" art of the American cinema is most demonstrable in "its fertility when it comes into contact with new elements," integrating them into its distinctive "style of cinematic narration."[72]

2. PUSHING THE PREMISES

Most of the four or five hundred theatrical films released each year continue Hollywood's narrative tradition straightforwardly, through practiced tactics of subject or style. The average filmmaker asks: What well-tested devices tell my story most effectively? Some filmmakers, however, have sought to refine the tradition, to explore its principles more thoroughly. These creators ask, in effect: How can I raise the premises to new levels of achievement? How can I revive a defunct or disreputable genre? How can I extend ideas that the studio system has failed to explore fully? How can I make causal connections more felicitous, twists more unexpected, character psychology more involving, excitement more intense, motifs more tightly woven? How can I display my own virtuosity? When filmmakers succeed at such tasks, they reveal the range and flexibility of classical premises.

Many of the best-remembered films of the 1960s and 1970s did just that. *Chinatown* became the ultimate neo-noir movie partly because changing standards of screen morality gave a raw vision of urban corruption greater sway ("She's my sister! She's my daughter!"). In addition, the film boasted striking narrative strategies, including its clever use of the motifs of water and vision, its strict adherence to Jake Gittes's range of knowledge (allowing for maximal surprises), and its bleak ending. *Bullitt* (1968), *Butch Cassidy and the Sundance Kid* (1969), *The French Connection* (1971), *The Last Detail* (1973), *Jaws* (1975), *Star Wars* and later *Airplane!* (1980), *Raiders of the Lost Ark* (1981), *E. T. The Extraterrestrial* (1982), *Tootsie* (1982), *Ghostbusters* (1984), *Back to the Future* (1985), *Terminator 2: Judgment Day* (1991), *Jurassic Park, Sleepless in Seattle* (1993), *The Lion King* (1994), *Forrest Gump* (1994), and other well-remembered films might best be thought of as efforts to set the bar ever higher. They have become contemporary classics by virtue of their ability to play by the rules, while also showing that those rules harbor inexhaustible potential.

New Niches: From Genre Ecology to Worldmaking

At the start of the 1960s, Hollywood's most high-profile films were historical costume pictures (*Cleopatra*, 1963; *Dr. Zhivago*, 1965), adaptations of Broadway plays, especially musicals (*The Music Man*, 1962; *The Sound of Music*, 1965), World War II epics (*The Longest Day*, 1962), and adaptations of trashy bestsellers (*The Carpetbaggers*, 1964). The new generation undertook few projects in these genres. Although Mike Nichols directed *Who's Afraid of Virginia Woolf?* (1966), and Coppola directed *Finian's Rain-*

bow (1968) and wrote *Patton* (1970), most young directors tackled genres that had attracted little notice in the studio era.

Crime films, for instance, were a staple of B-production in the 1940s and 1950s, but many of their directors, like Anthony Mann and Nicholas Ray, graduated to A-genres. There was room for a revival of the crime movie, now sold as a high-budget product with souped-up versions of traditional appeals. *Bonnie and Clyde* (1967) gave the outlaw-lovers genre a sheen lacking in Poverty Row predecessors like *Gun Crazy* (1949). *Bullitt* came to prominence for both its low-affect protagonist and its thrilling car chase through San Francisco, and soon *The French Connection* offered a still more alienated hero and a more hair-raising ride. *Bonnie and Clyde, Bullitt,* and *The French Connection* were among the year's top-five box office hits, something no crime film had achieved before, and *The French Connection,* astonishingly, won five Academy Awards (Best Picture, Best Director, Best Actor, Best Screenplay, and Best Editing). The genre had become top-drawer, and thereafter crime films would compete to display ever more rousing fights and pursuits.

Horror films, with few exceptions, had been even lower in the hierarchy than crime movies. Despite the achievements of Tod Browning, James Whale, and Jacques Tourneur, it was hard to argue that any peer of Hitchcock or Hawks had toiled in the nether regions. Still, horror remained vigorous in the low-budget sector, achieving a peak of popularity in George Romero's *Night of the Living Dead* (1968).[73] Occult fiction and nonfiction were creeping onto bestseller lists. At the A-level the breakthrough film was *Rosemary's Baby* (1968), adapted from Ira Levin's novel. This film paved the way for another William Friedkin triumph, *The Exorcist* (1973). The top-grossing film of its year and Warner Bros.'s most profitable film up to that time, it was nominated for ten Oscars and won two. The obscene language and grisly facial effects stunned audiences, but the film elevated itself with an obviously expensive, slow-burning prologue in Iraq, a disquieting music track (*Tubular Bells* and concert works by George Crumb), and themes of Catholic sacrifice and redemption. It made gruesome horror respectable.

The phenomenal success of *The Exorcist* accompanied the blossoming of horror in popular fiction (e.g., Tom Tryon's *The Other,* 1972, and Stephen King's *Carrie,* 1974). *Jaws* (1975), *King Kong* (1976), *Jaws 2* (1978), and *Alien* (1978) were among the top box-office grossers of their years. By 1980 horror had moved up the genre ladder. Ambitious directors like Steven Spielberg, John Carpenter, Brian De Palma, Wes Craven, Joe Dante, David Cronenberg, and Sam Raimi became eager to outshock their competitors. In ensuing decades, the genre attracted major talents, including Coppola (*Bram Stoker's Dracula,* 1992), Neil Jordan (*Interview with the Vampire,* 1994), Nichols

(*Wolf,* 1994), Tim Burton (*Sleepy Hollow,* 1999), and even, arguably, Martin Scorsese in his remake of *Cape Fear* (1991). Horror became what the Western had been for the studio era: a genre ranging from the lowest to the highest budget levels and affording plenty of room for individual expression.

Science fiction underwent a comparable upgrade. The genre was associated primarily with drive-in movies and cheap TV, but big-budget efforts like *The War of the Worlds* (1953), *Forbidden Planet* (1956), *The Time Machine* (1960), and *Fantastic Voyage* (1966) hinted at greater respectability. *2001: A Space Odyssey* (1968) made science fiction metaphysically serious by using strategies similar to those later employed by *The Exorcist*—striking special effects, a score culled from experimental music—but added brooding silences and a teasing conclusion. *2001* became the benchmark against which later science fiction directors had to define their work. *THX-1138* (1971), *Soylent Green* (1973), and *Logan's Run* (1976) set Orwellian plots in the dehumanized future, while *Silent Running* (1972) humanized its astronaut and his robotic pal. Stanley Kubrick had developed motion-control technology to create a ballet of space vehicles, but *Star Wars* (1977) used it for swooping dogfights. In the infinite spaces where Kubrick felt a terrifying silence, Lucas heard the trumpet call of adventure; instead of a space odyssey, a space opera. Innovations often took the form of genre-blending. The SF family adventure (*Close Encounters of the Third Kind*), the SF horror film (*Alien*), the SF war movie (*Aliens,* 1986), and SF noir (*Blade Runner*) all opened new niches that sustained variants for decades, from *The Terminator* (1984), *RoboCop* (1987), and *Alien Nation* (1988) to *Starship Troopers* (1997), *Pitch Black* (2000), *Equilibrium* (2002), and beyond.

The *Star Wars* series fostered the reemergence of fantasy, another minor genre of the studio years. After *The Wizard of Oz* (1939), fantasies had largely been the province of animated film, of special-effects master Ray Harryhausen (*The Seventh Voyage of Sinbad,* 1958), and Disney heroic fantasies (*Twenty Thousand Leagues under the Sea,* 1954) and fantasy farces like *The Shaggy Dog* (1959) and *The Absent-Minded Professor* (1961). The bigger-budget *Planet of the Apes* (1968) spawned one of the earliest franchises (racking up four sequels in 1970–1973). George Miller (*Mad Max,* 1979), Ron Howard (*Willow,* 1988), and other beginning directors indulged in heroic fantasy, while the ever-venturesome Ridley Scott tried it in *Legend* (1985). The Disney legacy is evident in *Ghostbusters* (1984), *Back to the Future, Beetlejuice* (1988), *The Addams Family* (1991), and *The Mask* (1994). New special-effects technology made fantasy comedy popular for G-rated fare (*Honey, I Shrunk the Kids,* 1989; *Casper,* 1995; *Flubber,* 1997) and teenage pictures. Heroic fantasy took some time to escape its ties to pulp magazines and children's books, but in 2003–2004 it found a place near the top of the genre heap with the Oscar-winning final installment of *The Lord of the Rings*. As I write this, studios are developing C. S. Lewis's Narnia stories and Philip Pullman's *His Dark Materials* into fantasy franchises.

Comic-book movies were scarcely a genre in the studio era, but they became a central one with the arrival of the blockbuster. Before the 1970s nearly all live-action adaptations of cartoon strips and comic books had been B-pictures. (An exception is the protocamp *Prince Valiant*, 1955.) When it became evident that the audience for megapictures was largely teenagers, major productions began drawing on comic-book characters, and *Superman: The Movie* (1978) proved that such projects could attract large audiences. Paradoxically, while Hollywood was investing in the genre, readership of comic books plunged and never recovered; young viewers evidently preferred their superheroes on the screen. As the century turned, Marvel Comics announced that it was less interested in publishing comic books than in generating characters to be spun off into media franchises.[74] In earlier decades, virtually no top-drawer director would make a comic-book movie, but the contributions of Warren Beatty (*Dick Tracy*, 1990) and Sam Mendes (*Road to Perdition*, 2002) testified to the genre's triumph as much as the box-office earnings of *Batman* (1989), *Men in Black* (1997), *Blade* (1998), *X-Men* (2000), and *Spider-Man* (2002) did. A new generation of fans like Kevin Smith and the Wachowski brothers began creating movies that virtually were comic books (*Dogma*, 1999; the *Matrix* trilogy, 1997, 2003), and "graphic novels" like *Ghost World*, *American Splendor*, and *Sin City* transmogrified into indie movies.

Once the new genres were established, ambitious directors could tweak them in idiosyncratic ways. Tim Burton gave a Gothic-absurdist twist to demonic possession (*Beetlejuice*, 1988), to mad scientist horror (*Edward Scissorhands*, 1990), to comic-book fantasy (*Batman* and *Batman Returns*, 1992), and to flying-saucer invasion (*Mars Attacks!* 1996). M. Night Shyamalan became the Hitchcock of the supernatural thriller, replacing the master's sardonic humor with a suffocating dread. *The Sixth Sense* (1999) infuses a ghost story with hopeless yearning; *Unbreakable* (2000) creates a melancholy superhero; *Signs* (2002) steeps its alien-invasion tale in grim religiosity; and the inhabitants of *The Village* (2004) live in the shadow of forest monsters. While Burton's scenes can barely contain their manic grotesquerie, Shyamalan seeks a hushed atmosphere in which an out-of-focus figure in the background or the sound of a snapping bramble can trigger anxieties. Both directors use the intensified-continuity style I'll describe in the next essay to put their own stamp on genres that rose to prominence in the blockbuster era.

Action movies fill acreage at our video stores, though the term apparently didn't become common until the late 1970s. Today the genre includes films about crime, war, and adventure, but the final category included distinguished representatives during the studio years. *The Black Pirate* (1926), *Gunga Din* (1939), *Four Feathers* (1939), *The Sea Hawk* (1940): these are prototypes of the adventure movie, and although they were classics, there remained room for young talent to bring new skills and technology to the genre. Some premises of the adventure film of our period were laid down by mission-team items like *The Guns of Navarone* (1961), *The Train* (1964), and *Where Eagles Dare* (1968), but the new version of the genre was crystallized in *Raiders of the Lost Ark*. Spielberg and Lucas cite a love of Saturday-matinee serials as their inspiration, but another influence would seem to be the James Bond films.[75] "Steven and I come from the visceral generation," remarked Lucas. "We enjoyed the emotional highs we got from movies and realized that you could crank up the adrenaline to a level way beyond what people were doing."[76] Again, it was a matter of raising a B-genre to the A-level by enhancing production values and making it an occasion for directorial virtuosity. The hairbreadth escapes that open *Raiders* are pulled off with a crisp panache utterly foreign to B-serials, as well as to most 1960s studio efforts.

Other minor genres were rehabilitated. Children's films, again Disney territory, were reinvented as auteur statements (*E. T. The Extraterrestrial*) or displays of technical wizardry (*Who Framed Roger Rabbit?*, 1988). Could one make the teen picture, associated with the despised *Beach Party* cycle at American International Pictures (AIP), a vehicle of personal expression? In *American Graffiti* (1973) Lucas proved you could, and directors who developed the genre included John Hughes (*Pretty in Pink*, 1986), Michael Lehman (*Heathers*, 1989), and Cameron Crowe (*Say Anything . . .*, 1989). Parody was rare in the studio era, confined mostly to variety-show skits on radio and television, but it flourished in feature films by Mel Brooks (*Blazing Saddles*, 1974), Woody Allen (*Take the Money and Run*, 1969; *Sleeper*, 1973), and the directorial team of Jim Abrahams and David and Jerry Zucker (*Airplane!*, 1980). Most recently, the biography, long a stuffy prestige item (*Wilson*, 1944; *MacArthur*, 1977), has been revived with lesser-known eccentrics as the subject. So we get biopics about a pornographer (*The People vs. Larry Flynt*, 1996), a triple-X star (*Wonderland*, 2003), a world-class imposter (*Catch Me If You Can*, 2002), and a game-show host who may be a CIA hit man (*Confessions of a Dangerous Mind*, 2002).

Of course, some directors sought to work in well-worn genres, but for ambitious filmmakers this could be tricky. It was hard to improve on your predecessors, so new angles of approach needed to be found. One tactic was to deflate one's sources. The Western, a central genre into the 1960s, suffered assaults from two sides. The cycle of comic Westerns—*Cat Ballou* (1965), *Support Your Local Sheriff* (1969), and *Support Your Local Gunfighter* (1971)—treated the conventions with amiable disrespect. At the other extreme, there was a cycle of debunking Westerns. Sergio Leone and Peckinpah redefined the genre's conception of heroism by revamping the stereotype of the "good bad man" into the just-barely-good bad man. *Soldier Blue* (1970), *Little Big Man* (1970), and others sought to expose the genre's racism. By the mid-1970s, major filmmakers found the Western played out, and even Leone and Peckinpah didn't return to it. For every *Dances with Wolves* (1990) and *Unforgiven* (1992), there were many misfires. Despite audiences' well-established indifference, however, directors at the dawn of the new millennium struggled to revive the genre (*Open Range*, 2003; *The Missing*, 2003; *The Alamo*, 2004).

When we ask why virtually no great Westerns or musicals or domestic melodramas are made anymore, one reason may be that our directors and writers can't find anything to add to the classic statements in those genres. All the best possibilities seem to have been mined.[77] Accordingly, lesser genres of the past can become important today because they offer more room for originality and ingenuity. Of course, directors may have gravitated toward them out of personal affinity—if they lacked fondness for the genre, their attitude might be Altmanesque—but regardless of their taste, the "genre ecology" that filmmakers confronted helped push them toward sparsely populated niches.

As these genres came to the fore, older directors who could not adapt faded from the scene. The mid-1970s decline of so many veterans isn't wholly due to age and distance from younger tastes. Most of these directors had no skills in the new genres. A few who did, like Don Siegel, could keep going a bit longer. Somewhat younger filmmakers rolled with the punches. The versatile John Boorman began his career with the Beatles rip-off *Catch Us If You Can* (1965) and achieved enough prestige to direct *Deliverance* (1972), but he was not above dabbling in the rising genres of science fiction (*Zardoz*, 1974), horror (*Exorcist II: The Heretic*, 1977), and heroic fantasy (*Excalibur*, 1981).

It may also be that many older directors weren't able to grasp the central importance of intense and extended physical action in these new trends. The 1930s had prized rapid pacing, but by the 1950s Hitchcock, Ford, Hawks, and

John Huston weren't kinetic directors by modern standards. Fuller, Mann, Richard Brooks, and Robert Aldrich had a stronger commitment to vivid physicality, but they weren't suited to the rehabilitation of lowly genres like horror and science fiction; for their generation, war films and Westerns were the salient action genres. In the next essay, I'll examine what Geoff King has called the "impact aesthetic" as a stylistic option, but here it's worth noting how it sustained the new genre ecology. The shark pursuit in *Jaws* and the truck stunts of *Raiders* display an aggressiveness quite foreign to the relaxed, noodling rhythms of the animal hunt in *Hatari!* or the sobriety of the cross-border chase climaxing *Torn Curtain* (1966). To compare *Rio Bravo* (1959) with a film inspired by it, *Assault on Precinct 13* (1976), is to gauge the extent to which up-to-date visceral violence, even handled with a certain rigor, demanded a harsh directorial sensibility. Still, Hitchcock's increasingly ghoulish murder scenes (*Psycho* [1960]; *Torn Curtain* [1966]; *Frenzy*, 1972) and the shock tactics of post-*Psycho* films like *What Ever Happened to Baby Jane?* (1962), along with *Bonnie and Clyde* (1967) and *The Wild Bunch* (1969), probably did help push Friedkin, Spielberg, and others toward genres that showcased what would come to be known as "energy."

Granted, what we might call energetic pacing was a distinguishing mark of studio-era Hollywood, especially of comedies, gangster films, and musicals. At Warner Bros. Darryl F. Zanuck demanded that *The Crowd Roars* (1932) be told "in the modern manner of compressed drama. . . . What we want to achieve is the rapid story progression that we had in *The Public Enemy* and *The Dawn Patrol.*"[78] Surprisingly, however, from 1930 to 1960, most films averaged 2 to 4 minutes per scene, and many scenes ran 4 minutes or more. During the 1950s, A-movies tended to move rather slowly. Hawks and Hitchcock liked leisurely exposition, even when they employed dramatic curtain-raisers like the bar fight in *Rio Bravo* and the rooftop chase in *Vertigo*. The screenwriter for *Family Plot* (1976) objected to the rather large chunk of backstory laid out in the séance opening the movie, but Hitchcock stuck to it.[79]

The veterans looked outdated in a period of helter-skelter storytelling. In films made after 1961 most scenes run between 1.5 and 3 minutes. This practice reflects the contemporary screenwriter's rule of thumb that a scene should consume no more than two or three pages (with a page counting as a minute of screen time). The average two-hour script, many manuals suggest, should contain forty to sixty scenes.[80] In more recent years, the tempo has become even faster. *All the Pretty Horses* (2000) averages 76 seconds per scene, while *Singles* (1992) averages a mere 66 seconds. One reason for this acceleration would seem to be the new habit of getting into and out of scenes quickly. Instead of setting up the locale and characters gradually, as was done in most A-pictures of the 1960s and 1970s, filmmakers nowadays often cut straight from the falling action of one scene to the rising action of the next.

Similarly, post-1960 movies rely somewhat more on crosscutting than did 1930s–1950s films. An opening is likely to introduce characters in swift alternation (Mom at home/Dad driving to work/Mom at home/Dad arriving at work) rather than in separate episodes (Mom at home followed by Dad at work). By switching unpredictably across locales, crosscutting keeps the viewer riveted to the screen. Rapid shifts of setting, recalling 1920s silent cinema, are likely to dominate the film's last act in particular, largely because of the deadline or "ticking clock" that governs the outcome.

Promoting minor genres, filling them with visceral action, and picking up the pace are some common innovations made by modern Hollywood. Less widespread, but becoming very striking in recent years, is what we may call "worldmaking." More and more films have been at pains to offer a rich, fully furnished ambience for the action. In the studio era, set designers and dressers were concerned about creating a reasonably concrete milieu, but in the period we're considering, this effort was carried to a new level. The first strong push, I believe, was provided by Kubrick's *2001: A Space Odyssey*, which was researched as no science-fiction film ever had been. Its sets teemed with casually inserted props donated by the likes of Bell Telephone, the Defense Department, and General Dynamics. The trappings are as overwhelming as the fancy Star Gate optics: Kubrick had given thought to what an astronaut's meal might look like, or how VoicePrint identification would work. As if in reply to the antiseptic primness of Kubrick's spaceship, Ridley Scott demanded a grubbier but no less detailed environment for *Alien*. He pressed further in *Blade Runner*, moving Deckard, the replicants, and Rachael through neo-neo-brutalist cityscapes, rooms strewn with detritus, and trembling, hazy light. The minutiae accumulate into a kind of information overload, so that in straining to pick out the protagonist and to hear recognizable English in the Babel of CitySpeak you may not notice that the citizens carry illuminated umbrella handles through perpetual acid rain. Scott called his strategy "layering" and remarked that "a film is like a seven-hundred-layer cake."[81]

Layered worlds, complete with brand names and logos, became essential to science fiction, but the tactic found its way into other genres too. Perhaps because 1970s location filming turned Hollywood away from spotless sets, filmmakers sought richly articulated worlds that were grimy. Pressrooms in 1950s newspaper movies are far less messy than that in *The Paper* (1994) and *All the President's Men* (1976), which contains trash from the real

Washington Post office. One need only compare the airy and tidy sets of *Ben-Hur* (1959) to the minutiae-stuffed locales of *Gladiator* (2000).

Star Wars signaled the marketing potential of massive detailing. Lucas remarked in 1977 that inventing everything from scratch—clothes, silverware, customs—created a "multi-layer reality": "In films, you generally have a given culture, a given time-period, some social factors to which the film's story refers. I had nothing."[82] Unlike Kubrick and Scott, though, Lucas unrolled his story across a series of films, and from the outset this world spilled off the screen. Lucas, who published a comic book and a novelization of *Star Wars* before the film was released, understood immediately that cross-media worldmaking was one way to extend the studio idea of a B-series.[83] Audiences who had visited Disneyland and had seen comic-book characters become TV heroes were ready to enter a self-contained universe straddling many media.[84] The richer the world, the more likely fans were to explore it. The *Star Wars* tale became a saga, its universe like that of an Advent calendar, where something new can be imagined behind every window. The feature films provide the story's anchoring moments, but spin-offs, prequels, and detours could be found in ancillaries—novels, comics, board games, videogames, and theme-park rides. "You can spend your entire life perfecting a new world when you create its every piece," Lucas remarked.[85] He tinkered with his universe, eventually reissuing the first *Star Wars* trilogy with more cross-references jammed into its frames.

Story comprehension was now multidimensional: a novice could follow the basic plot, but she could enjoy it even more if she rummaged for microdata in the film or outside it. By the turn of the century, several filmmakers were taking worldmaking even further. The makers of the *Lord of the Rings* trilogy shrewdly anticipated the demand for more ample treatment of Middle Earth by publishing tie-in books that gave background on characters and history. The creators of *The Matrix* were more daring, spreading key plot points across animated films and videogames.[86] To track the films fully, one would have to enter the Matrix through many media portals. Remarking on the eagerness of prospering young professionals to plunge into these imagined worlds, a British newspaper noted: "We are all nerds now."[87]

Archnerd Quentin Tarantino was in the lead. *Pulp Fiction* (1994) conjured up a city thick with references to movies and TV shows (*Saturday Night Fever, Happy Days*) and fictitious brand names (Red Apple cigarettes, Big Kahuna burgers). Tarantino admired novelists like Larry McMurtry, who "moves characters from book to book": "When I sell my movies, I retain the rights to characters so I can follow them. I can follow Pumpkin and Honey Bunny or anybody and it's not *Pulp Fiction II*."[88] He must have been delighted when Steven Soderbergh's *Out of Sight* (1998) suggested that it took place in the same Elmore Leonard Florida as *Jackie Brown* (1997): an FBI agent played by Michael Keaton appears in both films. With the *Kill Bill* movies (2003–2004), Tarantino cobbled together a hermetically sealed universe out of Asian action pictures, Eurotrash exploitation, and Japanese anime. Movie references, instead of ornamenting a freestanding storyline, coalesced into a virtual world. Anything, even the mere presence of actor Sonny Chiba, turned into an homage. Unlike Lucas, who quietly modeled *Star Wars* space battles on World War II combat movies, Tarantino signaled his sources in order to tease pop connoisseurs into a new level of engagement. Websites, both authorized and amateur, cataloged the dozens of films cited in *Kill Bill*'s two "volumes."[89] After completing volume 2, Tarantino remarked that he was reluctant to leave this world behind, and he floated the prospect of an anime prequel and a live-action sequel.[90] André Malraux spoke of art history as having become *le musée imaginaire,* the museum without walls; Tarantino gave Geek Chic an imaginary video store.

Density of another sort characterizes one more strategy for elaborating classical premises. In *Storytelling in the New Hollywood,* after outlining principles of classical narrative patterning, Thompson analyzes several films that display an extraordinary degree of "unobtrusive craftsmanship": "The glory of the Hollywood system lies in its ability to allow its finest scriptwriters, directors, and other creators to weave an intricate web of character, event, time, and space that can seem transparently obvious."[91] One prototype is the wedding party that opens *The Godfather.* Running about 26 minutes, this sequence introduces nearly all the major characters and most of the dramatic issues that will occupy the film. Sonny bickers with his wife and seduces another woman. Michael assures Kay that he isn't part of his family's business. Johnny Fontane asks Don Vito to help him with the Hollywood producer Woltz. Tom Hagen reminds Don Vito that they will meet with Sollozzo next week. The more one looks, the more foreshadowing one finds. Michael's being late for the wedding portrait establishes his distance from the family business. He explains to Kay how Luca Brasi helped with his father's business, setting up Luca's role in spying on Sollozzo for Don Vito. Even the first conversation we see, the Godfather's discussion with the undertaker who demands vengeance for his daughter's abuse, plays a role later: the grateful undertaker will make Sonny's perforated corpse presentable. The wedding celebration assembles all the dramatis personae, and the sequence, alternating the garden party with the machinations in Don Vito's study, creates an omniscient narration smoothly linking characters and anticipating the trajectory of the rest of the film.

In analyzing ten other films from the post-1960 era, Thompson shows that some go beyond standard causal cohesion. They take an almost swaggering pride in loading every rift with ore. Each scene has several purposes; lines of dialogue point forward in unexpected ways; visual and aural motifs, often discernible only after several viewings, quietly knit together. In *The Silence of the Lambs* (1991), for instance, a welter of subtle motifs lies alongside more marked ones. Everybody notices the recurring death's-head moth, but few viewers probably catch the butterfly-patterned wallpaper in the first victim's bedroom. We recall the motif of the lambs because they function as Clarice's "inner motivation," but Thompson points out that Hannibal Lecter's drawing of Florence's Duomo "as seen from the Belvedere," expresses his yearning for a cell with a "beautiful view" *(belvedere)* while also pointing to the killer's lair in Belvedere, Ohio.[92] There is also the progression of names:

> The beginning of the setup presents the protagonist as "Starling," then "Clarice," then "Starling, Clarice M." In contrast, the epilogue begins with a man at the podium, announcing: "Clarice M. Starling." Clarice steps up to receive her badge as a special agent at the graduation ceremony. By now she has achieved her two goals, to catch the serial killer and to become an FBI agent. The motif of names thus traces the progress of her growth. The epilogue begins with her full name, in correct order, being given for the only time in the film.[93]

Thompson goes on to show patterns of implication arising from Lecter's use of names, including the revealing anagrams he concocts for Clarice's investigation.

In these ways *Silence of the Lambs* takes traditional Hollywood principles of unity to another level. The film becomes "maximally" classical—more classical, we might say, than it needs to be. Thompson shows that the same qualities operate in *Groundhog Day* (1993), in which Phil, the cynical weatherman who has survived dozens of iterations of the same day and has earned Rita's love, is framed in front of a quilt whose groundhog pattern creates a halo around him (Fig. 1.7). Several of Thompson's exemplary movies, such as *Tootsie* (1982), *Back to the Future* (1985), *The Hunt for Red October* (1990), and *Hannah and Her Sisters* (1986) illustrate the hyperclassical strategy. Likewise, *Die Hard* (1988) has become a touchstone of the action genre, but it's also a model of the tightly woven screenplay, developing in both dialogue and imagery a cluster of motifs (glass, fear of heights, references to classic Westerns and TV shows, oppositions of New York/California, America/Europe, and Asian/black/white).[94]

The density may be auditory as well. In *American Graffiti* Lucas real-

1.7. In *Groundhog Day:* Phil's halo of alert groundhogs.

ized that the compilation pop soundtrack, initially motivated as broadcast from Wolfman Jack's late-night show, could create an echo chamber amplifying the story action. When Curt first sees the evanescent blond in the T-Bird, the Wolfman is spinning, "Why Do Fools Fall in Love?" Later, when Curt glimpses her but fails to catch up, we hear, "Ain't That a Shame?" The nerd Toad picks up Debbie to the tune of "The Great Impostor" and "Almost Grown." As John pretends to try to seduce the underage Carol, we hear "You're Sixteen (You're Beautiful, and You're Mine)." The echo effects continue until the Climax. Steve is reunited with Laurie to "Only You." As dawn breaks, Curt is abandoned by the blond to "Good Night, Sweetheart," itself rhyming with the song that kicks off the night's antics ("We're gonna rock, rock, rock until broad daylight"). These are not one-off correspondences but rather traces of a broader formal principle of unremitting, if sometimes barely audible, musical commentary.[95] By bleeding a song from one scene to another, the radio music bathes the action in an auditory zoosphere, a soundscape through which all the characters cruise. American graffiti is written not on walls but on the airwaves.

Where might this trend toward maximal design come from? Thompson hazards that the process of multiple rewrites over years of development allows various creators to add layers to the mix. I suspect as well that these felicities are addressed to other filmmakers, as marks of virtuosity in the trade. In addition, with many films designed to appeal to a wide range of viewers, there are pressures to sprinkle in details that might be caught by only a few. "It really is not necessary," remarks one screenwriter, "for everything in the movie to be understandable by every member of the audience. It's only necessary to make sure that everything in the movie *can* be understood."[96] Contrary to arguments that traditional storytelling forms have crumbled, these fully loaded movies suggest that some of the *most* classical films have appeared since the 1960s.

The Me I Always Wanted to Be

Jerry Maguire (1996) seems the ideal date movie. It offers sports for the men, romance for the women, and heartwarming humor for all. It seems "pure Hollywood," recycling many clichés: the predatory agent, the wisecracking sister (heir to Joan Blondell and Eve Arden), the cool image of Tom Cruise (Ray-Bans now hiding a black eye). Yet it is far more complex than any time-killing romantic comedy needs to be. Out of the premises of classical construction, writer-director Cameron Crowe has fashioned an intricate plot and a rare density of implication and motif. He need not apologize for being belated; he hasn't betrayed the legacy of Ernst Lubitsch and Billy Wilder.[97] *Jerry Maguire* is a masterpiece of tight "hyperclassical" storytelling.

The customary double plotline of work and love organizes the action. Jerry, a smooth sports agent, suffers a momentary attack of conscience and composes a "mission statement" demanding more concern for the players he represents. What happened, he asks, to our love of the game? Now it's all about money. The manifesto gets him sacked from the firm, but with him goes the accountant Dorothy Boyd, who's attracted by the idealism expressed in his statement. When Jerry loses his top client, his fiancée Avery abandons him, and he draws closer to Dorothy, a single mother with a winning son. Eventually the couple marries, but Jerry, good as he is at his job, has had only superficial relations with women. He bonds with little Ray but increasingly shuts Dorothy out. Jerry faces the standard pair of conflicts: external, as a freelancer struggling with rival agents and temperamental clients, and internal, as a failing husband who married his wife for her loyalty and because of her little boy. What he wants is success, but what he needs is love.

This would be enough of a through-line for most movies, but Crowe adds a parallel plot. Rod Tidwell, a wide receiver for the Arizona Cardinals, becomes Jerry's only client. Rod is an affectionate family man, and his deep love for his wife, Marcy, counterpoints Jerry's forced displays of affection for Dorothy. But Rod has become a "money player," showing tenacity and skill but no love of the game. Rod's contract is about to lapse. Needing to plan for his family's future, he decides not to re-sign, hoping for a big offer at season's end. He is Jerry's opposite: strong at intimacy, taking less than full joy in his work.

The two plotlines knot at a climactic Monday night game, with Jerry on the sidelines and the Tidwell family watching the TV broadcast. In a daring play, Rod falls. He lies silent on the field. Eventually, to the crowd's relief, he rises and exuberantly does something he swore he would never do: he dances with the ball. He emerges as the game's hero, and Jerry, realizing that he has no one with whom to share his pride in Rod, rushes home to Dorothy to affirm his love for her.

Crowe effortlessly maps this fairly complex plot across the four-part structure traced out by Thompson. The Setup (33 minutes) concludes with Jerry's departure from the firm, accompanied by Dorothy and two goldfish he's scooped out of the tank. The Complicating Action (another 31 minutes) functions as a countersetup and piles on the problems. Jerry's business is struggling, he loses the star quarterback Cushman, and Avery dumps him. Worse, he drunkenly makes a pass at Dorothy. At the film's midpoint, a sozzled Jerry staggers out to a taxi proclaiming: "I'm back!" The couple's romance is launched on a comically downbeat note.

The Development (32 minutes) interweaves Jerry's courtship of Dorothy with the trajectory of Rod's movement toward free-agent status. When the Arizona offer proves feeble, Dorothy decides to take another job, but Jerry forestalls that by asking her to marry him. She accepts, and this propels the action toward the Climax. This finale (running another 32 minutes) falls into two phases. In the first part, Jerry's marriage to Dorothy deteriorates while Rod plays doggedly, always at risk for injury. The final phase centers on the Monday night game, the scene of Rod's regeneration and the trigger for Jerry's declaration of love to Dorothy. Each man has passed through his darkest moment and triumphed. Having two major plots, the film permits itself two epilogues. Tidwell gets the fat contract he wanted, and as Jerry's business starts to recover he and Dorothy are united and launch a real marriage.

Here the central character grows in self-knowledge, but in a deeper way than the perfunctory exorcism of "ghosts." Jerry could put his talents to good use—the spontaneous idealism of his mission statement shows that—but he excels at superficial charm, and he falls back on this until Dorothy or Rod calls his bluff. *Jerry Maguire* illustrates how Hollywood dramaturgy can foreshadow personality change by presenting the character as having contrary impulses at the outset. "I love him," Dorothy tells her sister, "for the man he almost is." To become that man, Jerry must shed his glibness and speak from the heart. The "lord of the living room," the silver-tongued closer, must haltingly plead for love by echoing the words signed by a deaf-mute: "You complete me."

Likewise, the film reworks the familiar duality of love versus money in fairly complex ways. The two sides of Jerry's character, slick professionalism and earnest idealism, play out this tension. Dorothy sacrifices money for ideals, putting her career and son at risk, because Jerry's mission statement calls her to higher values. Thereafter she must often steer Jerry back

1.8. *Jerry Maguire:* The signature gesture of a confident man.

1.9. On videotape a former girlfriend returns Jerry's gesture.

1.10. The awkward married couple, joined by the happily married Rod.

1.11. In bed, Jerry blocks Dorothy with Ray.

to the principles he articulated. At first, by contrast, Rod seems concerned only with the size of his salary. "Show me the money!" he makes Jerry holler. Later, Rod explains to Jerry that he has only five years of play left, and so he needs a nest egg to keep his family secure. Rod expresses his goal in what he calls the Kwan: "It means love . . . respect . . . community . . . and the dollars too—the entire package."

As in the studio era, people are characterized through facial expression and movement. Jerry's signature gesture, two index fingers lifted to command attention, is marked, mocked, and deflated (Figs. 1.8–1.9). When he returns to his office after being fired, his body flails, undercutting his defiant plea for others to join him. Sunk in self-pity and hiding behind sunglasses, Jerry calls himself a cautionary tale, but Rod's glare and commanding demeanor put him in his place. The wedding's aftermath is dominated by the newlyweds' awkward courtesy and smiling discomfort. They are standing at opposite ends of the room, and Rod brings them together in a forced coziness, as his plotline will eventually unite them permanently (Fig. 1.10).

Then there's the delicate arc of Jerry's bonding with the boy Ray. They meet at an airport luggage conveyor, and Jerry discovers that he enjoys Ray's swinging from his and Dorothy's arms. Later, Jerry and Ray tease one another by exchanging absurd questions. They find a deeper rapport when, alone together on the sofa, they talk hesitantly about their fathers. (We learn that Jerry's father worked for a charity, giving Jerry a heritage of selfless effort.) Underscoring Jerry's emerging fatherly role is a sudden phone call from Rod, who's shown in the bathtub with his little boy. On another night, when Jerry comes to pick up Dorothy for their date, Ray kisses him, something he's done with no man but his father. The next morning Jerry sits down casually to pour Ray's cereal. Shrewdly, the script makes Jerry's growing love for her son confirm Dorothy's hopes for Jerry, but once they're married Jerry uses Ray as a buffer against her. This is, again, expressed through gesture. Jerry interrupts a serious talk with Dorothy by bringing the boy into their bed and hugging him close (Fig. 1.11).

Pause on any scene, and you'll observe how many threads of action are initiated or brought up to date through word and image. Jerry asks Avery for loyalty; he marries Dorothy because she is loyal; Marcy asks Rod's younger brother to be loyal to the family. In three separate scenes before Dorothy packs for San Diego, we hear her mention the prospect of leaving (once offscreen and almost inaudibly). Ray is forever asking to go to the zoo; in the last scene the family is returning from it. As Dorothy and Jerry leave the office in the elevator, they see a deaf couple signing, and Dorothy interprets. The line itself ("You complete me") will be repeated, but, just as important, Dorothy's ability to interpret reveals her capacity for devotion. (She learned signing in order to communicate with her favorite aunt.) Rod criticizes a TV sports show where "everybody cries," but of course he winds up there in his epilogue, sobbing out his thanks to his family.

Throughout, actions are foreshadowed, recalled, given fresh tints of meaning by varied repetition. During the battle of the phones, Jerry tries to win the loyalty of his clients before his rival, Bob Sugar, can entice them, and Crowe succinctly characterizes the two men by crosscutting their deal-making styles. Jerry tries to be reasonable, but Sugar is a shark, lying about Jerry and blackmailing one client. At the end of the sequence, Jerry's sagging prospects are pictured in the dwindling number of blinking lines on his speakerphone; eventually all go out. At the house Dorothy shares with her sister Laurel, the divorcées' therapy group may seem to be a gratuitous jab at women who can't hold men, but they form a Greek chorus commenting on the action. After Jerry has drunkenly called on Dorothy, they discuss the new definition of stalkers—"men who come over uninvited." At the climax of the romance plot, just before Jerry bursts in to confess his love for Dorothy, the women are reflecting on how hard it is for people to change.

1.12. Action and reaction in the same shot: Jerry tells Dorothy he's broken up with his girlfriend.

1.13. Jerry reveals his love of the game, while the money-grubbers look on.

Hollywood's wide-ranging narration keeps Dorothy's and Jerry's trajectories complementary throughout the film, making sure we realize how the actions of one affect the other. Cutting within scenes yields a comparable control of information, adding layers of character reaction to the core situation. Jerry proposes marriage to Dorothy alongside the rental truck. After seeing Jerry's sidelong glance at Ray, we're confirmed in the hunch that he is cruelly leading Dorothy to believe that he loves her as deeply as she loves him. But the pathos is mixed with humor, as we cut to Laurel, watching from the kitchen and demanding softly that Dorothy abandon Jerry. A comparable effect of omniscience can be achieved within one shot. Jerry turns away from Dorothy as he confesses that he and Avery have broken up, and we get the benefit of her reaction (Fig. 1.12). Subtler still is the comparison of Jerry with his adversaries, Avery and Bob Sugar, at the climactic game. In a single framing, we see him enjoying the game, oblivious to their grim calculations of profit (Fig. 1.13).

Jerry Maguire, like the "hyperclassical" films Thompson analyzes, teems with recurring motifs. In a world where professionals work the phones, it's not surprising that Jerry learns of Sugar's treachery when he answers a call for Cush. When characters refer to Jerry's memo, he reminds them with hesitant stuffiness that it's a "mission statement." A rock-and-roll critic, Crowe has learned the *American Graffiti* lesson; the pop songs create clusters of implications. Jerry celebrates Cush's allegiance by singing along with "Free Fallin'," but he is indeed in free fall, for Cush's father will betray him. The mariachi band that serenades Jerry and Dorothy at the restaurant shows up at the wedding to accompany Rod's rendition of "What's Goin' On," a plea for love and family harmony that will prove ironic: this marriage seems to be over before it starts. Music eventually gets linked to the goldfish Jerry rescues from the agency. At first the fish indicate how little support he has from his co-workers ("They're going with me") and how little his bosses respect him ("These fish have manners"). Afterward, as Jerry stares drunkenly at the fish on Dorothy's mantelpiece, they become a memento of his failure ("So we meet again"). Later the goldfish in the bowl by Ray's bedside suggest that now Jerry is responsible for the boy too, and he turns helplessly toward the fish: "It was just a mission statement." Earlier Cush has strummed the Nirvana song "Something in the Way" on the guitar, singing, "It's okay to fish because they haven't got no feelings." The line contrasts with Jerry's solicitude toward the goldfish while evoking the ways they have reflected his shifting emotions.

Two motifs create particularly subtle echoes. Tacked up in the Cardinals' locker room are morale-boosting slogans that comment on Jerry's efforts to get Rod to "help me help you." One sign reads "A positive anything is better than a negative nothing," confirming Jerry's attempt to get Rod to lighten up. Another sign, seen mostly in mirror reflection, declares, "Success consists of simply getting up one more time than you fall" (Fig. 1.14). The maxim applies to Jerry's refusal to quit and foreshadows Rod's rise in the climactic game. A second motif involves the first image we see: planet Earth. Jerry's voice-over introduces this with a casualness that already suggests a breezy Master of the Universe (Fig. 1.15), so we're not surprised to find a stylish globe in Jerry's office (Fig. 1.16). But when he loses Cush as a client and Avery rejects him, a banner at the sports meeting becomes ironic: "This is my planet" (Fig. 1.17). In later scenes, the tiny globes scattered across Dorothy's coffee table unobtrusively mark Jerry's new and humble place in the scheme of things (Fig. 1.18). Like the groundhogs rampant behind Phil in *Groundhog Day*, minor details of setting comment on the action.

The Godfather reminds us that one mark of the hyperclassical film is an opening passage packed with dangling causes and forward-pointing motifs. *Jerry Maguire* is launched by a brisk montage sequence that is practically a movie in itself. After Jerry introduces us to the earth, he surveys a range of young athletes. One, a girl boxer, is thinking of her former boyfriend, he tells us; this anticipates Avery slugging *her* ex, Jerry himself. Jerry's commentary picks out Cushman as the most promising young athlete, setting up critical events in parts one and two. Overall, the opening scenes link Jerry to kids, an important preparation for his bonding with Ray. More specifically, he doesn't see them as just dollars on the hoof; when a boy hits a home run, we get a shot of his face and hear Jerry remarking, "Check out what pure joy looks like." Jerry's idealism is fueled by his belief in sports as the arena of rapturous accomplishment, and it will trigger not only his controversial memo but also his criticisms of Rod Tidwell, the paycheck player.

1.14. On the wall, the advice that Rod will follow at the climax.

1.15. Jerry Maguire's opening shot: "So, this is the world," he tells us offhandedly.

1.16. Jerry's office features, in frame center, his own world.

1.17. Jerry brought low, with the convention sign mocking him from above.

1.18. Tiny globes appropriate to Jerry's new status are scattered around Dorothy's coffee table.

"I'm the guy you don't usually see; I'm the sports agent." Jerry glides out from behind a bank of monitors showing the grinding danger of football (anticipating Tidwell's injury at the Climax), pauses confidently, and strides through the lobby. He is by turns arrogant, glad-handing, and bootlicking. He squeezes a coach for a high salary. Whisked to an agency meeting, we see Jerry arguing with his peers (and seated beside his future nemesis, Bob Sugar). If we listen carefully we can hear his boss tell him, "You've gotta be tough"—foreshadowing the firm's reaction to Jerry's touchy-feely memo. Overall, this portrait of a shark in a suit counterbalances the more idealistic side of Jerry we heard in his voice-over during the kids' montage.

Three minutes into the movie we see Jerry's conflict between pursuing the bottom line and admiring pure sportsmanship. A string of disturbing incidents shows adult players dashing children's ideals. One player is accused of statutory rape, and another can't autograph unauthorized baseball cards. Most elaborately, a hockey player suffering his fourth concussion demands to play to earn his bonus, and Jerry shrugs off his little son's worries. Late at night, in a Miami hotel, Jerry has a crisis of conscience ("Breakdown? Breakthrough!"). This is a crucial passage. Torn by fragments of earlier speeches (most insistently, a doctor's insistent questioning of the unconscious hockey player: "Do you know your name?") Jerry faces the perennial problem of the Hollywood protagonist: "Who had I become?"

At the film's start Jerry's cocky narration had announced, over the earth: "Okay, so this is the world," but now he confesses: "I hated my place in the world." He starts to type out a "mission statement" for sports agents. It calls agents to a higher duty, to ignore the dollars and to dedicate themselves to personal attention. Crowe mildly mocks Jerry's pretensions ("I wrote and wrote and wrote and wrote and wrote, and I'm not even a writer"), but the presentation is largely sympathetic: "It was the me I always wanted to be." Character change is presented as returning to what you were before the world corrupted you. Jerry rediscovers his inner kid, defined as one who serves others: "I was my father's son again." When he strays from the path, Dorothy reminds us of his latent idealism, loving him for the man he almost is.

The motif of childhood is reiterated when Jerry sprints to a copy shop to have the mission statement designed and printed. "Even the cover looked like *The Catcher in the Rye.*" The offhand reference typifies the compact design of the whole prologue. Salinger's novel is an attack on the "phonies," the inhabitants of a world Jerry no longer wants to live in. The novel's protagonist, Holden Caulfield, dreams of being the catcher, the protector of children who would otherwise fall into danger. Jerry's idealism is reinforced by the literary reference, but the tone isn't solemn; Crowe manages to keep poking fun at Jerry's slightly naive self-importance. (*Catcher* might be the only book he's ever read.)

Nine minutes into the film, the script launches a series of rapid reversals. At daybreak Jerry tries to retract the memo he's shipped to the firm. Too late. He returns fearing the worst, hesitating by the elevator (through which he will eventually leave forever). But coming in, he's applauded by the agency staff. He's relieved. "I was thirty-five. I'd started my life." Then for the first time we stray from his range of knowledge and hear two colleagues, while applauding him, speculate that he'll last no more than a week. This becomes a dangling cause, put on hold while the script shifts from the career plot to the romance plot. The upcoming scenes will introduce Dorothy and Ray (on a plane, riding in coach while Jerry rides in front), portray Avery as brutally self-regarding, and show Jerry discomfited by the video at his bachelor party. Next day, he will be fired, and the film's Setup will end with his failure to convince his clients to come with him.

Scattered throughout this minimovie are still other motifs that will bloom throughout. The talented kids of the opening are recalled in Ray's unexpected ability to throw a baseball in the epilogue, leading to a last bit of humor as Jerry muses on his stepson's career potential—and providing the here-we-go-again wrap-up so beloved by classical cinema. In Miami, lashed by self-doubt, Jerry writes his mission statement because he has "so much to say and no one to listen." Talking will be an important element in the film. Jerry finds it easier to talk with little Ray than with Dorothy, and after a quarrel, Rod will shout after him, "You think we're fighting but I think we're finally talking." But Rod also reminds us that talking is "a primitive form of communication." It will be the dialogue exchanged by deaf-mute lovers that inspires Jerry finally to open his heart to Dorothy. The prologue sets up the benign narrational presence of Dicky Fox, Jerry's mentor, whose advice is channeled into Jerry's memo: "The key to this business is personal relationships." Dicky will get the movie's last word, smiling kindly and saying—to the novice Jerry, to us—"I love my wife. I love my life. And I wish you my kind of success."

The opening is enriched by understated stretches of music. The giddy world of agentry is accompanied by the Who's "Magic Bus," an upbeat paean (I'm told) to drugs. The Durutti Column's sober "Requiem" accompanies Jerry's plunge into despair, before another Who song, "Getting in Tune," conveys his euphoria at becoming his father's son again. By launching Jerry's story with the "Magic Bus," which describes a man going to visit his beloved, the movie rhymes that sentiment with the final song, Bob Dylan's "Shelter from the Storm," which depicts a man finding refuge with a loving woman. All these songs create another layer of evocation, running underneath Jerry's breathless commentary and a flurry of precise, rapid-fire imagery.

The deft economy of *Jerry Maguire* is wholly grounded in the precepts of orthodox filmmaking. The movie reminds us that the conventions of the classical tradition, from the goal-oriented protagonist and summary montages to dialogue hooks, appointments, and evocative motifs, are inexhaustible resources in the hands of gifted filmmakers. Indeed, few films from any era display such filigreed coherence and bear it so lightly.

3. SUBJECTIVE STORIES
AND NETWORK NARRATIVES

Hollywood's output, from routine efforts to richly detailed worlds and hyperclassical movies, adheres to long-standing principles of storytelling. Is this system therefore rigid and unbending? No. Hollywood has always valued innovation, for both artistic and economic reasons. The talent pool has to be refreshed, people long to see something different, and the right kinds of novelty can sell.

Any temptation to see the studio aesthetic as unadventurous should be scotched by recalling all the dynamic storytelling experiments that emerged in the years 1940–1955. After two trailblazing flashback movies, *Citizen Kane* and *How Green Was My Valley* (both 1941), Hollywood offered unreliable flashbacks (*Crossfire*, 1947; *Stage Fright*, 1950; *The I Don't Care Girl*, 1953); flashbacks-within-flashbacks (three layers in *The Locket*, 1946); and scenes playing out present action in the foreground and past action in the background (*Enchantment*, 1948; *Payment on Demand*, 1951). An opening sequence might lead us to erroneous assumptions that are corrected only at the climax (*Mildred Pierce*, 1945). Long stretches of the story might be presented through the eyes of the protagonist (*The Lady in the Lake*, 1947; *Dark Passage*, 1947). The action might slip unobtrusively into a dream sequence or a would-be dream sequence (*Laura*, 1944). The tale might be narrated by several characters (*The Killers*, 1946; *All About Eve*, 1950; *The Bad and the Beautiful*, 1952), by an antagonist whom we never see (*Letter to Three Wives*, 1949), by a dead man (*Laura*; *Sunset Boulevard*, 1950), or by an Oscar statuette (*Susan Slept Here*, 1954). It was an exhilarating period, but all these innovations called on the canons of classical storytelling. However creatively a movie twisted causation or temporal order or point of view, its revisions were always intelligible to mainstream audiences.

Something similar happened from the mid-1960s to the early 1970s. Influenced by a wave of imported European films, directors began to explore oblique and ambiguous storytelling. Admittedly, a few films, like *Point Blank* (1967), *2001: A Space Odyssey* (1968), *The Last Movie* (1971), and *Slaughterhouse-Five* (1971) demanded patient deciphering and offered perplexing endings. More commonly, though, a movie's daring devices would eventually be explained. In *Petulia* (1968), *They Shoot Horses, Don't They?* (1969), and *Images* (1972), the ambivalent time frames and bursts of enigmatic imagery sort themselves out. Even this limited experimentation became rare as the 1970s wore on. Directors moved toward a realism driven by characterization and mood and framed within familiar genres (*The Last*

Picture Show, 1971; *The Last Detail,* 1973; *Alice Doesn't Live Here Anymore,* 1975).

Another era of experimental storytelling was launched in the 1990s, when a fresh batch of films seemed to shatter the classical norms. Movies boasted paradoxical time schemes, hypothetical futures, digressive and dawdling action lines, stories told backward and in loops, and plots stuffed with protagonists. It seemed filmmakers were competing to outdo one another in flashy nonconformity. Offbeat storytelling became part of business as usual, and screenplay manuals offered tips on writing unconventional scripts.[98] *The Simpsons,* on the cusp as ever, packed parodic experiments into 22 minutes, and a straight-to-video kid's movie like *The Lion King 1½* (2004) offered a clever play with point of view.[99]

Yet the mainstream filmmaker who embraced the new complexities of plotting faced a problem. How could innovations be made comprehensible and pleasurable to a wide audience? The extremes of indie risk taking, such as Jim Jarmusch's *Stranger Than Paradise* (1983) or Richard Linklater's *Slacker* (1991), would likely seem unintelligible or pointless. Charlie Kaufman has explained that his original script for *Eternal Sunshine of the Spotless Mind* (2004) needed to be changed because executives worried that his exposition was too confusing: "That was a big discussion with the studio, always. How long can you keep the audience confused before they turn off, as though there's some kind of mathematical formula to it; are we going to lose people if we hold off this thing?"[100] As with the experiments of the 1940s and 1960s, most storytelling innovations since the 1990s have kept one foot in classical tradition. Because of the redundancy built into the Hollywood narrative system, unusual devices could piggyback on a large number of familiar cues. *Eternal Sunshine,* as Kaufman doubtless realizes, tells of boy meeting girl, boy losing girl, and boy getting girl.

Complexity and Redundancy

Why did narrative experimentation surge back in the 1990s? Our immediate impulse—to look for some broad cultural change as the trigger—should be held in check long enough to consider more proximate causes. One factor was the off-Hollywood cinema that began to surface with films like *Blue Velvet* (1986) and *She's Gotta Have It* (1986). The boom in independent production had created a crowded field, and product differentiation was needed. Plot maneuvers could boost the standing of a low-budget film with no stars. *Pulp Fiction* proved that tricky storytelling could be profitable, particularly if it offered a fresh take on genre ingredients. (Hence the string of self-consciously quirky movies centered on crime or romance that followed.)

Soon the major companies realized that there was an audience for offbeat stories, especially if stars wanted to play in them, so *Unbreakable* and *Eternal Sunshine of the Spotless Mind* became reasonable bets.

At the same time a generational shift was taking place. The New Hollywood had been raised on Old Hollywood and 1960s art movies, but the Newest Hollywood brought TV, comic-book, videogame, and pulp-fiction tastes to the movies, and a free approach to narrative came along. The twists in *The Sixth Sense* (1999), *The Game* (1997), and *Fight Club* (1999) would not have been out of place in Rod Serling's *Twilight Zone* TV series. The young audience was drenched in modern media, from cable TV to computers, and viewers knew the standard moves of mainstream storytelling. They were ready to embrace innovations, especially if they built on the conventions of fantasy and science fiction (such as time travel, plays of objective and subjective perspectives, and "what-if" premises like that governing *What Women Want*, 2000). In harmony with their audience, the rising generation of directors grasped the narrative possibilities afforded by the home-video revolution. Thanks to videocassettes, fans could study clever plotting at length, and a director could drop in details apparent only in repeat viewings and freeze-framing. By 2001 a critic could write of tracking *Memento*'s backward structure, "Oh, will this ever be fun to do on DVD!"[101]

Filmmakers seeking models of daring storytelling didn't have to look far. Hollywood has long been a stylized filmmaking tradition, and Josef von Sternberg, Fritz Lang, Orson Welles, and other directors put formal problems at the center of their work. The most commercially successful experimenter was Hitchcock, who was willing to confine a story to a single cramped locale (*Lifeboat*, 1944; *Rope*, 1948; *Rear Window*, 1954), kill off his protagonist (*Psycho*), and intertwine story lines connected by happenstance (*The Trouble with Harry*, 1955; *Family Plot*, 1976). Hitchcock is virtually the patron saint of young filmmakers who want to tinker with storytelling. Another central inspiration was Hollywood's 1940s–1950s experiments, particularly the noirs. "For me," notes Christopher Nolan, director of *Memento* (2001), "film noir is one of the only genres where the concept of point of view is accepted as a fairly important notion in the storytelling, and where it's totally accepted that you can flashback and flashforward and change points of view."[102] Likewise, some canonized works of the 1970s sparked directors' imaginations. Altman's *Nashville* (1975) and *A Wedding* (1978) influenced the "converging fates" films of later years, as did the more mainstream *Network* (1976). Nor should we underestimate the cumulative influence of bold entries in the next decade, such as Coppola's *One from the Heart* (1982) and *Rumble Fish* (1983); Terry Gilliam's *Brazil* (1985); David Cronenberg's

Dead Ringers (1988); and Woody Allen's *Zelig* (1983), *Hannah and Her Sisters* (1985), and *Crimes and Misdemeanors* (1989). Even the less prestigious horror and fantasy cycles of the 1970s and 1980s may have made directors more receptive to time-scrambling and games with point of view.

Other models came from waves of imported "art films." Directors of the 1990s were aware of the 1960s classics, such as Fellini's *8½* (1963), Bergman's *Persona* (1966), and British pictures like *The Loneliness of the Long-Distance Runner* (1962) and *This Sporting Life* (1963). Later, Robert Bresson (*L'Argent*, 1983), Andrei Tarkovsky (*Nostalghia*, 1983), Wim Wenders (*Wings of Desire*, 1987), Christine Edzard (*Little Dorrit*, 1987), Krzysztof Kieślowski (*The Decalogue*, 1988–1989; *The Double Life of Veronique*, 1992; the *Three Colors* trilogy, 1993–1994), Wong Kar-wai (*Chungking Express*, 1994; *Ashes of Time*, 1994), and, of course, Godard (from *Sauve qui peut [la vie]*, 1980 onward) put adventurous storytelling back on the agenda. For 1990s American filmmakers, the movie-consciousness characteristic of modern Hollywood again emerges as a sense of belatedness, of coming late to several mature traditions. Soderbergh exemplified the resulting pluralism. He remade a noir classic (*Criss Cross*, 1949) in *The Underneath* (1995), and he essayed a brand of art cinema in *Kafka* (1991) and in a 2002 remake of Tarkovsky's *Solaris* (1972). Not surprisingly, he idolized Richard Lester, another commercial director with experimental flair.[103] Soderbergh's deadpan absurdity in *Schizopolis* (1997) owes something to Lester's *How I Won the War* (1967) and *The Bed Sitting Room* (1969), while *Out of Sight* (1998) and *The Limey* (1999) recall the mosaic time scheme of *Petulia* (1968).

Whatever the causes and influences, adventurous plotting became a new arena of competition in the professional community. Today, a scriptwriter or director gets points for taking a chance in storytelling. Soderbergh and Linklater have run parallel indie/studio careers, while Robert Zemeckis, Joel Schumacher, and Spielberg have tackled somewhat risky projects like *Cast Away* (2000), *Phone Booth* (2003), and *The Terminal* (2004). The trend is likely to continue, now that *Reservoir Dogs* (1992), *The Usual Suspects* (1995), and the like have become classics dissected in film schools. My colleagues who teach filmmaking tell me that students often hit on eccentric formal schemes before they have worked out the story action. ("I want to begin and end my film with exactly the same scene, only it'll mean something different the second time.")[104]

Most of the daring storytelling we find in modern American film offers legible variants on well-entrenched strategies for presenting time, space, goal achievement, causal connection, and the like. Nothing comes from nothing.

Every new artistic achievement revises existing practices, and often the "unconventional" strategy simply draws on *other* conventions.

In *JFK* (1991), for example, Oliver Stone recruits a dazzling array of techniques to present several versions of the Kennedy assassination—first ominously offscreen, then replayed with different details filled in. Backstory events are presented in swift montages accompanied by witnesses' voice-overs. A scene may shift between color and black and white, or mix 35mm footage with 16mm and even 8mm. Yet these disjunctive techniques are situated within an orthodox plot. The protagonist, Jim Garrison, struggles to achieve his goals within the work/romance plotlines (his investigation hurts his marriage) and within a sturdy six-part structure (two Complicating Actions, two Developments). As in many detective tales, the narration is almost entirely limited to the investigator's range of knowledge; the memories of witnesses emerge only when Garrison or a staff member is interrogating them. The climactic trial resolves the two plotlines, allowing Garrison to make a prima facie case for a government cover-up and letting his wife and son realize that the family's sacrifice has served a noble purpose.

Given this stable structure, Stone can mix reconstructions, documentary material, and replays of earlier moments in the film, and even here the organization is less disjunctive than it might be. His technique of interrupting scenes with spurts of associated imagery harks back to Alain Resnais's *Hiroshima mon amour* (1959) and to American films inspired by European models. In *The Pawnbroker* (1964) abrupt and initially mysterious flashbacks disrupt present-day scenes, and *The Conversation* (1973) replays shadowy events in a way that is akin to *JFK*'s reprises. Stone draws as well on documentary technique, notably the collage style of Emile de Antonio (*In the Year of the Pig*, 1968) and Errol Morris (*The Thin Blue Line*, 1988), in which voice-over commentary is reinforced or undercut by the images we see.

Similarly, the interplay of black-and-white and color footage has been a modern convention since *A Man and a Woman* (1966) and *If . . .* (1968). By the early 1990s interpolated black-and-white footage could denote flashbacks or hallucinatory scenes (e.g., *The Fugitive*, 1993). Stone claims: "We clearly differentiate between fact and theory in the film. Any person familiar with film technique knows that when we cut to something like Ruby picking up a bullet in the hospital in black and white, it's a hypothetical image. . . . The uses of different film formats are viable techniques which film critics have always recognized."[105] Once Stone invokes this convention he can confound it to his benefit. The historical exposition during the opening credits presents an array of archival footage, both color and black-and-white. Everything we see here can be taken as veridical. Then obviously staged

1.19. To the unwary, this handheld shot of
Abraham Zapruder filming Kennedy's motorcade
might seem to be documentary footage (*JFK*,
opening sequence).

1.20. *JFK:* Governor Connolly is hit in a restaged
shot; the dirty splice recalls the infamous splice at
frame 207 of the Zapruder film.

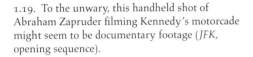

black-and-white footage shows the prostitute Rose Cheramie dumped from
a car and writhing on a hospital bed, warning that men are going to kill the
president. Is Stone here setting up the contrast he mentions, suggesting that
this scene should be taken only as a possibility? No, because then in the motorcade's ride through Dealey Plaza, he intermingles some documentary
shots, some obviously staged ones, and some less noticeably so (Fig. 1.19),
and all freely mix color images with black-and-white ones. The seven-minute
overture segues from a clear and pure collection of actuality footage to a
looser mingling of actuality and fiction, often with no definite markers as
to which is which.

The ensuing film plays with many hypotheses about who directed the
assassination and what the ultimate purposes were. Neither Garrison nor
the narration seeks to pin down the full details of the conspiracy. Instead
the film supports Garrison's effort to introduce doubt about Oswald's guilt
and to propose the rival hypothesis that Kennedy was caught in a three-
way crossfire. During the final phase of the trial, the visual narration vali-
dates Garrison's account by putting his hypothesis on the same visual level
as the prologue. Restaged action we know to be historically accurate, such as
John Connolly swiveling in the presidential limousine, is now presented in
black and white, but a color shot shows Garrison's postulated marksman
on the grassy knoll. Stone even sticks fake splices into his fictional footage
(Fig. 1.20). By intercutting his reenactments with Abraham Zapruder's
original 8mm footage, Stone clinches Garrison's closing argument. The narration mounts a counterhistory, building on familiar schemas drawn from
classical filmmaking and adjacent traditions.[106]

The court testimony stirs up murky suspicions, but in rendering Garrison's investigation and conclusions *JFK* remains translucent. It thereby illustrates a more general principle of current Hollywood experimentation:

the more complex the devices, the more redundant the storytelling needs to be. Unusual techniques need to be situated in an especially stable frame. Another outstanding instance of this give-and-take is *Memento* (2001), at once one of the most novel and most conformist films of recent years.

Following the death of his wife, *Memento*'s protagonist Leonard Shelby is afflicted with anterograde amnesia, the inability to form memories. The film links this condition to a formal strategy of telling its main story backward. So one string of events first shows Leonard murdering a man, then shows the action that preceded the murder, then shows the action that preceded that, and so on. To complicate things, another string of events, consisting mostly of Leonard brooding in his motel room and talking on the phone, unfolds in chronological order and alternates with the reverse-order scenes. The forward-moving sequences lead up to the last event we see in the reversed scenes (which is the first event in that string if we arrange the scenes in chronological order). This bold innovation exacts its costs. Writer-director Christopher Nolan must keep us focused on Leonard's amnesia, on which the film's premise turns. In addition, the plot must clarify which stream of action is moving backward, and which forward, and the film must help the viewer link the retrograde scenes in some coherent fashion. Nolan uses several classical devices to assure redundancy on all these fronts.

Throughout the opening stretches, Leonard's mental condition is reiterated. He tells the motel clerk, "I can't form new memories," and the clerk points out that he has explained this several times before. Leonard reexplains his affliction to the bartender, Natalie, and other characters remind him of it. Within five minutes of the film's opening, Leonard's discipline of writing notes to himself is shown and thereafter is commented on ("those freaky tattoos," Natalie calls them). And of course Leonard's counterpart, Sammy Jankis, has the same ailment. A hero bereft of short-term memory motivates the constant repetition of information; Leonard may forget, but we're never allowed to. As for the parallel-track plotlines, the traditional color/black-and-white dichotomy clearly marks the difference. (The plot would be much harder to follow if both streams of events were in only one format.) Beyond this, the Sammy Jankis flashbacks use a different black-and-white lighting scheme than the present-tense motel scenes, and Leonard's flashbacks showing his wife alive and moving about their house are filmed in soft, handheld imagery rather than in the saturated, locked-down shots of the reverse-order sequences.

Within the backward stream of action, Nolan deploys a host of cohesion devices to keep us oriented to the plot's progression. Scenes are linked by physical tokens: photos, facial scratches and bruises, a broken car window, a license plate, a motel room key, and a flurry of notes on pads, cups, coasters, and Leonard's flesh. Closure operates retrospectively, but the events still cohere through cause and effect. We see Leonard burn a book and a clock in one scene, and in the next scene the book and clock sit on a nightstand. Appointments, deadlines, dangling causes, and dialogue hooks cooperate. At the end of one scene in color, Leonard sees "Remember Sammy Jankis" written on his wrist, and at the beginning of the next scene, a black-and-white one, he's on the phone in his motel explaining, "I met Sammy through work." In addition, Nolan has carefully repeated the closing and opening moments of most reverse-order scenes, often with the same shots and voice-over, so that when we return to that track we can recall where we left off. Thus the moment when Leonard notices the Sammy Jankis memo on his wrist is shown twice: at the end of one scene, forming the dialogue hook just mentioned, and before that, at the start of the previous color sequence (in story order, the subsequent piece of action). As if all this weren't enough, virtually every piece of writing we see is read aloud to us by Leonard, and an extensive inner monologue provides a flow of commentary reiterating the key motifs. Seldom has an American film been so daring and so obvious at the same time.

Nolan's real achievement, it seems to me, is to make his reverse-order plot conform to classical plot structure and film-noir twists. In the very first scene, our hero kills the mysterious Teddy and thus apparently achieves his goal. But if the Climax is settled at the start, where's the suspense? Soon the film shows that Leonard's true goal is to kill "John G.," the burglar who purportedly raped and killed his wife. The Setup (ending at about 24 minutes) concludes with a new problem: perhaps Teddy is not John G. If not, hasn't Leonard killed (i.e., won't he later kill) the wrong man? The Complicating Action (running about 30 minutes) draws Natalie into his scheme and sets up a new goal, that of helping her eliminate the drug dealer, Dodd. The Development (another 30 minutes) mobilizes delaying scenes—Leonard recalls his wife, burns mementos, hires a hooker to reenact the wife's death—and introduces doubts about Leonard's sanity ("Maybe you should start investigating yourself"). The same portion presents Natalie as film noir's classic treacherous woman. Teddy warns Leonard not to trust her, and at the turning point of the Development, we watch her deceive the forgetful Leonard and announce, "I'm going to use you." Unfortunately, he can't write down her confession of betrayal, so he won't remember it. This must be the first time a femme fatale dooms her lover by hiding all her pens and pencils.

In *Memento*'s climactic 30 minutes, Leonard kills Natalie's boyfriend, Jimmy, after which Teddy proclaims that he has used Leonard for this purpose, as he's used him to kill others. This portion also presents, in the chronological exposition, Sammy Jankis's fate. Leonard recounts that Sammy's wife, suspicious that he was faking amnesia, let him repeatedly inject her with her insulin. (Most critics and fans seem to agree that the Jankis story is Leonard's projection of his own situation and hints at the way his wife really died.) If story events had been presented in chronological order, Teddy would at the start have explained fully how he duped Leonard into killing Jimmy and others, providing us with all necessary exposition. In reverse order, however, Teddy's explanation serves as a climactic revelation, resolving many uncertainties. By following the classical four-part pattern, Nolan makes his rewound plot provoke curiosity and suspense.

Unlike 1960s European films, which often postpone explaining their unexpected narrational tactics,[107] *Memento* announces its premise in miniature in its first seconds, when a reverse-motion rendering of Leonard's killing of Teddy culminates in a Polaroid snapshot image slowly vanishing. The (fairly arbitrary) tie between short-term memory loss and the plot's reverse structure is secured early on when the motel clerk tells Leonard that his affliction is "all backwards." As in *JFK*, complex storytelling requires large doses of redundancy. In fact, the redundancy can precede the movie itself. *Memento*'s publicity announced the reverse-order structure in the website (otnemem.com) and promotional ancillaries.[108] The making-of video, headlined "How to begin a story that starts at the end?" is filled with comments like that of composer David Julyan: "It plays forward and backward at the same time." In such ways, DVD bonus material can redouble the repetitions within the plot.

Memento is often considered a "puzzle film," and the emergence of this category in recent years testifies further to new Hollywood's pride in intricate narrative maneuvers. Viewers seem to apply the notion fairly broadly, invoking it whenever a film asks us to discuss "what really happened," to think back over what's has been shown, or to rewatch the film in the search for clues to the key revelations.[109] We can go a little further and trace a rough spectrum of puzzle movies. In the mildest instances, the story world is presented as consistent and objectively existing, but there are gaps in our knowledge about it. The narration withholds information, often not signaling that it's doing so. So the plot may depict a hoax *(The Game)* or a confidence trick *(House of Games,* 1987). Here our range of knowledge is confined principally to a single character, and the late-arriving information comes as the sort of surprise conventional in the mystery or detective genre. Comparable plot twists can be found in the supernatural thriller. *The Sixth Sense* (1999) is an extreme case, because the piece of information withheld is, to say the least, fundamental. Still, this information remains a fact about the story world, and, as in the detective film, the revelation is as much of a surprise to the protagonist as it is to us. In such movies, the narration is likely to replay scenes at the Climax so as to put them in a new light; redundancy confirms the concealed premise. Intrigued viewers may rewatch the film to see *how* they were misled—typically, how the telling skipped over certain information. Precedents for these twist films would be such classic essays in duplicity as *You Only Live Once* (1937), *Fallen Angel* (1945), and *The Blue Gardenia* (1953).

In such films, the narration is unreliable, but the unreliability consists largely of omissions and misdirections. In the core cases of the puzzle film, the narration is more flagrantly misleading. Typically, it presents actions that seem to be taking place, but sooner or later we're encouraged to doubt the actuality of those events. The usual revelation depends on subjectivity: something we've taken as objective turns out to be a character's fantasy or hallucination. The device goes back at least to *The Cabinet of Dr. Caligari* (1920) and was revived in *Occurrence at Owl Creek Bridge* (1962). It was a common tactic of 1960s art cinema, on display in *8 1/2* (1963), *Persona* (1966), and many other movies. The revelation may occur partway through, as in the case of *A Beautiful Mind* (2002), or at the climax, as in *Fight Club* (1999) and *The Others* (2001). I'll have more to say about the subjectivity stratagem later.

Even to speak of revelations may be going too far, for some films create a lingering doubt. After the film ends, there may be a zone of indeterminacy within which we cannot say definitely what took place. In *Memento*, it seems to me, we can only suspect that the Sammy Jankis story is Leonard's projection of his own killing of his wife; the film doesn't provide enough redundancy to let us ascertain this. Still, many matters, such as Leonard's shooting of Teddy, don't seem to be in doubt. Something similar is going on in *The Conversation* (1974). That the company president was killed by the young couple is quite definite, but the details of the murder as shown to us may only be Harry Caul's extrapolations.

When the zone of indeterminacy includes more central facts, the puzzle element increases. *The Usual Suspects* (1995) equivocates about both small and big matters. It refuses to specify whether everything that Verbal Kint tells the customs investigator is a lie. Did the other crooks in the gang say and do everything that Verbal reported? Is the driver we see at the end to be identified as Mr. Kobayashi? We cannot know, but it matters little to our understanding of the story's progression (and faute de mieux, what we are shown must serve as the default). More seriously, although we know that Verbal Kint is not who he purports to be, we cannot say that he is Keyser Soze with the confidence we could summon up if we had more redundant clues. Verbal probably is the mastermind (*soze* means "verbal" in Hungarian), but we aren't given solid corroboration in the way that the lying flashback in Hitchcock's *Stage Fright* (1950) is acknowledged and corrected by the liar himself.

These puzzle films draw their strength from certain genres (mystery, horror, neo-noir) that feature self-conscious, ludic narration. We're expecting to be misled, and so we must be ready to have our expectations drastically revised. We're guided through the games of gap making and gap filling by genre conventions, the redundancy built into mainstream storytelling principles, and our familiarity with adjacent traditions: short stories by H. P. Lovecraft, Saki, and O. Henry as progenitors of the twist tale, art films as arenas of subjective/objective ambiguity. As the zone of indeterminacy widens, however, our reliance on classical closure wanes, and we must call on more rarefied comprehension skills to play with the ambiguities the films offer. We can assume that in *Blowup* (1965), the hero photographed something compromising in the park and that later he found a dead man there. But because the action is restricted to his range of knowledge, he learns no more, and we are as stymied as he is at the end. *Blowup* is a detective story without a solution. In rare cases, like *Last Year at Marienbad* (1961), the entire movie's action seems indeterminate, and then we lose all moorings. We can't be sure that any events or states of affairs count as veridical, and the narration is revealed as thoroughly unreliable. Completely indeterminate movies are rare in American cinema; *Point Blank* (1967) may count as one, and perhaps only David Lynch currently makes them.[110]

So an intriguing range of novelty has become feasible in our puzzle films, just as it was in the 1940s and 1960s. In the pages ahead, I will review a few more offbeat options explored in modern American movies: the maladjusted protagonist, degrees of character subjectivity, scrambled time schemes, multiple protagonists, and plots based on converging fates and social networks. Many invite re-viewing, teasing the spectator to discover the hows and whys of their construction. At the same time, these strategies exploit the redundancy built into the classical norms and often mobilize some underused resources of studio-era moviemaking. And although the innovations look fresh on the movie screen, many rely on our acquaintance with story schemas circulating in popular culture at large.

Antiheroes and Mental Spaces

James Stewart and John Wayne would seem to incarnate the classic cinema's beau ideal, ordinary guys who happen to be heroic. But we ought to recall that in the 1950s, they portrayed some fairly demented characters. As Elwood Dowd, a mild-mannered alcoholic, Jimmy found his best friend in Harvey, an invisible giant rabbit. He played a man driven by vengeance in *Winchester 73* (1950), a bounty hunter lusting for reward money in *The Naked Spur* (1953), and a detective engulfed in delusional passion in *Vertigo* (1958). The Duke stretched himself too, portraying a ferocious patriarch in *Red River* (1948) and a mad warrior hoarsely shouting for blood in *The Searchers* (1956). Or think of *In a Lonely Place* (1950), in which Humphrey Bogart plays an embittered, sadistic screenwriter perfectly capable of committing a sex murder. Ladies were given no less flavorful parts: Bette Davis chewing the scenery as the matriarch of *The Little Foxes* (1941), Joan Crawford competing with her daughter in *Mildred Pierce* (1945) and with a younger rival in *Possessed* (1947). Hollywood's 1940s love affair with popularized Freudianism yielded those near-psychopathic principals of thrillers (*Hangover Square*, 1945), gangster films (*White Heat*, 1949), cop movies (*Where the Sidewalk Ends*, 1950), and melodramas (*Leave Her to Heaven*, 1945). In movies drawn from plays by Clifford Odets (*The Big Knife*, 1955) and Tennessee Williams (*Baby Doll*, 1956; *Cat on a Hot Tin Roof*, 1958), virtually every character seemed to suffer from deep psychological problems. Parker Tyler, the undisputed connoisseur of this trend, notes, "Like all generalities phrased for readers of *The Saturday Evening Post* and *Reader's Digest*, normalcy and happiness, whether considered under the spiritual aegis of astrology or psychoanalysis, are very relative conditions."[111]

Hollywood's current concern with giving its heroes and heroines a character arc usually doesn't yield neurotic extremes of behavior. Most of our protagonists, from Jerry Maguire to the waitresses in *Mystic Pizza*, display forgivable flaws—impetuosity, shyness, naïveté, disillusionment after failed love affairs. They are basically nice people, and the films show them becoming nicer. One way to innovate, then, is to push your protagonist to extremes. He might be quirky to the point of delusion, like Brewster McCloud or Donnie Darko. He might be shy to the point of passive-aggressive mania, like Barry Egan in *Punch-Drunk Love* (2002). He might be torn between rage and otherworldly asceticism, like Travis Bickle (*Taxi Driver*, 1976) or Jimmy Fingers (*Fingers*, 1978), or so driven by fantasies of success that he has skipped several stages of socialization, like Rupert Pupkin (*King of Comedy*, 1983). Perhaps your hero is an overbearing raconteur who seems to have lost his grip on reality (*Big Fish*, 2003), or an adman who retreats into fantasy when he loses his job (*American Beauty*, 1999). Maybe he robs banks just to get his boyfriend a sex-change operation (*Dog Day Afternoon*, 1975). His pathology may manifest itself as emotional numbness (*Falling Down*,

1993) or charming indifference to his horrendous crimes (*The Minus Man*, 1999). Because a policeman's lot is a thankless one, the lineup of scarred cops stretches from *Dirty Harry* (1971) to *Narc* (2002) and *Dark Blue* (2002). The forces of justice in *L. A. Confidential* (1997) consist of a preening shakedown artist, a brownnosing college boy, and an obedient thug.

Men seem more prone to these frailties than women, but occasionally a seriously warped heroine graces our movies. She may be as deeply neurotic as her 1940s sisters, falling prey to hallucinations (*The Others*, 2001) or mysterious ailments (*Frances*, 1982; *Safe*, 1995). She may, despite her correct upbringing and apparent prudence, pursue risky sex (*Looking for Mr. Goodbar*, 1977; *In the Cut*, 2003) or a traumatizing affair (*Girl, Interrupted*, 1999). When she commits murder, she may be a serial killer (*Monster*, 2003) or just a very ambitious career woman (*To Die For*, 1995). Just as Jack Nicholson and Robert De Niro deglamorized men in earlier decades, Christina Ricci seems to be presenting today's young women as mischievous alcoholics and nymphomaniacs (*The Opposite of Sex*, 1998; *Prozac Nation*, 2001). Unstable women can partner with unstable men, notably in lovers-on-the-run films. Sylvia Sidney and Henry Fonda in *You Only Live Once* (1937) behave like model citizens compared to the couples in *Bonnie and Clyde* (1967), *Badlands* (1973), and *Natural Born Killers* (1994).

This willingness to deheroicize protagonists probably owes something to the new demands for character flaws. One screenplay manual posits, alongside the heroic protagonist, other options: the outsider (Mozart in *Amadeus*, 1984), the mad character (McMurphy in *One Flew Over the Cuckoo's Nest*, 1975), and the victim (*Enemies: A Love Story*, 1989), all of whom can change in the course of the story.[112] The rise of the horror and fantasy genres may have encouraged more stars to play dark and damned heroes, as Cruise does in *Interview with the Vampire* and as Nicholson does in *The Shining* (1980) and *Wolf* (1994). Character-driven films of the New Hollywood like *Carnal Knowledge* (1970), *The Last Detail* (1973), and *Shampoo* (1975) made filmmakers aware of alternatives to the "externally" driven protagonist. For example, *Five Easy Pieces* (1970) reflects the influence of European art cinema in portraying an antihero who lacks a clear-cut goal. Robert Eroica Dupea is two people. In the south, Bobby talks with a broad drawl and kicks back with good old boys and his big-haired girlfriend, Rayette. Summoned to his home up north, Robert puts on a tailored jacket, speaks with upper-class fastidiousness, and rejoins his brother and sister, talented but socially awkward musicians. Characters, milieus, and motifs are organized around his two personalities: Tammy Wynette tunes versus classical pieces, the waitress Rayette versus the pianist Catherine, dusty oil fields versus the moist forests of Oregon. This plot is nearly all "inner motivation." An external action seems to start when Robert thinks he wants to dump Rayette, but Catherine rejects him because he can't love anyone. He hates both rednecks and intellectuals because he hates himself, and at the climax he confesses to his father, mute and blank from his heart ailment, that he can't find peace. His life doesn't add up. Robert moves around, "not because [he's] looking for anything much," but because he wants to leave wherever he is. At the finale Bobby abandons Rayette at a gas station and hops a truck to Alaska, where, he's been told, things are cleaner.

Though well suited for episodic treatment, the maladjusted protagonist is more often fitted into a goal-driven structure. *Man on the Moon* (1999) revives the figure of the troubled and troublesome genius. Andy Kaufman's dream—to be "the biggest star in the world" and play Carnegie Hall—is jeopardized by his fairly unusual notion of entertainment. He's a comedian who confesses to having no sense of humor and creates an alter ego (Tony Clifton) of surpassing obnoxiousness. Conceiving humor as a series of pranks, put-ons, and non sequiturs, Andy seems forever the little boy we see at the start teaching his sister nonsense songs. He carries around a plastic snot bubble he can attach to either nostril, he compulsively rearranges food on his plate, and he's moved by Howdy Doody and singing-cowboy movies. "You're insane," his agent tells him at the start of his career. "But you might also be brilliant." It's the purpose of the plot to show that both claims are true. Almost despite himself, Andy wins a role on *Taxi* (end of Setup), but then he undermines the show and worries that his concert audience has become comfortable with him (Complicating Action as counter-setup). So Andy reinvents himself as a wrestler who will fight only women, thereby meeting the woman he marries (Development). After learning he has cancer, Andy mounts a new show—at Carnegie Hall, naturally—that encapsulates his frankly childish conception of entertainment (Climax). At the close of the concert, complete with the Rockettes and Santa, he invites the audience out for milk and cookies. Andy's epiphany occurs when he visits a gray-market Philippines cancer clinic and discovers to his pleasure that the miraculous cures are faked with chicken parts, just the kind of dumb trick to delight a kid.

Like the problematic protagonist, subjective sequences have a long history. The dream inserts of the earliest films were refined in the elaborate dream and fantasy sequences of 1920s European cinema. Then and now, these portions of the film are usually demarcated by technical markers like soft focus, distorted decor, slow motion, and slurred sound. Stretches of subjectivity have remained a mainstay of modern Hollywood cinema, from the

1.21. *The Insider:* As his world collapses, the hero sits in a hotel room, imagining himself in his yard watching his daughter.

wide-angle delirium of *Seconds* (1966) to the warped landscapes surrounding the melancholic protagonist of *The Insider* (1999; Fig. 1.21) and the memory erasure of *Eternal Sunshine of the Spotless Mind.* But we've already seen that another long-standing convention works to *conceal* the fact that we're in somebody's mind. Ever since *The Cabinet of Dr. Caligari* (1920), films have tricked viewers into believing in the reality of scenes that turn out to be mere delusions. The tactic is a favorite of horror and fantasy cinema, as in *Carrie* (1976) and *Identity* (2003), but it is available to any genre. In *Shattered Glass* (2003), the flashback episodes seem to be framed by the protagonist recounting his triumphs to an adoring journalism class, but eventually we learn that there is no audience, only an empty classroom. Artier fare treats subjectivity with more ambivalence. The phantasmagoric city of *Mickey One* (1965) and the revenge quest of *Point Blank* (1967) could be construed as each protagonist's fantasy constructions. The Climax of *The Rapture* (1991) induces us to wonder whether we are witnessing the Final Days or the descent of the heroine into lunacy. The uneasy visions haunting the hero of *Jacob's Ladder* (1990) can be read as genuine threats or hallucinations induced by chemical experiments in the Vietnamese jungle; at the end, the narration suggests that nearly everything we've seen has been a dying man's vision of a potential future. Such endings invite dedicated viewers to lock into puzzle-film mode and to rescan the movie for clues and narrational gambits.

   A Beautiful Mind (2001), pure Oscar bait, illustrates how a careful director and screenwriter can manipulate subjective states within the canonical four-part structure. Setup: John Nash, the inspired but socially awkward mathematician, breaks through with his discovery of competitive equilibrium and wins a place at MIT's prestigious Wheeler Center. Complicating Action: Nash is recruited by a government agent, Parcher, to help break Russian codes and prevent a nuclear attack. This intrigue consumes about 40 minutes, with the turning point revealing to us that Parcher and his entire enterprise are a hallucination born of Nash's schizophrenia. Even more startling, Nash's college roommate, Charles, is revealed as imaginary too. Development: Nash struggles to recover, supported by his wife, Alicia, but threatened at every step by the return of Parcher, Charles, and Charles's equally phantasmic niece, Marcy. Climax: Nash returns to teaching, gains a measure of lucidity, and is awarded the Nobel Prize.

Director Ron Howard lures us into Nash's fantasy world through some devious means. At the start of the movie, Nash is fascinated by reflections and refractions (Fig. 1.22), and he scribbles his equations on panes of glass as light streams in on him (Fig. 1.23). Nash's visit to the Pentagon is filmed with flamboyant camera movements and compositions (Fig. 1.24), motivated as expressing his thrill in finding the "governing dynamics" of the Russian codes. The glowing patterns of numbers that he plucks out of the code arrays once more equate bursts of light with bursts of genius (Fig. 1.25). The motif becomes recast as romantic imagination when Nash shows Alicia the outline of an umbrella in the stars (Fig. 1.26). Yet these mild flights of fancy also serve as decoys. Having been given fleeting access to Nash's mind, we're likely to take as objective the more radical hallucinations that aren't so evidently marked off. The sinister agent, Parcher, trails Nash, but he vacates the frame in a timely fashion when others appear. Just as casually, the film plants the phantasmagoric Charlie in the college life of the Setup. Charlie comes staggering into Nash's lodgings with a completely plausible hangover. In later scenes he inhabits Nash's space and hands him swigs from what seems to be a tangible whisky flask. Yet he's never seen outside Nash's ken or mingling with others. The plot motivates this situation by making Charlie an English major, somebody unlikely to hang around with math geeks. There are some cunning dialogue hooks too, as when Charlie invites Nash out for beer and the next scene shows Nash carousing with his math pals, while Charlie stands alone far from them. The revelation that Charlie is a phantom strikes us with considerable poignancy, because he has helped Nash achieve success. A touching scene shows John thanking Charlie for his friendship but warning him that henceforth he will be ignored.

The first half of the film is restricted to Nash, but once the Development incorporates Alicia's range of knowledge, the narration becomes more objective. We learn to take Charlie and Parcher as delusions, even when they're standing among a real crowd or badgering Nash when he's alone. Thanks to shifts in point-of-view cutting, scene after scene reconfirms them as figments of his imagination. Eventually the romance plot triumphs, and Alicia wins John to the light by teaching him the well-worn lesson that the heart

1.22. *A Beautiful Mind:* Sparkling reflections in a drinking glass morph into the pattern of a necktie.

1.23. Daylight stamps Nash's equations onto his frantic face.

1.24. A giddy deep-focus image presents Nash scrutinizing the Russian codes.

1.25. Once again, numbers in light: the patterns Nash discerns are illuminated in the code arrays.

1.26. Nash guides Alicia's hand to trace an umbrella in the stars.

is more real than the mind. As Nash haltingly gains lucidity, his demons don't vanish, but he learns to ignore them. In the final moments he simply turns his back on Charlie, Parcher, and Marcie to follow Alicia out of the Stockholm foyer.

By setting Nash, head down, all stammers and tics, on the margins of groups, the narration deceives us from the start by making us think that he's merely eccentric. Apparently we have another vulnerable Hollywood protagonist who must come out of his shell. The film's first half doesn't raise the issue of hallucinations, whereas the second half allows us to move knowingly into and out of his troubled but beautiful mind. This strategy, purely classical, not only leads us to enlightenment but allows the heroic misfit to arouse our compassion. The narration's sleight of hand is anticipated in the film's ad tagline, "He Saw the World in a Way No One Could Have Imagined." Hollywood's traditional storytelling structure meets the challenge by imagining for us what its maladjusted hero sees with firm, vivid, and redundant clarity. As luck would have it, Ron Howard's production company is called Imagine.

One can, however, imagine differently, as two of David Lynch's experimental narratives indicate. *Lost Highway* (1997) inexplicably morphs its initial protagonist into another character, each played by different actors. The plot eventually folds in on itself, with the new protagonist leaving the message that the original one heard at the film's start. *Mulholland Drive* (2001) does the same, although now the double is played by the same actor, while some characters from early scenes reappear in different relations to her. If complex storytelling demands high redundancy, Lynch has been derelict in his duty. The films' phantasmagoric body-switches occur without explanation in a milieu soaked in dread and threatened violence. The eerie mix of horror-film atmospherics and radiant naïveté may urge us to construe each film as presenting the fantasies of a possessed protagonist, but the cues are not nearly as firm as they are in *A Beautiful Mind*. Instead, the absence of definite reference points allows Lynch to rehearse a few obsessive scenarios of lust and blood without settling on which are real and which are imagined.

Time and Time Again

Rearranging the order of story events has been a mainstay of Hollywood plotting since the earliest years.[113] In the 1940s, while screenplay manuals were warning writers to avoid flashbacks, films were filling up with them.[114] Two decades later, spurred by Resnais and other Europeans, U.S. directors employed not only flashbacks but enigmatic glimpses of future story events. In *Petulia* (1968) fragmentary flash-forwards anticipated the end of the affair, and *They Shoot Horses, Don't They?* (1969) peppered its plot with forecasts of a stylized trial. The flash-forward device is particularly interesting because it announces an overt narration. Unless a character has ESP (a possibility raised in thrillers like *Don't Look Now*, 1973), visions of the future can be attributed only to some narrating process outside the characters' world. Far-reaching flash-forwards remain rare, though we find local instances in the brief intercutting of the end of one scene with the beginning of the next, as in *The Godfather* and *Hannibal* examples I've mentioned.

Occasionally we encounter flash-forwards that are initially presented as a character's anticipation of an action, to be eventually played out objectively, in the manner we've already seen (*Yentl*, 1983; *Bound*, 1996).

Today, flashbacks are quite common; and most, as in the studio era, are triggered as character memory. Group-centered melodramas like *The Joy Luck Club* (1993) and *How to Make an American Quilt* (1995) have come to rely on people recounting their lives, which the film's narration dramatizes for us. Audiences have learned to follow abrupt flashbacks in a film's opening stretches, accepting them as a character's recollection or recitation of backstory events. The black-and-white flashbacks scattered through the Setup of *The Fugitive* (1993) provide concise and arresting exposition. Other uses of the device can be more intricate. *Six Degrees of Separation* (1993) and *Basic* (2003) embed flashbacks within other flashbacks. *The End of the Affair* (1999) presents two sets of parallel and complementary flashbacks, showing some events from alternative points of view and many out of chronological order. *The Sweet Hereafter* (1997) threads an array of time schemes around the central school bus accident, weaving them across the personal story (also studded with flashbacks) of the lawyer prodding the grieving parents to mount a lawsuit. In *Dead Man Walking* (1995), the jumps back in time arise from a standard narrating situation—a man on Death Row recounting his crimes—but black-and-white flashbacks suggest inconclusive and hypothetical possibilities, while eventually color is used to present the events as they really happened.

More and more, though, flashbacks aren't motivated by character memory or reconstruction. This is a change from traditional practice, in which a framing situation would present a character recounting or reflecting on the past. Even in the studio era, however, character memory was little more than an alibi for temporal reordering.[115] Scenes were reshuffled to kindle suspense or curiosity, and few efforts were made to represent consistent or plausible memories. (Characters often "recalled" scenes that they weren't present to witness.) Today the narration will often simply juxtapose one chunk of time with another, though still marking the flashback with an intertitle, a dialogue hook, or a vivid optical transition and burst of sound. Now, it seems, audiences' familiarity with flashback structures allows filmmakers to delete the memory alibi and move straight between present and past.

One step toward this fluidity was Kubrick's *The Killing* (1956), which presents the events around a racetrack heist by following one character to a decisive moment, then skipping back earlier in the day to follow another. In Lionel White's original novel, *Clean Break* (1955), the time shifts are handled through chapter divisions and omniscient narration. Kubrick's film employs a more overt and self-conscious device, a clipped voice-over that raps out the time of day in a manner reminiscent of documentaries. Again, the plot's complex structure calls forth redundancy. But Quentin Tarantino points out that rearranging blocks of time as *Clean Break* does is common in prose fiction:

> Novels go back and forth all the time. You read a story about a guy who's doing something or in some situation and, all of a sudden, chapter five comes and it takes Henry, one of the guys, and it shows you seven years ago, where he was seven years ago and how he came to be and then like, *boom,* the next chapter, boom, you're back in the flow of the action. . . . Flashbacks, as far as I'm concerned, come from a personal perspective. These [in *Reservoir Dogs*] aren't, they're coming from a narrative perspective. They're going back and forth like chapters.[116]

In this spirit *Reservoir Dogs* was dedicated to Lionel White, yet the film follows Hollywood tradition by overtly marking the flashbacks. They are signposted by intertitles ("Mr. White," "Mr. Blonde," "Mr. Orange") and dialogue hooks ("I blasted my way out" followed by shots of the gunfight). *Pulp Fiction* (1994) offers somewhat purer instances of the chapter-division flashback, each labeled with an orienting title. Large blocks rather than mere interpolations, these flashbacks recall Richard Stark's four-part noir novels, in which a first batch of chapters presents a suspenseful situation, the next sections backtrack to show what led to it, and the final part returns to the present for the climax.

Tarantino's debt to pulp fiction reminds us that many storytelling innovations in contemporary American cinema have precedents in other popular media. To take an extreme case, it's tempting to think of *Memento* as a dumbed-down version of the retrograde plotting seen in Harold Pinter's 1978 play *Betrayal* and its film version (1983). Isn't a reverse-order structure something tolerated only in highbrow drama and art cinema? Actually, well before *Memento* hit the screens, a fall 1997 episode of *Seinfeld* ("The Betrayal") told its story in reverse. Back before Pinter, George F. Kaufman and Moss Hart employed the device in the 1934 Broadway play *Merrily We Roll Along,* adapted as a musical show by Stephen Sondheim in 1981. In the novel *Goodbye to the Past* (also 1934), W. R. Burnett moves the action from 1929 steadily back to 1873. Like *Memento* and Tarantino's films, all these works announce their deviant structure. The *Seinfeld* episode specifies days and times at the head of each scene; the text of Kaufman and Hart's play explains the device and lists the scenes' epochs; *Goodbye to the Past* takes as its epigram Kierkegaard's dictum "Life can only be understood backwards; but it must be lived forwards." Again, formal experiment demands overt prompting.

Plots revolving around a secret have always encouraged flashbacks, and a good many of the 1940s time-juggling movies were mystery thrillers and detective movies. So are recent examples like *Memento* and *Pulp Fiction*. Partway through Soderbergh's *Out of Sight* (1998) the plot replays the opening scene of the protagonist's arrest, but now we know the reasons behind his attempted bank robbery. In a neat trick, Soderbergh's new arrangement tallies with the demands of canonical script structure. If the lead-up to the robbery were in its chronological place, the romance plot wouldn't get launched until the Complicating Action. The reshuffling of scenes introduces the cop Karen Sisco in the Setup, making her both love interest and tandem protagonist. Analogous experiments in reordering can be found in Asian films, such as Wai Ka-fai's *Too Many Ways to Be No. 1* (Hong Kong, 1997) and Hong Sang-soo's *Ah, Su-Jeong!* (South Korea, 2000), but the American instances tend to be more explicit about their construction, signaling an out-of-order block of scenes by superimposed titles, freeze-frames, or voice-over commentary. The neo-noir *Confidence* (2003) begins with an echo of *Sunset Boulevard* (1950) as the hero introduces the extensive flashback by remarking, over a shot of his body lying in an alley, "So I'm dead."

American film of the 1990s also revived the device of repetitive flashbacks, replaying a situation with fresh emphasis or varying points of view. Classical Hollywood had done this through what we might call multiple-draft flashbacks, dramatizing characters' different versions of events, usually framed by a trial (e.g., *Thru Different Eyes*, 1929) or an investigation (*Crossfire*, 1947). After Kurosawa's *Rashomon* (1950) refused to present any witness's testimony as the accurate version, Hollywood responded in a comic vein with *Les Girls* (1957), which gives three versions of a dance troupe's breakup and concludes with a placard filling the screen, "What Is Truth?" But most recent American films have avoided the incompatibilities of multiple-draft flashbacks and have simply returned to an earlier scene to provide supplemental information. Following in the steps of *The Killing*, *Jackie Brown* (1997) replays the climactic money exchange according to different characters' range of knowledge, thereby filling us in on exactly how the scam was pulled. *One Night at McCool's* (2001) contrasts two aspects of the meeting that initiates the story action. Repetition of key scenes from new angles or with enhanced knowledge sometimes crops up in the "network narratives" I'll explore shortly, as when *Go* (1999) returns to earlier chains of events in order to plug gaps and introduce branching story lines.

I've remarked that long-range flash-forwards are uncommon, but they have taken on a new role with the 1990s interest in alternative-futures or forking-path plots. Here the film presents a turning point in a character's life and proceeds to dramatize the outcomes of different courses of action. The most influential recent example is Tom Tykwer's *Run Lola Run* (1998), but precedents can be found in Resnais's *Smoking/No Smoking* (1993) and Kieslowski's *Blind Chance* (1987). In Hollywood, *Back to the Future II* (1989) allows Marty McFly to visit different futures, but later films preview alternative outcomes without benefit of a time machine. *Sliding Doors* (1998) intercuts two possible futures for its heroine, while *The Family Man* (2000) leaves one mostly offscreen. Again a potentially avant-garde device finds a home in popular media. Charles Dickens and O. Henry experimented with alternative plot resolutions, Resnais adapted his films from plays by Alan Ayckbourn, and thanks to split-screen compositions, an episode of TV's *Malcolm in the Middle* depicts two futures simultaneously. Today's viewers have likely learned to follow branching story options from computer menus, videogames, and the *Choose Your Own Adventure* books they read as children.[117] The 1990s popularization of chaos theory doubtless prepared the way too. Now *The Butterfly Effect* (2004) can rewind back and forth among no fewer than five rival outcomes.

It isn't just local hooks between scenes that allow us to understand films with scrambled time sequences. As we'd expect, everything, sooner or later, hangs together by virtue of causal coherence. We can understand who among the Reservoir Dogs is the traitor because we can assign each scene to the botched heist, to the preparation for it, or to the aftermath. The school bus disaster of *The Sweet Hereafter* provides a reference point allowing us to understand each scene as either preparing for it or following from it. As we've seen, the temporal disorder and ambivalent subjectivity in *Memento* are smoothed down by causal links. Thompson has shown that mainstream Hollywood can stretch to accommodate even the time-warping repetitions of *Groundhog Day* (1993) as long as they rest on a clear pattern of goal orientation and cause and effect.[118] Screenwriting manuals that encourage the new "nonlinear" trends in plotting still demand intelligible exposition, unified strings of events, and vivid turning points.[119]

When classical storytelling asks us to compare characters or situations, we're typically given a causal framework. Jerry Maguire's failing marriage is contrasted to Rod Tidwell's thriving one with respect to each man's goal-directed actions. But what about plots that reverse the priorities, stressing parallels at the expense of causal connections? Apart from *Intolerance* (1916), in which Griffith sought to bring out abstract similarities among four historical epochs, Hollywood has discouraged this sort of construction. *The*

Godfather Part II (1974) is the major recent exception. The film steadily jux-taposes the rise of two men to Mafia power: Michael Corleone in the years after World War II and his father, Vito, in the prewar era. Both father and son are driven by vendetta morality. The opening portions show Vito flee-ing Don Ciccio, who has murdered Vito's father and mother. The parallel segment presents the strafing of Michael's family compound at Lake Tahoe. At the film's double climax, Vito returns to his hometown and takes vengeance on Don Ciccio, while Michael wipes out his enemies in a blood-bath. The parallel structure also throws differences into relief. Vito builds his empire by expanding his circle of friends and helping the weak. Michael strips himself of personal ties, divorcing his wife, bullying his sister, and murdering his brother. The film ends by juxtaposing Vito's family waving happily from the train leaving Corleone with a shot of Michael, alone and brooding in shadow. He has protected his father's power but thrown away whatever human values justified it. Perhaps only the success of *The God-father* could permit its sequel to explore such large-scale parallels, but it's significant that within each strand the action is causally coherent. Vito's de-cision to eliminate Fanucci in Little Italy becomes a step toward consolidating his power, while Michael's plan to control gambling in Cuba is part of his Jacobean revenge scheme. As in *Intolerance* (1916), the epochs that alter-nate with one another contain arcs of purposeful action.

American independent cinema has been bolder, occasionally offering par-allel stories in which causal connections are minimized. Murray Smith has shown that *Mystery Train* (1989), *Slacker* (1991), and *Night on Earth* (1993) employ spatial and temporal links to create parallel situations, while *Flirt* (1995) brings its three stories abreast by having the same dialogue played out in each one.[120] *The Hours* (2002) intercuts three women in three eras (1921, 1951, and 2001), and although slender causal connections among them are eventually revealed, the dominant impression is of thematic parallels—the temptation of suicide and the difficulty of accepting life and love.

Serendipity and Small Worlds

We're used to hearing that a new movie is *Die Hard* on a boat or *Jaws* in a spaceship, but in its day *Stagecoach* (1939) was known as *Grand Hotel* on wheels. The 1932 film, derived from Vicki Baum's novel and a successful Broadway adaptation, gathered several characters at Berlin's magnificent Grand Hotel. It laid down some basic conventions: in one locale, a star-packed cast portrays characters linked by contingency. The plot is woven out of ill-fated romances, cross-class comparisons, intermingled causal lines, and con-trasts between dramatic crises and mundane routine. In the decades we're considering, *The VIPs* (1963) continued the tradition, and other films modified it. *The Poseidon Adventure* (1972) and *The Towering Inferno* (1974) plunged their assorted characters into life-or-death situations. Kenneth Tynan remarks, "No literary device in this century has earned so much for so many people. Unite a group of people in artificial surroundings—a hotel, a life-boat, an airliner—and, almost automatically, you have a success on your hands."[121]

Grand Hotel plots are variants of what is nowadays called the "ensemble" movie, and this format became unexpectedly salient in the 1960s. Once pictures had to be sold as one-off events, producers mounted star-packed features that could protect big investments. A vast and instantly recognizable cast seemed suitable for historical epics (*How the West Was Won*, 1963), prestigious dramas (*Judgement at Nuremburg*, 1961), and adaptations of novels usually described as "sprawling" (*Advise and Consent*, 1962; *Hotel*, 1967). Some big films assigned stars to cameo roles (most risibly in *The Greatest Story Ever Told*, 1965), while others created plots with more than one protagonist (*Ship of Fools*, 1965; *Airport*, 1970). Sometimes, as in *The Towering Inferno*, one or two characters get primary emphasis, but minor story lines involving second-string stars fill a lot of screen time.

Such tales prod us to reflect on the variety of ways a film can use a protagonist. The single hero or heroine is our default case. Many romantic comedies give the couple roughly equal importance (e.g., *You've Got Mail*, 1998). When two protagonists share a goal, such as combating crime (the *Lethal Weapon* partners), we can speak of *dual* protagonists. Occasionally adversaries can be elevated to the status of co-protagonists, as in *Amadeus* (1984). Or two principals' actions may be coordinated, even though they have quite different goals (e.g., *Citizens Band*, 1977; *Desperately Seeking Susan*, 1985; *The Hunt for Red October*, 1990). Kristin Thompson calls these *parallel* protagonists.[122] The synchronization of the two leads' stories can be thematic rather than causal, as in the hourglass symmetry of Woody Allen's *Crimes and Misdemeanors* (1989). One story line, somber and dramatic, shows the ophthalmologist Judah reluctantly deciding to have his mistress, Dolores, killed. At first he's tormented by remorse, but he comes to accept and even forget his crime. A more comic line of action centers on Cliff, a frustrated documentary filmmaker whose marriage is unraveling. He is drawn to the television producer Halley, but she winds up marrying his brother-in-law, Lester, an obnoxious TV celebrity. The plots are joined by the figure of the rabbi Ben, Cliff's other brother-in-law whom Judah is treating for an eye disorder. Concretely, two celebrations—one early, one late—bring the lines of action together. At the first party, Judah and Cliff don't meet. In the film's epilogue, the wedding party of Ben's daughter, Judah and Cliff talk for the first time, each musing on his situation. One man has betrayed his devoted mistress, another has been betrayed by his would-be lover. Their meeting at the end evokes the crimes that go unpunished and the misdemeanors that destroy love.

When plot structure and narration emphasize three or more protagonists, things get more complex. As we've seen with *Where the Boys Are* (1960), the plot can fit the fates of several characters to the four-part structure, but usually some get slighted. This imbalance was characteristic of the cycle of three-person plots that included *On the Town* (1949), *How to Marry a Millionaire* (1953), *Three Coins in the Fountain* (1954), and *It's Always Fair Weather* (1955). We might better think of these ensemble films as presenting not three equal protagonists but one or two expanded subplots. These movies give sidekicks and confidantes a bit more to do than they have in a lone-protagonist film. The structure lingers in ensemble pictures like *Dead Poets Society* (1989), where the chief protagonist may emerge as the person who has the most to lose and who takes the strongest action.[123]

In other ensemble films, several protagonists are given equal emphasis, based on screen time, star wattage, control over events, or other spotlighting maneuvers. Yet some plot phases and character arcs may be abbreviated, as Evan Smith notes:

> Each story thread is shorter, less developed, than a conventional plot line. . . . While most threads boast a recognizable beginning—middle—end (three-act development), others, brazenly, do not. Key plot points, even entire acts, are compressed, combined, or omitted altogether. Meet Character A, after he has already launched into his second act and is already pursuing some quest to its final resolution. . . . Meet Character B, sample her life, witness the event that sends her running, and then . . . her story suddenly ends, just stops, without resolution.[124]

In Lawrence Kasdan's *Grand Canyon* (1991), the married couple Mack and Claire and the brother-sister pair of Simon and Vanessa are given roughly equal emphasis. Their lines of action follow Thompson's four-part template, but other plotlines show Mack's son falling in love with a girl he meets at camp, Vanessa's son becoming alienated, and Mack's friend Davis vowing to stop making ultraviolent movies. The subsidiary characters don't encounter all the customary obstacles and setbacks, yet their wants are developed beyond the limits of a traditional subplot, providing thematic echoes or counterpoints. It seems likely that audiences' familiarity with soap operas and the longer-running story arcs of prime-time television shows like *Hill Street Blues* readied them for such multiplot pictures.

When the plot lifts more than a couple of characters to prominence, how to keep things unified and understandable? One strategy is to tie the characters together by a circulating object, such as the coat of tails in *Tales of Manhattan* (1942), the rifle in *Winchester 73* (1950), a car in *The Yellow Rolls Royce* (1964), and a currency note in *Twenty Bucks* (1993). Usually, though, characters are connected more intimately. They can mingle in the same locale, as in the hotel movies *Grand Hotel, Week-End at the Waldorf* (1945), *Hotel Berlin* (1945), *Plaza Suite* (1971), and *Four Rooms* (1995). *Smoke* (1995) links customers in a tobacco shop. A space-based ensemble film is almost always restricted in time as well. *American Graffiti* (1973), *Drive-In* (1976), and *Dazed and Confused* (1993) present clusters of small-town youths living through a few hours, while *Do the Right Thing* (1989) concentrates on a single day in a neighborhood. Amid running gags and one-off vignettes, *Car Wash* (1976) traces several threads in one workday: an aspiring singing duo, a lonely cashier, a cowboy with clap, a hooker waiting for nightfall, and, most elaborately, a youth's efforts to win a radio contest and persuade a ravishing woman to date him. Of course, such plots typically also bind people by more than proximity: the characters are lovers, friends, co-workers, or relatives, as in extended-family films like *Parenthood* (1989) and *Hannah and Her Sisters*.[125] Even strangers can be hooked up through what one manual calls an "event frame," a common fate or significant occasion.[126] When the circumstances are dire, we have the disaster film,[127] while *A Wedding* (1978) and *Gosford Park* (2001) assemble their protagonists around a celebration and a weekend holiday respectively. *200 Cigarettes* (1999) cuts to and fro among several young people headed toward a New Year's Eve party. Event frames multiply in *Four Weddings and a Funeral* (1994), which focuses the action on the five ceremonies announced in the title.[128]

If there's no overarching event frame, unacquainted characters might be granted more autonomy, pursuing their own lives but intersecting occasionally by sheer accident (most often a *traffic* accident: it's dangerous to take to the roads in today's movies). This version of the ensemble plot has come to be known as the "converging fates" device. Crisscrossed fates may launch the plot, as in *It's a Mad Mad Mad Mad World* (1963), when an auto crash unleashes several characters in search of buried treasure.[129] More commonly, convergences emerge in the middle or at the end. *Honky-Tonk Freeway* (1981) intercuts several drivers' trips south, all in pursuit of personal goals. Along the way some characters meet at gas stations and rest stops, and all gather at the Climax, when a Florida mayor sabotages the highway and diverts traffic to his tourist-starved town. *Nashville* (1975) is a more famous example, stressing the sheer contingency of the encounters before bringing nearly all the characters together at the final concert. The multi-frame composition of *Time Code* (2000) lets some characters intersect in one quadrant while keeping divergent story lines alive in other screen areas.

Again, this plot pattern has several precedents. The 1946 Warner Bros. release *Three Strangers* begins with a chance meeting among three people who, one remarks, "really have nothing to do with one another." After they agree to share a lottery ticket, the stories diverge. The lottery venture affects each one differently, and closure is created when the characters reunite on the evening that the lottery results are announced. Some overseas imports were likewise based on tangential and obscure convergences. Jacques Rivette traced interconnecting lives of members of theater troupes in *Paris Belongs to Us* (1961) and *L'Amour fou* (1969). Jacques Tati's *Play Time* (1967) consists largely of accidental encounters replayed throughout Paris in a single day and night. Edward Yang's *Terrorizers* (1986) starts with a mistaken phone call that crucially affects many lives. Closer to home, the intersecting-fates pattern was already available in popular fiction, notably in Thornton Wilder's best-selling *The Bridge of San Luis Rey* (1927). Opening with a bridge collapse that kills five people, the novel traces each person's life up to the fatal moment.

We might expect that converging-fates plots, which riddle their scenes with coincidence, work against the primacy of causal connections. Don't accidents now supplant foreshadowing and kindred tactics of tight construction? Actually, as with most innovations, other principles serve to smooth over any disparities. However independent the lines of action may be, each tends to be shaped by the usual goals, obstacles, appointments, deadlines, and the like. And unlike coincidences in real life, movie coincidences create "small worlds" in which characters will intersect again and again, especially if the duration and locale of the action are well circumscribed. *Go* shows three characters working together before each goes off on an adventure, but they're eventually reconnected through common acquaintances. Circulating-object plots like *Twenty Bucks* tend to create convergences by having characters from one story line return as walk-ons in others.

Some genres have even conventionalized the role of chance. Comedies have long incorporated bad luck and awkward timing, and these can motivate converging fates. *Two Days in the Valley* (1996) traces the unfortunate mishaps linking an insurance scam, a cop's vendetta, a failed double-cross, an aborted suicide, and the meeting of two dog lovers. Greg Marcks's black comedy *11:14* (2003) presents a cascade of accidents that connect in freakish, Rube Goldberg fashion. New romantic comedies may treat coincidences as fate's way of announcing that two people are destined to be together (*Sleepless in Seattle,* 1993; *Serendipity,* 2001). At a loftier level, the accidental meetings in *Nashville* (1975) and *Pulp Fiction* (1994) become a thematic concern, emphasizing either pure contingency ("If Vincent hadn't gone to the toilet at just that moment . . .") or the hand of destiny ("It serves a paid killer right that . . ."). The one-off intersections in *Magnolia* (1997) are motivated partly by the sense that chance meetings are themselves inevitable, reinforced by a prologue announcing that eerily apt things happen all the time. Coincidences, in short, are wholly acceptable in stories *about* coincidence. As Aristotle remarked, "It is likely that some things should occur contrary to likelihood."[130]

Sometimes the very overtness of the converging-fates strategy can make the plot cohere. Convergence is revealed not just through the selection of events but also through narrational strategies of ordering and emphasis. After all, in any story, some fairly chancy occurrence gets the ball rolling, and major characters tend to assemble at the climax. When a multiple-protagonist plot brings strangers together, the more that the narration emphasizes their separate lives, the more we expect significant encounters among them. If our people start to converge, even by chance, then we can feel a satisfying omniscience. Their intersection seems inevitable just because we've been following them from the start. This effect is especially vivid in a thriller like *The Family Plot,* in which the innocent couple searching for a missing heir confounds another couple's kidnapping scheme, so we expect a confrontation when each pair realizes what the other is up to. The narration can create a still stronger sense of inevitability in the manner of *The Bridge of San Luis Rey,* putting the climactic convergence at the start and flashing back to show events leading up to it.

Most often, of course, the lead characters aren't utterly unknown to one another. But as the number of protagonists grows, their connections can get pretty complicated. A is B's friend, C's brother, D's landlord, and E's lover, while E is D's sister and B's employer. . . . What we might call "network narratives" are built out of just such attenuated links, and they present a particular craft challenge. "Really, universally," Henry James remarks, "relations stop nowhere, and the exquisite problem of the artist is eternally but to draw, by a geometry of his own, the circle within which they shall happily *appear* to do so."[131] For smaller social networks the plot can draw this circle by circumscribing time and locale and focusing on one or two chains of cause and effect, as in the comic crime thrillers *Lock, Stock, and Two Smoking Barrels* (1998), *Snatch* (2000), and *interMission* (2003). *Nashville* and *Short Cuts* (1993) indicate that a plot of more widespread links can also be unified by thematic comparisons. John Sayles, like Altman a director specializing in network narratives, provides moral cross sections of entire communities in *City of Hope* (1991), *Lone Star* (1996), and *Sunshine State* (2003). *Magnolia* evokes pervasive father-child parallels by tracing the connections radiating out from the dying patriarch Earl Partridge and the TV show he produces. His wife's mental health is collapsing, and his estranged son has become a Man Power guru. More remotely, a boy starring on Partridge's quiz show is bullied by his father, while the show is hosted by a man with a cocaine-abusing daughter. All these films show as well that network narratives centering on intimate and long-lasting relationships—those of friends, lovers, family—may draw on converging-fates devices too.

Network narratives have a long history in the novel, from Dickens's *Our Mutual Friend* to David Mitchell's *Ghostwritten*, although soap operas and ensemble-cast TV series probably yielded more proximate models for cinema. The form's recent popularity may also owe something to the emergence of network theory in the 1980s and 1990s. Scientists began to explore the nature of small worlds and the connectedness of apparently random phenomena, from cricket-chirping rhythms to the organization of the Internet.[132] As chaos theory came to be called the "butterfly effect," popular culture conceived network theory as "six degrees of separation." After 1990 the phrase passed into common use, thanks largely to John Guare's play and the Six Degrees of Kevin Bacon game, and it seems to have inspired artworks both high and low. An installment of Daniel Clowes's comic book *Eightball* features twenty-nine interconnected tales in a single day in one town.[133] Whatever new shapes degrees-of-separation plots take, most remain coherent and comprehensible, thanks to the principles of causality, temporal sequence and duration, character wants and needs, and motivic harmony that have characterized mainstream storytelling (not just in cinema) for at least a century.

Just how transparent a network plot can be is evident in *Love Actually* (2003). The time: the five weeks before Christmas. The locale: mostly London (and a Portuguese village, and a Milwaukee bar). The core lines of action: the prime minister (played by Hugh Grant) is falling in love with his tea girl, Natalie. His sister, Karen, is worried that her husband is being seduced by his secretary. Karen's friend, the widower Daniel, is trying to help his little boy woo the girl of his dreams. The writer Jamie, only remotely connected to this batch, is smitten with his Portuguese housekeeper. All four undergo critical changes in their love lives, and each stands at the center of a cluster of friends, relations, and employees.

The plot delivers love triangles, sketchy vignettes, and abbreviated goal-achievement pathways.[134] Sarah, an employee of Karen's husband, has eyes for a co-worker, but her affair with him is blocked by the incessant demands of her retarded brother. Other characters are even further removed from the main story lines. Before Jamie loses his girlfriend and flees London for the holidays, he attends Peter and Juliet's wedding. At that wedding we see a waiter, Colin, who, like Jamie, heads overseas—to America, where an English accent ought to attract girls. Colin confides his plan to his pal Tony, who knows another gradually forming couple, John and Judy, who work as stand-ins in pornographic films and who are therefore three steps distant from Jamie. Hovering over all is the wrecked rock singer, Billy Mack, who sings a dreadful holiday cover of "Love Is All Around." Billy is unconnected to any of the other principals, but the unexpected ascent of his tune on the charts adds a satiric event frame.

Director-writer Richard Curtis keeps these proliferating plots in check using several classical devices. The conventions of romantic comedy, with the first fumblings, inevitable misunderstandings, abrupt separations, and bursts of passion, help us thread our way through the maze of relationships. The film falls neatly into four parts of around 30 minutes each, with every major line of action receiving due elaboration. For example, during the Setup Daniel's son, Sam, confesses his romantic problem. Then Sam learns that Joanne is leaving for America (Complicating Action). He decides to accompany her song in the Christmas concert and devotes himself to endless practice (Development). After playing backup drums for her number, Sam chases her to the airport for a final farewell (Climax). In the epilogue, set in Heathrow's arrivals terminal, Sam greets Joanne on her return. To top things off, Curtis gathers several other story lines in the terminal. The porn couple is there with Tony to greet Colin, who returns from the States accompanied by buxom women. Jamie and his housekeeper, Aurelia, meet Peter and Juliet. Karen and her children greet her errant husband, Harry, and Daniel now has a girlfriend in Carol, another parent at Sam's school. Most important, the prime minister arrives with Natalie, whom he's married. Has any other film jammed so much resolution into a single epilogue? As we might expect, that closure is prefigured in the prologue, a series of documentary shots of people arriving at Heathrow while voice-over narration comments on the power of love.

This opening monologue, spoken by the prime minister, partially motivates the degrees-of-separation structure: "Love actually is all around." One could argue that the prime minister's romance is the overarching one, given the amount of time dedicated to it, the comedy revolving around his social station, his voice-over narrating presence, and Hugh Grant's star power. The burned-out Billy Mack ties things together too, because scenes tracking the success of his song tend to start each major part, and in the Climax even he finds love with his portly manager. As sometimes happens in a classical film (not merely a "postclassical" one), characters comment on the structure of the plot that enmeshes them. Daniel encourages his son when the boy thinks Joanna has ditched him: "You've seen the films, kiddo. It ain't over till it's over." But Sam has already anticipated his father's advice. "You know," he says just before the Climax, "the thing about romance is people only get together right at the very end."

It's worth noticing that converging-fates tactics and network narratives can combine with other sorts of formal artifice. *Full Frontal* (2003) inter-cuts two levels of reality, a film and the offscreen lives of the players, their friends, and their relations, all linked through various degrees of separation. *Thirteen Conversations About One Thing* (2001) blends converging fates and repeated flashbacks to reveal varying attitudes toward happiness. In *21 Grams* (2003) Alejandro González Iñárritu treats a traffic accident as a turn-ing point in three characters' lives, but unlike his earlier converging-fates film *Amores Perros* (2000), here he scrambles temporal sequence in each plotline. Yet all these movies make themselves accessible through classical devices. *Full Frontal*'s prologue picks out its main characters and explains their relationships through snapshots and voice-over testimony, and differ-ences in format (film/video) clearly segregate the movie-within-the-movie from the goings-on behind the scenes. *Thirteen Conversations* uses chap-ter titles, seasonal clues, and repeated scenes to help us straighten out its chronology. In *21 Grams,* the Setup is tantalizingly fragmentary, but the plot becomes steadily linear, presenting more sequential scenes and fewer flashbacks as it proceeds. We arrive fairly soon at a stable event frame: a fa-tal hit-and-run shatters the lives of the driver, the victim's wife, and the man who gains the victim's transplanted heart. *21 Grams* achieves closure, and it motivates this, in the approved manner, as at once random and determined. The mathematician protagonist remarks, "There are so many things that have to happen for two people to meet. That's what mathematics are."

My concentration on American experiments in narrative shouldn't lead us to ignore comparable efforts abroad. Indeed, roundabout storytelling has resurged internationally. Network tales have become common in European and Asian cinema, and they're often combined with juggled time frames and point-of-view ploys. Lucas Belvaux's *Trilogy* (2003) presents three films in three genres tracing various pathways taken by its core characters. The Finnish film *Joki* (*The River,* 2001) captures various lives during an hour, each tale punctuated by the same sonic boom. Lee Chang-dong's *Peppermint Candy* (South Korea, 2000) essays a reverse-order murder mystery, and François Ozon's 5 × 2 (2004) follows a couple's disintegration in reverse, from divorce to first meeting. It's to be expected that Hollywood would borrow from such overseas experiments, perhaps adding redundancy and happier endings, as in remakes like *Vanilla Sky* (2001) and *Wicker Park* (2004).

The innovations I've been considering are all enhanced by DVD. An already twist-packed film can be revised as a director's cut, piling on complications and begging for comparisons with the original release. (The video versions of *28 Days Later, Identity,* and *The Butterfly Effect* contain endings that diverge from those in the theatrical releases.) Now that we can rake every frame at leisure, we may expect more puzzle films and forking-path plots, more details demanding a freeze-frame. Paul Thomas Anderson doubtless hopes that video viewers of *Magnolia* will search out all instances of the numerals 8:2, the film's reiterated references to the plague of frogs in Exodus. Some films will offer a choice about what story line to pursue. The DVD version of *Timecode* (2000) allows us to listen to any image quadrant. In the straight-to-DVD release *Real Time: Siege at Lucas Street Market* (2001), a hostage crisis is captured in surveillance-camera and news-report views that we can change at will. Teased by these exercises in interactivity, however, we will still apply the schemas of classical story comprehension, and the films will be engineered to satisfy them.

By insisting on the ways that daring films make themselves accessible, I don't mean to shrug off their ambitions. The point is that these experiments take place within a tradition, one that demands a balance between innovation and adherence to norms. The norms can be recast in a great many ways, but they can't be jettisoned without leaving the tradition behind. Hollywood storytelling fosters creative renewal within flexible but firm limits.

4. A CERTAIN AMOUNT OF PLOT: TENTPOLES, LOCOMOTIVES, BLOCKBUSTERS, MEGAPICTURES, AND THE ACTION MOVIE

It's a little bit like a musical. The visual effects sequences are like the dance numbers, but they have to have a certain amount of plot or they don't work either, and then in between all that you have sixty or seventy minutes of a two-hour movie where you explain why we should care about these characters and what they're going through.

ROLAND EMMERICH[135]

The action film has become the emblem of what Hollywood does worst. The weekly reviewer sees the all-engulfing special effects, the formulaic conflicts of cops and their superiors or the rogue male and the soulless bureaucracy, the car crashes and fistfights and bomb blasts and concludes that American cinema is sinking fast. The film academic is likely to search out the contradictions of capitalism or the crisis of masculinity (evidently one of the longest-running crises in history). Instead of interpreting these movies as symptoms of something, though, we can ask how much they stray from the norms of traditional filmmaking. Do they announce the breakdown of Hollywood storytelling?

For some scholars, these movies betray the classical tradition by elevating plot over character. But few studio-era films in any genre offered probing character studies, and the adventure movie was always heavily oriented toward plot. Our action picture is heir to nineteenth-century adventure fiction and to film serials, from *What Happened to Mary?* (1912), *Fantômas* (1913), and *The Perils of Pauline* (1914) to *Panther Girl of the Kongo* (1955). We don't expect psychological depth from Alexandre Dumas, Eugène Sue, Robert Louis Stevenson, Edgar Rice Burroughs, or Zane Grey, so why should we expect it from *The Black Pirate* (1926), *The Most Dangerous Game* (1933), or *Beau Geste* (1939), let alone from *48 HRS* (1982) or *Raiders of the Lost Ark* (1981)? What's surprising is that today's screenwriters create *more* psychologically complex characters than the genre has typically required.

In action films, we're told, spectacle overrides narrative, and the result works against the "linearity" of the classical tradition. All the stunts and fights make the film very episodic. But these claims are untenable because narrative and spectacle aren't mutually exclusive concepts. Aristotle long ago indicated that spectacle *(opsis)* is a manner of showing forth plot *(muthos)*.[136] Every action scene, however "spectacular," is a narrative event, and it can advance characters' goals and alter their states of knowledge. When a frantic auto pursuit yields clues, or when gunplay kills the hero's best friend, these are matters of causal import. "In action films," Murray Smith points out, "the plot advances *through* spectacle; the spectacular elements are, generally speaking, as 'narrativized' as are the less ostentatious spaces of other genres."[137] Just as important, if we look at the construction of action movies, most aren't significantly fragmentary. They are outfitted with all the standard equipment of goals, conflicts, foreshadowing, restricted omniscience, motifs, rising action, and closure.[138]

Granted, action set pieces are central to the genre, but like the dance numbers in a musical, they can be integrated with long-running lines of action. What may mislead theorists is that chases and fights, like musical numbers, can be expanded indefinitely. We can always add a baby carriage innocently wheeled into the car's path or another adversary popping out to punch the hero. Granted as well, the length of some action sequences isn't warranted by their role in furthering or enriching the main action, as when the Humvee pursuit in *The Rock* (1996) sacrifices economy to momentary thrills. But— such is the nature of narrative—any story event can be expanded to any length; witness the aimless conversations of some European films. In principle, any twist of an action set piece can be integrated with the overarching plot dynamics. In *Die Hard* (1988), every combat contributes to the thrust and parry of McClane's struggle with the "terrorists" occupying the skyscraper. Despite occasional indulgences, most American action pictures are more tightly woven than they need to be.

To get perspective, critics might examine some of Hong Kong's outstanding action films, from the Shaw Brothers classics like *Crippled Avengers* (1978) to the extravaganzas of Jackie Chan (*Police Story*, 1985), Yuen Kuei (*Yes, Madam!*, 1985), and Tsui Hark (*The Blade*, 1995). These tend to be much more episodic than their Hollywood counterparts, centering on violent or comic set pieces while ignoring character change and motivic texture. For all its debt to Hollywood action cinema, Johnnie To's *Breaking News* (2004) focuses entirely on the tension of an apartment-house siege and spares nothing for backstory, subplots, or inner demons. Hong Kong plots compensate for causal slackness with the audacity and virtuosity of their action sequences and with other principles of unity, such as parallelism and reel-by-reel construction.[139] Powerful in communicating the body's grace, strain, suffering, and exaltation, most of these films lack the psychological intimacy of even a *Die Hard*.

"Do *Volcano* (1997), *Mission: Impossible* (1996), and *Independence Day* (1996) need 'classical Hollywood narrative construction,' when it is precisely the fragmentation of their narratives into soundtrack albums, somatic theme-park jolts, iconic emblems stuck on T-shirts, and continuous loops of home entertainment that are really what is being sold?"[140] This question, posed by writer-producer James Schamus, is intriguing because all these films *do* display classical construction. Here, as in other genres, shotgun merchandising campaigns don't seem to shatter protocols of storytelling. You can sell films in lots of different ways, and the films stay unified.

But are the films *experienced* as unified? Researchers studying the reception of *Judge Dredd* (1995) found that fans were happy to list things they liked: "Lots of blood." "Yeah." "Explosions." "Good effects." "Dead bodies." Q: "Anything else? Plot, anything like that?" A: "We don't watch it for that! We watch it for the action, well, I do, anyway.". . . "I was watching it for the action, I didn't really get any story."[141] On the basis of this feedback, the researchers concluded that *Judge Dredd*'s narrative was relevant only to a small segment of viewers. Once more, though, the film is classically constructed. A flawed protagonist who thinks he epitomizes the law must confront the fact that he was created in an extralegal experiment (internal plot). At the same time he must rid the city of his amoral brother, Rico, born from the same experiment (external plot). The action unfolds in four distinct parts plus epilogue, and the problems are resolved in a cliffhanging finale when Dredd's pistol, the Lawgiver 2, answers to his voice command and not Rico's (a feature planted and reiterated earlier in the film).

Judge Dredd is a pretty thinly plotted movie, but it could have been far simpler. Why do filmmakers bother with classical construction if ardent viewers consider it dispensable, even distracting? I'd suggest several answers:

1. People may say they care little for plot, when in fact plot sinks to a level of minimal awareness. It may seem unimportant to viewers because it quietly leads them to concentrate on other things.

2. The audience isn't homogeneous. Scriptwriter Steven DeSouza (*Commando*, 1985; *Die Hard*) says he tries to work on several levels. Action suffices for the kids (such as, presumably, the interviewees in the *Judge Dredd* study), but he wants to reach "intelligent adults" too, so he tries to insert more subtle touches and bits of characterization.[142] It makes economic sense for big-budget films to layer their appeals in this way, broadening the potential audience.

3. Let's assume that audiences strategize to achieve pleasure. How could a filmmaker best accommodate them? For the subculture that worships stars, we might make a movie that records Mel

Gibson and Julia Roberts smiling coyly at each other for 90 minutes. For the viewers who love action, we might patch together
a film consisting wholly of explosions. But each of these options
would attract, to put it mildly, a restricted public. We know no
better way to gratify a broad range of tastes than through classical
construction, which blends star power, physical action, and a host
of other appeals into what we call an "interesting story."

4. As Roland Emmerich points out in the epigraph above, no action
    movie is all action. "Spectacle" is expensive, so the bulk of any
    picture will consist of stretches of sheer story, mostly conversa-
    tion. How else would one fill these stretches if not by appeal to
    the canons of mainstream construction? Proustian inner mono-
    logues, belletristic Godardian ruminations, and Warholian stares
    at sofas aren't feasible options. Nor, interestingly enough, are the
    looser canons of Hong Kong construction. The Hollywood default
    remains, as Emmerich says, characters we care about. And the
    readiest way to make us care about characters is to plunge them
    into a swirl of cause and effect, goals and obstacles, conflicts and
    resolutions, appointments and deadlines, patterns of restricted
    and unrestricted narration, recurring motifs and dangling causes
    and symmetrical closure—in short, all the resources of tradition.

5. Finally, as we saw in examining "hyperclassical" construction,
    films aren't made just for audiences but for other filmmakers.
    Professionals are expected to recognize the rules. The flying se-
    quences in *Top Gun* (1986), the writers assure us, were planned
    to advance the "story progression."[143] Moreover, a filmmaker
    can gain fame with fresh or elegant solutions to storytelling prob-
    lems. The best action films, DeSouza remarks, are smart.[144] *Jaws,*
    Road Warrior (1981), *Raiders, Die Hard,* and *Jurassic Park* (1993)
    have achieved renown partly because they smoothly integrate
    plot twists, character arcs, and recurring motifs. Even if audiences
    don't care about such fine points, many in the community of
    creators do. Prowess in craft yields not only professional satisfac-
    tion but also prestige, and perhaps a better job. Making smart
    action pictures pays off.

All these lines of defense still concede too much, because they make Hollywood storytelling into too much of a compromise. It isn't, I think, simply
a precarious tension of narrative versus spectacle, or a balance of one set of
tastes against another. It isn't just a shrewdly packaged jumble of disparate

appeals. The triumph of the classical cinema, as practiced in Hollywood and elsewhere, is that it is a coherent, flexible aesthetic system of great range and power—somewhat like, as I remarked earlier, perspective in Western painting. Classical storytelling flourishes in large part because it dramatizes certain enduring and widespread aspects of human action, and it presents those aspects in clear and forceful ways.

Whammo!

Chases, stunts, fights, and explosions have long been with us. They were a principal feature of the earliest shorts, adventure serials, and Western and slapstick features. In films of the Keystone Kops and William S. Hart, extended action in open spaces was quickly identified as a distinctively American contribution to film entertainment. After 1920 stunts and violence were integrated into more complex narratives. Buster Keaton's *Our Hospitality* (1923), Douglas Fairbanks's *Thief of Baghdad* (1924), and Harold Lloyd's *Girl Shy* (1924) display a consummate blend of thrilling action and story economy. For perfection of construction, an "action film" like Keaton's *The General* (1927) has seldom been equaled. Throughout the 1930s and 1940s, Westerns, crime films, and adventure movies mounted memorable action sequences, such as the jungle hunt in *The Most Dangerous Game* (1933), the charge in *The Charge of the Light Brigade* (1936), and the climactic pursuits of *Saboteur* (1942), *Naked City* (1948), and *White Heat* (1949). Action sequences benefited from the postwar return to location filming, particularly in lower-budget movies like *The Lineup* (1958), which opens with a screeching car chase through San Francisco. Spy films like *Goldfinger* (1964), crime films like *The St. Valentine's Day Massacre* (1967) and *Madigan* (1968), and Westerns like the Leone and Peckinpah entries pushed toward ever more flamboyant scenes of violent action.[145] They were joined by disaster films like *The Last Voyage* (1960), *The Poseidon Adventure* (1972), and *Earthquake* (1974), which traded on massive physical destruction.

In the 1980s, the action film as we know it emerged, partly because video stores needed a category in which to file films as different as *Road Warrior* and *Where Eagles Dare*. A cycle of politicized action films, starting with *First Blood* (1982) and including *Commando* and the Chuck Norris films, flaunted a grassroots patriotism suspicious of government agencies.[146] Auteurs emerged, notably Tony Scott, James Cameron, and John McTiernan. At the same time, the genre exploded in the low-budget sector. *Mortal Kombat* (1995), based on a video game, cost $30 million and grossed $66 million in its first two months. Jean-Claude van Damme and Steven Seagal became the cut-rate Stallones and Schwarzeneggers. In the early 1990s, an action film could be produced for $2 million or less and sell profitably to overseas cable and home video.[147] Other industries, notably Hong Kong's, began competing in the genre in the 1980s, and even Eastern European action pictures found favor in local markets.[148]

Because of the need to showcase exciting action, the film may display simpler plotting than a romantic comedy or neo-noir, but simpler is not necessarily more disunified. There are ample precedents for thin linearity in the tradition of action-adventure fiction. A novel like *The Three Musketeers* (1844–1845) shoehorns plenty of swordfights and pursuits into the broader plotlines of D'Artagnan's aspiration to become a musketeer and the struggle between court factions. The enduringly popular novel *The Mark of Zorro* (1919) shows how a swordplay plot can easily integrate romance and mystery.

Far from being a noisy free-for-all, moreover, the industry's ideal action movie is as formally strict as a minuet.[149] Many principles of unity have been laid out with remarkable precision in a manual by screenwriter William Martell.[150] Martell shows how strategies of contemporary script construction—act structure, ticking clocks, the "broken" hero—are worked out in the genre. He claims that the most important element of the action film is the villain's plan, and he insists that it be well motivated. He points out that in the first half the hero is likely to be reactive, whereas in the second half the hero seizes the initiative. Critics tend to praise films in which the hero somehow mirrors the villain, but Martell shows that this is a genre convention. He also categorizes various sorts of hero (Superman/Everyman) and outlines variants on the buddy-cop and fighting-team format, even pinpointing the exact moments when conflicts surface. Throughout, Martell refers to exemplars, most frequently *Die Hard,* "the model of what a genre script should strive for, and the barometer with which to measure all future action films."[151] Ironically, the genre considered most scattershot turns out to have the most widely recognized formulas of organization.

True, they *are* formulas, but that's just a derogatory term for norms. Few films fulfill these norms in imaginative ways, but that's true in every genre. The point is that these precepts are well-tested strategies for achieving clarity and arousing interest. In fact, action cinema displays the premises of Hollywood storytelling craft in a particularly pure form. Whether plain, like *The Bourne Identity* (2003) or fancy, like *Spider-Man* (2002), action movies tend to follow the four-part structure delineated by Thompson. Classical goal orientation defines the symmetrical quests of *Star Wars:* the Empire needs to find the rebel stronghold, the Jedi seek the plan for the Empire's battle station, and the two searches converge at the Climax. And one could hardly find clearer instances of escalating goals than these:

> A cruise ship is rigged with several explosive devices. When officials refuse to pay the extortion, a team of bomb-disposal experts is called in. But one is killed, and the squad chief is ready to capitulate: "Pay the man his money." Negotiations have broken off, however, so the team leader must disarm the bombs (*Juggernaut*, 1974).

> A former Green Beret is recruited to prove that the Vietnamese are holding MIAs, and when he arrives at the camp he rescues one. Vowing to return, he is betrayed and captured. He escapes, then saves the prisoners and wreaks vengeance (*Rambo: First Blood Part II*, 1985).

> A team is pursuing nuclear missiles stolen by terrorists. Retrieving all but one, they must then prevent the mechanism from being set off in Manhattan (*The Peacemaker*, 1997).

Of course, there will be appointments and deadlines, with a ticking-clock Climax. There may be converging story lines as well. In *Independence Day* (1996), the president and his family are initially in Washington, D.C.; the computer whiz and his father are in New York City; the former Vietnam pilot and his family live in the desert; and the air force pilot and his girlfriend live in Los Angeles. The threads wind together gradually until all the major characters unite in Area 51 and the Climax of the film is launched.

Even the cartoonish *Independence Day* fleshes out its alien-invasion story line with personal problems, deadlines, and recurring tags—chess, cigars, wedding rings, and fireworks. Once more, the action picture proves more tightly unified than it needs to be if visceral arousal were all that mattered. Foreshadowing and motivic development are common as well. The drinking contest early in *Raiders of the Lost Ark* (1981) shows that Marion can hold her booze, so she can later drink Bellocq silly. (The twist comes when he reveals that the wine is his family label: "I grew up on this.") The credits for *The Mask of Zorro* (1998) begin with the silhouetted figure's sword blade whisking through his familiar Z (Fig. 1.27) before the fiery signature becomes an abstract network of slashing diagonals (Fig. 1.28). The story's opening shot picks up this design by showing a penknife blade sawing inverted V-shaped holes in burlap, before eyes peer out (Fig. 1.29). Alejandro Murrieta, the boy who cuts the holes, will become the new Zorro, so the image at once picks up the zigzag motif, prefigures Zorro's domino mask, and creates an M-figure that recalls the family's initial. After the sadistic Captain Love kills Alejandro's brother, the motif returns neatly. During the film's final swordfight,

1.27. *The Mask of Zorro:* The emblematic Z . . .

1.28. . . . becomes an abstract graphic pattern . . .

1.29. . . . picked up in the slits of Alejandro's burlap mask. The M shape foreshadows both Zorro's mask and . . .

1.30. . . . the design that Zorro will slice into Love's cheek, at once a Z and an M.

Zorro carves an M in Love's cheek, a variant of the Z-trace that creates an image of vengeance in the name of family honor (Fig. 1.30).

Speed (1994) exemplifies the fairly well-crafted action picture. You can say it has three acts (bomb on elevator/on bus/on subway train), or Thompson's four parts (with a midpoint stakes raiser, the death of an innocent bus passenger, proving that the bomber is willing to kill everyone). The running motifs do causal work. The bomber is watching a televised football game featuring the Arizona Wildcats, and in phone conversation with Jack, the cop on the lethal bus, he refers to Annie, the woman driving, as a "wildcat." Only later will Jack realize that the bomber can see Annie's Arizona sweater, so there must be a video camera aboard. The "pop quiz" line answered by Jack's flippant "Shoot the hostage" at the film's start recurs at the end, but now Annie is the hostage, and Jack cannot follow his own maxim. Both motifs tie into a broader arc of Jack's character. At the beginning he's valiant but impetuous, and his mentor, Harry, warns him that he's going to have to learn to think if he's to survive. The bomber mocks Jack for the same reason: "Do not attempt to grow a brain." But when Jack concludes that the bomber is monitoring the bus, he devises a way to send looped video footage to the bomber while the passengers escape. At the Climax, Jack can use his recklessness strategically: with the subway train hurtling out of control, he realizes that he must accelerate. In the course of his adventure, Jack's boldness gets tempered by wiliness and prudence. This is not a moral education worthy of Henry James, but it's enough to bind the suspense and stunts into a reasonably well-contoured whole.[152]

Apart from its conformity to general storytelling norms, the action picture exhibits unique conventions. One is the hierarchy of antagonists whom the hero faces. In *Payback* (1999), Parker must work his way up the ladder from his double-crossing pal through a string of bosses and crooked cops to the top dog. "You go high enough," Parker says, "you always get to one man." Part of the humor of *Lock, Stock, and Two Smoking Barrels* (1998) is the continuous revelation of ever more fearsome villains. Another genre convention is a driving, propulsive narration. To the usual stock of dialogue hooks the action picture adds voice-over information pouring from offscreen radio and television broadcasts, often to provide a quick epilogue at the film's close (for example, in *Cop Land*, 1997). Action montages are likely to display eye-catching special effects, most recently "ramping" (slowed or speeded motion in the course of a shot). Fusillades of glossy graphics and hammering soundtracks in *The Last Boy Scout* (1991), *Spy Game* (2000), and *Man on Fire* (2004) have become the signature style of Tony Scott, who began his career in advertising design.

The genre supplies its characters with particular skills and tools, and these, once planted, play crucial causal roles. Early in *Blue Thunder* (1983) we're told that Murphy, a helicopter-bound cop, learned in Vietnam how to execute a 360-degree spin. The maneuver will save Murphy in the Climax. The hero of *Volcano* (1997) is a civil engineer transplanted from St. Louis, so when lava floods into Los Angeles he can arrange overturned buses and highway dividers like sandbags on Mississippi levees. The protagonist of *Paycheck* (2003), having previewed his future, provides himself with a kit of unprepossessing equipment that will eventually help him to escape tight corners. In *The River Wild* (1994), the heroine is a former guide who knows how to negotiate the treacherous rapids, and in a pinch she can wield oars as weapons. Her architect husband is a landlubber, but his building skills enable him to set a booby trap for the men who are holding his family hostage.

One convention might seem to play into the hands of scholars who separate spectacle from narrative. This is the whammo (aka whammy). The whammo is a burst of physical action, injected to keep things from turning into just a string of conversations. Said whammos, industry sources tell us, are supposed to arrive every 10 minutes or so. Hence the "whammo chart" attributed to various producers and television writers.[153] The idea of a whammo is pretty ill-defined, but in any case this rocking-horse rhythm seems to be rarely achieved. *Rambo*, everybody's idea of an action movie, dawdles for 15 minutes before presenting a mild whammo. The whammos start at about 33 minutes and then pile up at 36 minutes, 40 minutes, 50 minutes, 59 minutes, and 64 minutes. At 67 minutes the Climax begins, a fiery combat lasting over 18 minutes. In *The Peacemaker,* an opening dose of action occurs about 8 minutes in, but the next burst, an exciting car chase in Vienna, doesn't appear for half an hour, and another whammo hits 24 minutes after that. Again the Climax is one extended action sequence, a pursuit of the bomber through Manhattan lasting nearly 20 minutes. A strict whammo schedule seems less common than the convention that the Climax should be a rising surge of set pieces.

What the whammo chart ignores is the extent to which whammos usually advance the plot. And what comes between whammos aren't merely strings of gags or stretches of empty talk. In even the most unambitious action movie, a lot of time is taken up with mystery and anticipation. Between chases and fights, *The Peacemaker's* protagonists must decipher coded messages to figure out the terrorists' plan. The stunt driving in *Speed* is integrated into a tense uncertainty around efforts to disarm the bomb. In *Master and Commander* (2003), the downtime between nautical engagements is occupied not only with characterization but with strategizing and elaborate preparation.

Die Hard might seem to be the ultimate whammo movie, yet no fireworks start for 17 minutes, and thereafter combats come at intervals of 2 to 10 minutes. In all, the film provides about 53 minutes of physical action (generously defined; a lot of this consists of scowling men sneaking around), 18 minutes of that occurring in the Climax. That leaves, as per Emmerich's demand for a certain amount of plot, 73 minutes for suspense, male bonding, inventive insult, fumbling cops, fatally arrogant FBI agents, meddling TV reporters, puzzles about the gang's aims, parallels between business and crime, the fate of a Rolex, the redemption of a patrolman, the healing of a marriage, and making fists with your toes. A lot of the action movie's action is emotional and cerebral, and to make this satisfying the filmmakers resort to the causal thrust and motivic organization typical of classical storytelling.

Not all blockbusters are action movies, and not all action movies become blockbusters. Still, the action picture—as cop drama, fantasy adventure, or science fiction—remains the exemplar of the box-office triumphs of modern Hollywood. We've seen that there is much more to contemporary film than this pale and gaunt prototype. No less than other genres, the action picture sinks its roots into a long history of popular culture, so it would be surprising if it didn't share conventions with its peers and progenitors. Cameron

Crowe's admiration for the achievements of Wilder is echoed by screenwriter Steven DeSouza's regard for noir classics. Asked about the tendency for action heroes to fire off quips, DeSouza replies, "Go back even further, to a picture like *The Big Sleep*. Look at the wisecracks he makes throughout that movie. It's a long-standing American film tradition." And the urbane, conceited villain versus the troubled hero? "That kind of combination goes back as far as the Bogart pictures. Take a look at *The Maltese Falcon* and all of the hero's problems in that. His guilt over his partner's death, set against the arrogance and confidence of the Sidney Greenstreet character."[154]

Once more we confront the fact of belatedness. But this belatedness hasn't yielded a paralyzing self-consciousness, a collapse of narrative values, or a rejection of studio-era canons. DeSouza, like many of his peers, sees himself as continuing a worthy enterprise. The diversity and occasional power of modern Hollywood movies show that hacks, artisans, and gifted creators are maintaining a vibrant storytelling tradition very likely to outlive us all.

PART II

A Stylish Style

It is too easy to say that camera tricks and dazzling cuts are
no substitute for full-bodied characterizations. Too easy and
too misleading. We are simply too close to the popular cinema
of today to read it correctly. If American movies seem today too
eclectic, too derivative, and too mannered, so did they seem back
in the twenties, the thirties, the forties, and the fifties.

ANDREW SARRIS

. . . . . .

Portraits of two A-list directors:

Starting as an assistant to D. W. Griffith on *Intolerance* (1916), Woodbridge Strong Van Dyke II began directing in 1917 at age twenty-eight. Before his death in 1943, he made over eighty features, including *White Shadows in the South Seas* (1928), *Tarzan the Ape Man* (1932), *San Francisco* (1936), several Jeanette MacDonald musicals, and many entries in the *Thin Man* series. Van Dyke came on the set every day at 5:00 A.M., laid out his shots for the day, and often wrapped before 3:00. He filmed only what he needed of every bit of action. An MGM editor recalled, "He knew he would go to a close-up, pick up the end of the scene, another two shot, wrap and that's it. So you could only cut it in one way. And he never ran the film himself [to check the rushes]."[1] Because he signed his films W. S. Van Dyke, he became known as Wun-Shot Woody.

Brett Ratner started making music videos for Madonna and Mariah Carey, and he too was twenty-eight when he finished his first feature, *Money Talks* (1997). He went on to make *Rush Hour* (1998), *The Family Man* (2000), *Rush Hour 2* (2001), and *Red Dragon* (2002). By the end of 2003 his films had grossed nearly a billion dollars worldwide. "I'm not a master filmmaker yet. Sometimes I'm just trying to figure it out, so I start one place and then change my mind, and then I go back. I drive my editor crazy. I drive everybody crazy." His penchant for covering every scene from many angles disturbed *Red Dragon*'s producer, Dino DeLaurentiis. Ratner laughs: "He was on the set every morning at 7 A.M. with his arms crossed. He would be standing there like my father, like I'm going to get into trouble for being five minutes late to the set."[2]

Although Van Dyke was considered merely a solid craftsman, the tangy sobriety of his professionalism stands in contrast to Ratner's brashness. And Van Dyke's artisanal efficiency seems miles away from the paramilitary logistics of shooting even the most lightweight comedy today. Our films are so overproduced that the director seems less a creator than a harried executive, struggling to keep hundreds of special-effects wizards on track, shooting every scene from half a dozen angles to defer choices until the months of editing. We face, for better or worse, a marked change from the classic studio years. Granted, as I argued in the first essay, today's Hollywood has built its plots out of those principles governing studio pictures since the late 1910s. But what of the look of the movies? What can our frantic, aggressive megapictures owe to the poise and nuance of the great silent films or the 1930s classics? Surely the very existence of a Brett Ratner shows that we have a postclassical style?

How we answer that question depends on whether we're studying change or continuity, picking idiosyncratic or ordinary examples, contemplating the peaks or scanning the valleys. Most filmmakers, even the Ratners, follow the rules. As we'll see, the principles governing classical visual style have not been overthrown. To the extent that style has changed, it is due in large measure to the sense of belatedness I've already mentioned.

During the studio era, the rules for style were embedded in concrete practice. They were just the way you did things. If you were a director, your choices were constrained by tacit but strongly felt boundaries, matters of taste and judgment as much as anything else. You could move the camera, but you shouldn't cut in the middle of a movement. You could shoot extreme close-ups, but rarely. Every piece of action demanded one right spot for the camera, which it was your task to find. You didn't (for reasons of economy as much as professional pride) set up four cameras to grab action haphazardly. From this perspective, the casual setups and abrupt cuts that emerged in the 1960s could only look amateurish.

By then, however, young filmmakers had become conscious of the rules in a more abstract sense, as a codified set of preferred practices. Those who hadn't been to film school had made amateur films or worked in television, home to a visual rhetoric more standardized than Hollywood's. To those who wanted to experiment, tradition looked like a set of recipes. By the 2000s, a filmmaker like Gus Van Sant could recall that in the silent era "everything started to become the cinema language that we've been using" and confess that

> I was at the point where I couldn't read scripts or watch something like
> a Steve Martin comedy without noticing that it was just using the lan-
> guage of medium shot/wide shot/close-up without really knowing I

was using it. The film's cinema part was just a method that the director used to get the humor, comedy and the story across.[3]

Yet—and this shouldn't surprise us—successive generations of new film-makers did not reject the premises on which the system rested. They pledged themselves to the traditional purpose of using moving pictures to tell stories in a clear, arousing way. And as we've seen with narrative inno-vation, they often found inspiration in marginal, secondary, and rare op-tions within the tradition. Van Sant's distaste for continuity cutting led him to film *Elephant* (2003) in extended traveling shots—a choice that would not have surprised Max Ophuls, Stanley Kubrick, or the Alfred Hitchcock of *Rope* (1948) and *Under Capricorn* (1949).

A simple distinction helps us to understand the issues better. What has changed, in both the most conservative registers and the most adventurous ones, is not the stylistic *system* of classical filmmaking but rather certain technical *devices* functioning within that system. The new devices very often serve the traditional purposes. And the change hasn't been radical. Most of today's devices aren't spanking new; many were available to directors in the studio years. Since the 1960s these techniques have been promoted, com-ing to the foreground in ways not seen in earlier decades. As they've be-come more prominent and pervasive, these techniques have altered the tex-ture of our film experience, somewhat as the somber lighting, steep angles, and deep-focus photography of the 1940s changed Hollywood storytelling. Today's style is important to study because it has become the dominant way movies look in the United States and, indeed, in most other countries. It came into being and maintains its power by reworking earlier principles of cine-matic construction.

Those principles revolve around what's come to be called "classical con-tinuity" because they assure that the spectator understands how the story moves forward in space and time. Establishing and reestablishing shots sit-uate the actors in the locale. An axis of action (or "180-degree line") gov-erns the actors' orientations and eyelines, and the shots, however different in angle, are taken from one side of that axis. The actors' movements are matched across cuts, and typically the closest shots are reserved for the most significant facial reactions and lines of dialogue. Crosscutting may juxtapose various strands of action by alternating among them, shaped by dramatic relevance and often the pressure of a deadline.[4] U.S. directors settled on this synthesis of staging, shooting, and cutting techniques in the years after 1917, and its premises became the basis of an "international film language" for en-tertainment cinema. From the 1950s onward, this system was codified in handbooks and film-school curricula.[5] The new devices I'll be considering don't on the whole challenge this system; they revise it. Far from rejecting traditional continuity in the name of fragmentation and incoherence, the new style amounts to an *intensification* of established techniques. Intensified continuity is traditional continuity amped up, raised to a higher pitch of emphasis. It is the dominant style of American mass-audience films today.

How may we characterize this style's distinctive strategies? What historical factors brought it to prominence? How does it affect storytelling and the audience's experience? These are the questions I tackle in the pages that follow. Concentrating on visual technique, I want to track regularities in films from different directors and genres over the last forty years. These regularities aren't rigid commandments but a structure of options; even when Brett Ratner can't make up his mind, he's choosing between some relatively well-defined menu items. Postponing zeitgeist readings and roundabout interpretations, I aim at providing some pertinent explanations for both common and uncommon options. I try to locate some proximate causal forces within the problem-solving processes and craft norms of film production. I end this essay by reflecting on some of the style's overall functions and effects

1. INTENSIFIED CONTINUITY: FOUR DIMENSIONS

Four strategies of camerawork and editing seem central to the new style: rapid editing, bipolar extremes of lens lengths, reliance on close shots, and wide-ranging camera movements. Most of these techniques have been remarked on before, often by irritated critics, but none has been considered closely, and we haven't sufficiently appreciated how they work together to create a coherent set of artistic choices. Further, despite technological progress on many fronts, the choices available to filmmakers have narrowed since the studio era. The strategies I'll be discussing have become dominant, even domineering: increasingly filmmakers aren't encouraged to explore other options. This situation marks, as I'll suggest in the final pages of this essay, a loss of some expressive resources of studio-era cinema.

Picking Up the Pace

Everybody thinks that movies are being cut faster now, but how fast is fast? And faster compared to what? Pop journalism has tried to clue us in. "Your average movie," notes one writer in 1999, "has 600 or 700 cuts."[6] Hollywood practitioners commonly say that films typically average about 1,100–1,200 shots.[7] Both sets of figures underestimate the accelerating speed of today's editing.

In the 1920s, Hollywood films were cut quite fast, averaging four to six seconds per shot, but the arrival of sound put on the brakes. Between 1930 and 1960, most feature films contained between three hundred and seven hundred shots, so the average shot length (ASL) hovered between 8 and 11 seconds.[8] Even in the B-film range, one must look hard to find movies averaging less than that. The A-features that are cut very quickly often owe their pace to cramped production schedules or the need to patch together stock footage. *Tarzan Finds a Son* (1939) averages a hectic 3.6 seconds, largely because of its many cutaways to library shots of jungle creatures. At the other extreme, several films were built out of abnormally long takes. John Stahl's *Back Street* (1932) has an ASL of 19 seconds, while Otto Preminger's *Fallen Angel* (1945) averages 33 seconds per shot. Through the 1950s, Preminger, Vincente Minnelli, and Billy Wilder continued to employ lengthy takes.

In the mid-1960s, several filmmakers began accelerating their cutting rates.[9] Many A-films of the period contain ASLs of between 6 and 8 seconds, and some have significantly shorter averages. *Goldfinger* (1964), for example, clocks in at 4.0 seconds, *Mickey One* (1965) at 3.8 seconds, and *Head* (1968) at a remarkable 2.7 seconds. The pace accelerated in the 1970s.

Then, about three-quarters of films had ASLs between 5 and 8 seconds, and we find a significant number of still faster ones. As we'd expect, action films tended to be edited more briskly than other types (and Sam Peckinpah's seem to have been cut fastest of all),[10] but musicals, dramas, romances, and comedies didn't necessarily favor long takes. *The Candidate* (1972), *Slaughterhouse-Five* (1972), *Pete's Dragon* (1977), *Freaky Friday* (1977), *National Lampoon's Animal House* (1978), *Foul Play* (1978), and *Hair* (1979) all have ASLs in the 4-to-5-second range. Midway through the decade, most films in any genre included at least a thousand shots.

In the 1980s the tempo continued to pick up, but the filmmaker's range of choice narrowed dramatically. Double-digit ASLs, still found during the 1970s, virtually vanished from mass-entertainment cinema. Most mainstream films had ASLs of between 5 and 7 seconds, and, again, many films averaged between 4 and 5 seconds—not only action films like *Raiders of the Lost Ark* and *Lethal Weapon* (1987) but also dramas (*Stand by Me* and *The Right Stuff*, both 1983; *Amadeus*, 1984; *The Breakfast Club*, 1985). We also find more films with ASLs in the 3-to-4-second range. Most were action pictures or movies influenced by music videos, such as *Road Warrior* (1981), *Pink Floyd: The Wall* (1982), *Tron* (1982), *WarGames* (1983), *Streets of Fire* (1984), *Highlander* (1986), *Top Gun* (1986), *Near Dark* (1987), *Alien Nation* (1988), and *Black Rain* (1989).

At the close of the 1980s, many films boasted 1,500 shots or more. There soon followed movies containing two to three thousand shots, such as *JFK* (1991) and *The Last Boy Scout* (1991). *El Mariachi* (1993), the low-budget breakout by Robert Rodriguez, contains nearly 2,100 shots; *Demolition Man* from the same year has nearly 2,600. Soon the three-to-four-thousand-shot movie arrived (*Braveheart*, 1995; *Nixon*, 1995; *Armageddon*, 1998; *Any Given Sunday*, 1999). Several directors began pushing the ASL below 3 seconds. *The Crow* (1994), *U-Turn* (1997), and *Sleepy Hollow* (1999) come in at 2.7 seconds; *El Mariachi*, *Armageddon*, and *South Park* (1999) at 2.3 seconds. By century's end, the ASL of a typical film in any genre would run 3 to 6 seconds.[11]

Today, films are on average cut more rapidly than at any other time in U.S. studio filmmaking. Some films flirt with shot lengths reminiscent of late 1920s Soviet silent montage. Between 1961 and 1999, I can find only one film with an ASL of less than 2 seconds (*Dark City*, 1998, 1.8 seconds), but in the 2000s there's at least one every year (e.g., *Moulin Rouge* and *Requiem for a Dream*, 2001; *Pirates of the Caribbean*, 2003).[12] Although action films tend to be cut at a scorching tempo, fast cutting governs all genres.

Historical dramas like *Quills* (2000), absurdist exercises like *Adaptation* (2002), and romantic comedies like *Bridget Jones's Diary* (2001) and *Intolerable Cruelty* (2003) all average 5 seconds or less per shot. Who would expect that *Love Actually* (2003; 3.8 seconds ASL before the final multiframe bombardment) would be cut faster than *21 Grams* (2003; 4.6 seconds ASL)? The trend also rules animated films like *Monsters Inc.* (2001; 3.0 seconds ASL) and *Finding Nemo* (2003; 3.3 seconds ASL).

Although I know of no film averaging less than 1.5 seconds per shot, the weight of the norm has clearly shifted downward over the last four decades. A 6-to-7-second ASL, as in *The Others* (2001) and *Lost in Translation* (2003), now looks sedate, while only art movies like *13 Conversations about One Thing* (2001) and *Solaris* (2002) risk a 10-to-11-second average. Directors like Roman Polanski and Mike Nichols, who once favored exceptionally long takes, have joined the trend.[13] Nichols has explained that the prolonged shot "began to seem to me more self-regarding, and cutting (and cutting a *lot*) began to excite me and began to give me the pleasures that most directors have right away."[14] Only Woody Allen and M. Night Shyamalan have consistently chosen to build movies out of extended shots.

The quickening of editing has affected other techniques. While studio directors avoided cutting in the middle of a camera movement, today's filmmakers feel no hesitation. In the old days, the spots at which the camera started and stopped were as significant as the movement itself, but now tracks and pans are usually interrupted by cuts, denying us a sense of a steady progression toward a revelation. As if fast cutting weren't enough, filmmakers can create a percussive burst of images in other ways. Vehicles whiz through the foreground, breaking our line of sight. Whiplash pans and jerky reframings present two glimpses linked by a blur. Rack focusing (changing focus between foreground and background) can shift a shot's composition as crisply as a cut can. Directors not only cut on bursts of light, like flashbulbs or headlights; pulsations within a shot, yielded by disco strobes or cracks of lightning, can seem to boost the editing rate as well. These other techniques, filmmakers seem to believe, help the cutting to impart "energy," refreshing the screen, maintaining interest, building excitement.

Has rapid cutting therefore led to a "postclassical" breakdown of spatial continuity? Certainly, some action sequences are cut so fast (and staged so gracelessly) as to be incomprehensible. Todd McCarthy remarks that in *Armageddon* "director [Michael] Bay's visual presentation is so frantic and chaotic that one often can't tell which ship or characters are being shown, or where things are in relation to one another."[15] Nonetheless, many fast-cut sequences do remain spatially coherent, as in the *Die Hard, Speed,* and *Lethal Weapon* franchises. The illegibility of some action scenes, I'll suggest later, is partly traceable to misjudging what will read well on the big screen. More important, no film is ever one long action sequence. Most scenes present conversations, and here fast cutting is applied principally to shot/reverse-shot exchanges. How else could *Ordinary People* (1980) attain an ASL of 6.1 seconds, *Ghost* (1991) one of 5.0 seconds, *Almost Famous* (2000) one of 3.9 seconds, *Barbershop* (2002) one of 2.9 seconds, and *Runaway Jury* (2003) one of 2.0 seconds? Today's editors tend to cut at every line, sometimes in the middle of a line, and they insert more reaction shots than we would find in movies from the classic studio years.

By building dialogue scenes out of brief shots, the new style has become somewhat more elliptical, using fewer establishing shots and sustained two-shots. As Lev Kuleshov, V. I. Pudovkin, and other Soviet montage directors realized, classical continuity contains redundancies: shot/reverse-shot exchanges reiterate the information about character placement given in the establishing shot, as do eyelines and body orientation. For the sake of intensifying the dialogue exchange, filmmakers have omitted some of the redundancies provided by establishing shots. At the same time, though, fast-cut dialogue has reinforced certain premises of the 180-degree staging system. When every shot is short, when establishing shots are brief or postponed or nonexistent, the eyelines and angles in a dialogue need to be even more unambiguous, and the axis of action is likely to be respected quite strictly.

Going to Extremes

From the 1910s to the 1930s, the normal lens used in feature filmmaking in the United States had a focal length of 50mm, or two inches. Longer lenses, from 100 to 500mm or more, were commonly used for close-ups, particularly soft-focus ones, and for following swift action at a distance, such as the movement of animals in the wild. Shorter ("wide-angle") lenses, commonly 25mm or 35mm, came into use when filmmakers wanted good focus in several planes or full shots of a cramped setting. During the 1930s, cinematographers increasingly relied on wide-angle lenses, and after *Citizen Kane* (1941), lenses of 35mm to 40mm focal length came to be the standard ones.

Black-and-white films of the postwar period flaunted the short focal-length lens. Elia Kazan, Douglas Sirk, and others sought to employ it in CinemaScope films (Fig. 2.1), but the lens often exaggerated optical faults in the wide-screen process and, for color, required the crew to boost illumina-

2.1. The wide-angle lens for CinemaScope, with resulting distortion (*Wild River*, 1960).

2.2. A more typical early CinemaScope composition, with figures spread out tableau fashion (*Demetrius and the Gladiators*, 1954).

2.3. *The Hill:* Wide-angle distortion for expressive effect.

2.4. Panavision permitted controlled distortion in wide angle shots, suitable for the neo-noir *Chinatown*.

tion to blinding levels. So most anamorphic films made in color retained a less exaggerated look (Fig. 2.2). The Panavision process, however, allowed filmmakers to use wide-angle lenses more freely. At the same time, some directors were pushing black-and-white wide-angle imagery further. Sidney Lumet, for instance, shot all of *The Hill* (1965) with three wide lenses (24mm, 21mm, and 18mm), thereby warping foreground elements grotesquely (Fig. 2.3).[16] Although critics found this style, in the hands of Lumet, John Frankenheimer, Arthur Penn, Sidney J. Furie, and Brian Forbes, overwrought, a few directors applied it to color and Panavision in the early 1970s. The wide lens's characteristic distorting effects—bulging on the frame edges, exaggerating distances between foreground and background—are flaunted in *Carnal Knowledge* (1971) and *Chinatown* (1974; Fig. 2.4).[17] Thereafter, filmmakers using wide-screen formats commonly resorted to the wide-angle lens to provide looming close-ups, expansive establishing shots, views inside cramped quarters (like the front seats of cars, as in *The Sugarland Express,* 1974), and medium shots with strong foreground-background interplay (Fig. 2.5). In the 1980s and 1990s, action directors like John McTiernan and Paul Verhoeven coordinated the short lens with packed compositions

2.5. *The Deer Hunter* (1978): Wide-angle depth used much as in the 1940s and 1950s.

2.6. Cartoonish distortion thanks to wide-angle wide screen (*The Hudsucker Proxy*, 1994).

2.7. Split-focus diopter work in *The Italian Job* (1969).

2.8. The archetypal long-lens shot of the 1960s: Benjamin races to Elaine's wedding, apparently making little progress, in *The Graduate*.

and tight camera movements, while the Coen brothers saw its possibilities for caricatural comedy (Fig. 2.6). Directors who wanted extreme wide-angle imagery could also turn to the Super-35mm format: there a 17mm lens yielded a wider field and less distortion than the widest anamorphic one, the 28mm. At the limit, there was the split-focus diopter. Used in television commercials to present the product looming over distant figures, the lens became more common in feature filmmaking (Fig. 2.7).

The long lens proved even more enticing. Thanks to influential European films like *A Man and a Woman* (1966), the development of reflex viewing and telephoto[18] and zoom lenses, an influx of new directors from television and documentary, and other factors, directors began to include a great many more long-lens shots. Since the long lens magnifies fairly distant action, the camera can be placed quite far from the subject, an advantage when shooting exteriors on location. Even on interior sets, long lenses could save time, and as multiple-camera shooting became more popular in the 1970s, directors used long lenses to keep cameras out of each other's range. The long lens could suggest either a documentary immediacy or a stylized flattening, making characters appear to walk or run in place (Fig. 2.8).[19] The long-focus lens became an all-purpose tool, available to frame close-ups, medium

2.10. Planes are stacked with a painterly flatness, thanks to the long lens (*Heat,* 1995).

2.9. The long lens used for an establishing shot (*Jerry Maguire,* 1994).

shots, over-the-shoulder shots, and even establishing shots (Fig. 2.9). Robert Altman, Bob Fosse, Milos Forman, and other directors were likely to use long lenses for nearly every setup.

The new lenses yielded several stylistic by-products. When the long lens was employed for close-ups, its shallow depth of field automatically softened and glamorized faces. Its squeezed perspective suited the abstract pictorialism of films like *Scarface* (1983) and *Manhunter* (1986). Just as the Coen brothers were linked to the wide-angle image, directors like Michael Mann and Tony Scott became identified with the perpendicular telephoto shot (Fig. 2.10). For similar reasons, the long lens encouraged the self-conscious rack focusing that came to prominence in the 1960s; in later years this play with focus was orchestrated with figure movement to create shifting compositions in depth (Figs. 2.11–2.12).[20] The lens also facilitated what editors call the "wipe-by" cut.[21] Here a long-lens shot picks out a figure, and something closer to the camera (traffic, a tree being dollied past) slides into view. Then, as our view is completely masked, the cut comes, and when the obtrusion leaves the frame, we have a closer framing of the figure (Figs. 2.13–2.14).

From the 1960s onward, exploiting both extremes of lens lengths within a single film became a hallmark of intensified continuity. For *Bonnie and Clyde* (1967) Arthur Penn used lenses from 9.8mm to 400mm (Fig. 2.15).[22] Several movie-brat directors appreciated the advantages of long lenses but also wanted to maintain the 1940s tradition of deep-space shooting. So Francis Ford Coppola, Brian De Palma, and Steven Spielberg freely mixed long-focus and wide-angle lenses within scenes.[23] Robert Richardson, interviewing for the job of cinematographer on Oliver Stone's *Salvador* (1986) recalls Stone asking: "I have only one question for you. Can you cut a long lens

2.11. Rack-focus in *Die Hard* (1988): The shot shifts us between near and distant planes. At this point, the pistol Hans has hidden on frame right is in focus . . .

2.12. . . . but it drops out of focus when McClane orders Hans to follow him.

2.13. The famous wipe-by cut in *Jaws* (1975): Sheriff Brody watches the sea, and a figure walks across our vision, momentarily blocking him.

2.14. Cutting on the blurred foreground, the next shot enlarges Brody along the camera axis.

2.15. An exceptionally long lens captures the moment of C. W. Moss's father's betrayal of the gang in *Bonnie and Clyde*.

with a wide-angle lens?" Richardson thought, "Are you kidding? Of course you can. No problem."[24]

This revelation of new options can't be deplored, but again, it has turned out to constrain filmmakers' choices. Just as it's unlikely that today's director will build an entire film out of long takes, it's virtually unthinkable to shoot the bulk of a film with a 50mm lens, as John Ford, Ozu Yasujiro, and Robert Bresson did. A manual aimed at the beginning director states flatly: "If you are going to make it as a director of mainstream theatrical features, you have to force perspective"—that is, avoid the normal lens and

2.16. A typical sustained two-shot from Preminger's *Exodus*.

2.17. In George Cukor's *The Marrying Kind* (1952), an entire scene played out in a relaxed, spacious two-shot.

rely on extreme telephoto and extreme wide-angle lenses.[25] Only for retro exercises like *Far from Heaven* (2002) are filmmakers likely to deny themselves the resources of extreme lens lengths.[26]

Closer and Closer

Watching Otto Preminger's *Exodus* (1960; Fig. 2.16) in 2001, Harvey Weinstein of Miramax burst out: "Talk about minimalism. I mean, look at this. These scenes are just all master shots. There is no cutting within any of these scenes. I am sitting here, and I am amazed. . . . With everything shot in a master, never cutting to a close-up, everybody just wandering around in front of the camera, it's deadly dull."[27] Weinstein speaks for most of today's filmmakers. Any style that treats conversations in a sustained, fixed shot must be a perverse, boring minimalism. The master shot—a general view of the action, usually filmed as a complete run-through of the scene—is still part of production practice, but it has become steadily less important on-screen. Paul Schrader remarks, "The only reason to do the master is to have something you can show the editor."[28]

Directors who began their careers in the 1.33:1 format of the mature sound cinema tended to favor larger views when shooting in the wide-screen ratio, and Preminger, who had made the sustained two-shot central to his aesthetic in the 1940s, often staged conversations in static takes. His choice wasn't only aesthetic; he remarked that he hated to edit, and as a producer of his own films he believed that he could save time by shooting extended masters.[29] Vincente Minnelli, John Stahl, Billy Wilder, and a few others pursued a similar approach. Minnelli called it "pulling the scene through one camera."[30] Perhaps Weinstein would have sent these directors back to the set for reshoots, as Darryl F. Zanuck reputedly did when John Ford refused to give him glamorous close-ups of leading ladies.

From the 1930s well into the 1960s, even directors not committed to long takes used the master shot as the default framing. This practice led to stretches of scenes being played out in a *plan américain*, which cut off actors around the knees or mid-thighs. This framing also allowed for lengthy two-shots favoring players' bodies (Fig. 2.17). After the 1960s, directors often replaced two-shots with "singles," medium-shots, or close-ups showing only one player. This practice is one source of the quicker editing during the period. Of course singles were also a common option during the studio years, but there was a range of alternatives: some films used many singles, others very few. In recent decades, the options have narrowed. Long shots and *plans américains* have become rarer and briefer; scenes tend to rely on over-the-shoulder shots and singles. These close framings allow the director to vary the pace during editing and to pick the best bits of each actor's performance.[31]

Even within the period I'm considering, the changes can be noticeable. Both the 1966 and 1999 versions of *The Thomas Crown Affair* contain an early scene in which Crown sells a building to his competitors. Both films show essentially the same story action: Crown and his assistants sit at a table with the buyers. He signs his property over to them, then deflates their gloating by telling them that they have overpaid. The scene ends with an assistant rubbing in the rivals' defeat.

In the first version, directed by Norman Jewison, the sale scene lasts 42 seconds and consumes five shots, yielding an average of slightly more than 8 seconds. Although the scene starts with a close-up of Crown's hand checking his watch and then signing the deed, the conclusion of the business is presented in a distant master shot lasting 17 seconds (Fig. 2.18), the lengthiest take in the scene. This orienting view is followed by a long-lens *plan américain* of Crown rising to leave (Fig. 2.19), one reaction shot of the flustered buyers (Fig. 2.20), and a repeat of Crown's departing shot. As Crown moves briskly to his next appointment, Jewison will not devote a new shot to the scene's tagline: after Crown has left, an assistant stands up to wish the buyers luck (Fig. 2.21). The laconic handling makes Crown a no-nonsense deal closer.

By contrast, the Crown of John McTiernan's 1999 version toys with his adversaries, and with us. A wide master shot shows the boardroom for a mere three seconds before the scene moves into many closer views. Four wide-angle shots of two buyers alternate with long-lens shots of Crown scanning

2.18. *The Thomas Crown Affair* (1969).

2.19. *The Thomas Crown Affair.*

2.20. *The Thomas Crown Affair.*

2.21. *The Thomas Crown Affair.*

the document before his hand moves down to sign it (Figs. 2.22–2.23). Yet still he hesitates, creating (false) suspense. When he finally signs, more cutting shows his rivals' glee, followed by his explanation that they have paid $30 million too much (Fig. 2.24). In a reaction shot, their grins freeze. As Crown leaves, the camera glides rightward to pick up his assistant, who grins mockingly in tight close-up (Figs. 2.25–2.26). Not only has McTiernan used seventeen shots in place of five (yielding an ASL of 3.5 seconds), but he has presented much closer framings, with singles picking out Crown and his assistant. This Crown is an urbane and sadistic gamesman who will enjoy setting traps for insurance investigator Catherine Banning.

Admittedly, some of the differences between the two versions may stem from qualities of performance. Jewison's remote presentation is consistent with Steve McQueen's chilly star image, while the debonair Pierce Brosnan is more likely to banter with his prey. Yet stylistic variations of this sort are likely to stand out whenever we compare a contemporary remake with its source. The later version will almost invariably be faster cut than the original, and dialogue scenes will tend to play out in close singles or over-the-shoulder framings rather than in two-shots or roomy masters.

Jewison's *Thomas Crown Affair* also falls within our post-1960 period, and this boardroom scene is hardly typical of the whole film, which does rely

2.22. *The Thomas Crown Affair* (1999).

2.23. *The Thomas Crown Affair.*

2.24. *The Thomas Crown Affair.*

2.25. *The Thomas Crown Affair.*

2.26. *The Thomas Crown Affair.*

on close views in many scenes. The 1969 version also accelerates the visual tempo by its famous use of multiframe imagery, splintering a shot into several smaller copies or scattering different images throughout the 1.85 frame (Fig. 2.27). Still, our specimen shows that in the 1960s some filmmakers were varying their handling quite a bit from scene to scene, reserving big close-ups for certain parts of the action. Preminger pursued the same tactic in *Exodus*, when Dov Landau's climactic admission of collaboration brings him unusually near to the camera (Fig. 2.28). Significantly, this scene wins Weinstein's approval: "Man, the movie just really kicked into gear, didn't it?"[32] Today's filmmakers have less concern with saving close-ups across a film, though, as we'll see, they may lay down other constraints for themselves.

If a scene relies on rapidly cut singles, the filmmaker must find ways to underscore certain lines or facial reactions. The standard tactic is to differentiate shot scales, but, again, post-1960s filmmakers faced a compressed range of options. The 1940s filmmaker could treat a single figure in *plan*

2.27. Multiframe imagery in *The Thomas Crown Affair* (1969).

2.28. *Exodus:* The Jewish boy admits helping the Nazis in the concentration camps.

américain (knees or thighs up), or medium shot (waist up), or medium close-up (chest up), or standard close-up (full face), or extreme close-up (part of the face). Given this spectrum, a cut from a *plan américain* to a medium close-up could constitute a major shift of emphasis. But as *plans américains* and ensemble framings became less common, the norms were reweighted; in many films the baseline framing for a dialogue became a medium shot or an over-the-shoulder framing. So the filmmaker began to work along a narrower scale, from the medium two-shot to the extreme close-up single.[33] Thus in our 1999 *Thomas Crown* example, the heightening tension is signaled by the shift from moderately close views to still closer views, building to a tight single of Crown's assistant (see Figs. 2.22, 2.24, 2.26).

When widescreen processes were introduced, filmmakers often felt obliged to rely on long and medium shots, but by the late 1960s, thanks partly to Panavison's sharper, less distorting lenses, directors could present closer widescreen framings. Indeed, the wide format gives close singles a real advantage; the tendency to place the actor's face off center leaves a fair amount of the scene's locale visible, which lessens the need for establishing and reestablishing long shots. When actors change position, cutting back to the master shot may not be necessary. Now, with tight framings, performer movement is often a matter of "clearing" a medium shot. Actor A exits in the foreground, passing in front of B; hold on B for a moment before we cut to A arriving in another medium shot. The 1999 *Thomas Crown* does not use a more distant shot to show Crown leaving the meeting, as Jewison's version does. Instead, McTiernan lets Crown clear his single (see Figs. 2.25–2.26).

Currently the orienting long shot often serves to punctuate a scene. It can mark out a phase of the action or provide a visual accent that close-ups, because of their frequency, no longer muster. An editor remarks, "Dropping back to the master shot or even an establishing shot in the middle of a scene can let it breathe, or alternately can give it a beat that will then invest your close-ups with even greater force and intensity."[34] Indeed, a scene's most distant framing may well come at the very end, as a caesura. Most important, the pressure to use closer views has narrowed the expressive resources available to performers. In the studio years a filmmaker would rely on the actor's whole body, but now actors are principally faces.[35] According to Anthony Minghella, "dynamic blocking" doesn't entail choreographing several players in a wide view but, rather, letting one player step into close-up.[36] Mouths, brows, and eyes become the principal sources of information and emotion, and actors must scale their performances across varying degrees of intimate framings.

Finally, it's likely that contemporary cinema's reliance on close views has eased the transition to digital-video filming. On video, distant shots nakedly display all the format's flaws in resolution.[37] Accordingly, one selling point of digital shooting is that its close-ups are adequate for theatrical presentation. "When we were researching digital video," says the director of *Star Maps*, "we saw *Celebration* and thought, 'My God, all those close-ups look great.'"[38] Harvey Weinstein would probably agree.

The Prowling Camera

When we do find longer takes and fuller framings, the camera is usually in motion. Camera movement became standard in most films during the last years of silent cinema. With the coming of sound, filmmakers began to rely on the flamboyant tracking or crane shot, especially in opening scenes, and on those slight reframings that keep the compositions balanced. Today's camera movements are ostentatious extensions of the camera mobility that came to prominence during the 1930s.

Take, for example, the prolonged following shot, in which the camera tracks a character moving along a lengthy path. These virtuoso shots were developed in the 1920s, became prominent at the start of sound cinema (e.g., *Scarface*, 1932; *The Threepenny Opera*, 1931), and formed the stylistic signature of Max Ophuls. During the 1950s Orson Welles (*Othello*, 1952; *Touch of Evil*, 1957), Samuel Fuller (e.g., *Forty Guns*, 1957), and Stanley Kubrick (*Paths of Glory*, 1957) exploited bravura following shots. In more modern times, such camera moves appeared in ordinary films, such as the corridor conversations of *Hospital* (1971), but they also became identified with Martin Scorsese, John Carpenter, Brian De Palma, and other New Hollywood directors. Partly because of these influential figures, and thanks to lighter cameras and stabilizers like Steadicam, the shot pursuing one or two characters down hallways, through room after room, indoors and outdoors and back again, has become ubiquitous. When *Road Trip* (2000) boasts a complex shot trailing its hero through several crowded rooms, and music videos like Björk's *Hidden Place* and Lina's *Step Up* consist of a single endlessly moving take, we can assume that the technique has achieved saturation. At a higher level of ambition, there seems to be a competition among directors to see how lengthy and intricate they can make their traveling shots. The shot following Jake LaMotta from his dressing room, through the crowds, and into the ring in *Raging Bull* (1980) made De Palma sit up. "I thought I was pretty good at doing those kind of shots, but when I saw that I said, 'Whoa!' And that's when I started using those very complicated shots with the Steadicam."[39] Scorsese devoted three minutes to a couple's zigzagging passage through the Copacabana club in *GoodFellas* (1990), while the opening tracking shot of De Palma's *Bonfire of the Vanities* (1990) lasts five minutes. Not resting content, De Palma used digital effects to blend several takes into the seamless 13-minute shot that opens *Snake Eyes* (1998).

Other sorts of camera movement are common as well. Today's orienting shot will often be an inching track forward or sideways, creating a "moving master." The crane shot, which formerly marked a high point, now serves as casual embellishment. It enlivens montage sequences and expository moments; it can appear at any point in the scene. "If somebody goes for a piss these days," Mike Figgis remarks, "it's usually a crane shot."[40] The crane may be replaced by a soaring bird's-eye view, made increasingly easy by a new generation of aerial cameras mounted on miniature remote controlled helicopters.

The camera is likely to prowl even if nothing else budges.[41] During a dialogue the camera may slowly magnify a character's face through a zoom (the "creeping zoom") or a forward tracking shot (the "push-in"). The gradual enlargement may underscore a moment of realization or build continuous tension, as when a shot/reverse-shot passage is handled by intercutting two creeping zooms or push-ins. Or the camera may arc slowly around a single actor or a couple. A common way to present people gathered around any table—dinner table, card table, operating table—is to spiral around them. The circling shots might be long takes (the sisters' luncheon in *Hannah and Her Sisters*, 1985) or mere glimpses (the diner opening of *Reservoir Dogs*, 1992). The arcing camera also became a clichéd means of showing lovers embracing. De Palma gave the rotating clinch an overblown treatment in *Obsession* (1976),[42] and it was parodied in *Being There* (1979), when Chauncy Gardener learns how to kiss by watching a TV couple embracing in a florid 360-degree tracking shot. In *A Beautiful Mind* (2001), the circling camera becomes a deceptive motif, initially evoking the giddiness of John Nash's Pentagon visit but eventually associated with moments of schizophrenia.

Scenes tend to start with a camera movement, far or near. The crane is helpful here, as it was in the studio years: from a high angle, we see a car arriving, then we crane down as someone gets out and walks to a building. Alternatively, the camera may present an establishing shot while coasting along laterally. Whereas a 1930s scene might open on a close-up of a significant object and track back, contemporary filmmakers often begin with an arcing or sidelong movement past an unimportant foreground element, a building or car or tree. As if pulling aside a curtain, the camera slowly unmasks the action.

As a figure of style, the free-ranging camera may have been popularized by the late 1970s horror films, which implied that a hovering, slightly shaky camera might represent the monster's point of view. But the device certainly predates the horror cycle. The reiterated push-in emerged early in the decade, and it was often used for parallel shot/reverse shots or for building tension while two characters talk on the phone (*Mean Streets*, 1973; *Dog Day Afternoon*, 1975). Arcing shots also became fairly common at the same time, not only to show characters talking on the phone (*The Taking of Pelham 123*, 1974) but also to capture them dancing (*American Graffiti*, 1973), lying in bed (*The Heartbreak Kid*, 1972), or merely sitting at a table (*Carnal Knowledge*; *Sisters*, 1972; *The Sting*, 1973; *Murder on the Orient Express*, 1974). The arcing establishing shot was already in place in *Deliverance* (1973) and *Soylent Green* (1973), only to become insistent in *MacArthur* (1977) and *The Deer Hunter* (1978). The camera could circle important objects (the crystal rocket that will carry the infant Superman to earth in *Superman: The Movie*, 1978) or characters standing alone against a crowd (*The Candidate*, 1972; *Jesus Christ Superstar*, 1973). As with the creeping zoom or the push-in, a stretch of shot/reverse-shot cutting might alternate shots spiraling around each character in turn (*Rollerball*, 1975; *Coma*, 1978). Paul Schrader has suggested that autonomous camera movement, so prominent in films of European directors like Bernardo Bertolucci, became the hallmark of his generation of U.S. directors.[43]

In the 1970s and early 1980s, free-ranging camera movements typically appeared only a few times per film. Eventually, however, they constituted a default menu for shooting any scene. In planning his sequences, Scorsese says, "In most cases you can say, 'No matter what the location is, I know that the camera is going to track.'"[44] A 2003 directing manual states, in all seriousness, "a good objective for any first-time director would be to move his camera as much as possible to look as hip and MTV-wise as he can."[45]

Why do so many directors presume that the camera should move in many or most shots? The usual explanation is that a mobile framing, like quick cutting, boosts the scene's "energy."[46] Camera movement also separates the planes of the image and creates a more voluminous pictorial space. For this reason, Vilmos Zsigmond, an influential cinematographer during the 1970s, has claimed that the technique "gives you the third dimension, which is the way movies should be. If you lock down the camera, it's like seeing everything with one eye."[47]

The demand for frequent camera movement probably helped popularize handheld shooting too. Handheld shots can be found in silent cinema: the Odessa Steps sequence of *Potemkin* (1925) contains one, and Abel Gance's *Napoléon* (1927) highlights several in its snowball-fight sequence. Such shots occasionally appeared in postwar studio films, usually to convey realistic combat (*The Sands of Iwo Jima*, 1949; the prizefight dramas *Champion*, 1949, and *Killer's Kiss*, 1955). Soon the triple influence of cinema verité documentaries (e.g., *Primary*, 1960), French New Wave films (e.g., *The 400 Blows*, U.S. release 1959), and British films borrowing from the New Wave (e.g., *This Sporting Life*, U.S. release 1963) made handheld shots more acceptable in mainstream American movies. Since then the technique has usually appeared in one-off moments, but sometimes it defines entire films, particularly those pledged to raw realism (e.g., *The French Connection*, 1971; *Dog Day Afternoon*; *Traffic*, 2000; *21 Grams*, 2003). Oddly enough, any novice filmmaker, or any older filmmaker who wants to go back to basics, is likely to endorse the handheld camera for its "freedom from the rules," ignoring the fact that it's been an utterly conventional strategy for nearly forty years.

A fast cutting rate, the bipolar extremes of lens lengths, a reliance on tight singles, and the free-ranging camera are salient marks of intensified continuity. Virtually every contemporary mainstream American film will exhibit at least some of them. Although I've isolated these techniques for ease of exposition, each tends to cooperate with others. Tighter framings permit faster cutting. Long lenses pick out figures for one-on-one editing. Rack focusing does within the shot what cutting does between shots: it reveals areas of interest successively (rather than simultaneously, as in the deep-focus classics of Welles and William Wyler). The arcing camera can use either a long lens, allowing foreground elements to drift by in a blur, or a wide-angle one, deriving its strength from tightly timed shifts from plane to plane.

Granted, there is more to contemporary visual style than these devices. A complete inventory would have to consider at least the menu of color schemes (desaturated, high-contrast, monochrome), slow- and fast-motion imagery, and a bag of camera gimmicks, such as having an actor seem to float through a crowd by riding the camera dolly. It seems to me that these devices add decorative and expressive overlays to the story information transmitted by the basic intensified continuity techniques.[48] Subjectivity will continue to be a major alibi; *Requiem for a Dream* (2000) and *Spun* (2002) use outré devices to convey the frenzy of drugged states. Funereal palettes are routinely given to horror films and grim family dramas (e.g., *The Ice Storm*, 1997). The two expressive dimensions of subjectivity and atmosphere meet in the shimmering and oversaturated color of action pictures like *Man on Fire* (2004), to suggest both a hellish milieu and a psychically tormented protagonist. Sometimes filmmakers insert a one-off flourish—a helicopter shot, the "ramping" of normal action to slurred or accelerated tempo, an abrupt high angle. These decorative touches will tend to show up in just those stretches that have always welcomed self-conscious narration: montage sequences, intense climaxes involving suspense or strenuous activity, openings and closings of scenes, beginnings and endings of the film. At worst, they may just register as visual hiccups, glitches glossed over by an otherwise coherent narration.[49]

Not all filmmakers have assimilated the style in every respect. Like other *Star Wars* installments, *Episode I: The Phantom Menace* (1999) is cut quite fast,[50] but it avoids the ultratight framings and the roaming camera of *Armageddon* (1998) and *The Matrix* (1999). By contrast, M. Night Shyamalan employs close-framing techniques but keeps his shots lengthy (18.2 seconds in *Unbreakable*, 2000). But it is rare for filmmakers to avoid every device. Though John Cassavetes employs prolonged takes in *Love Streams* (1984), he relies heavily on arcing and lateral camera movements, as well as intensifying push-ins. We find locked-down, fairly distant camera positions in *Escape from New York* (1981) and *Sleepless in Seattle* (1993), but the former is nonetheless cut fairly rapidly and the latter favors telephoto framings. Taken separately or as a cluster, these four techniques constitute prominent and pervasive conventions of today's Hollywood style. In effect, contemporary cinema has cultivated certain options that were on the studio-era menu but dropped others—fixed-camera long takes, sustained two-shots, frequent long shots and mid-range framings, and images filmed with a 50mm lens.

2. SOME LIKELY SOURCES

I've drawn most of my evidence about intensified continuity from regularities in the films and comments by practitioners, but critics have also noticed these norms. In 1980 Richard Jameson observed that an overwrought style had become evident in the previous decade.[51] Two years later, Noël Carroll pointed to a tendency toward "strident stylization" since the mid-1960s.[52] I've already mentioned the critics' sense that movies are cut faster nowadays, with Todd McCarthy of *Variety* harping on the drawbacks of the style: "*Gladiator*, with its fast flurries of action and jump cuts, emphasizes the ferocious speed and urgency of every move in the arena, to the slight detriment of spatial unity and action continuity."[53] Of *The Bourne Supremacy* (2004), McCarthy writes: "One has to imagine that the lack of clarity, continuity and coherence in this furiously fought sequence is intentional," but he worries about the director's tendency to give action scenes "breathless bluster, insistent showiness and defiant disorientation."[54] Although McCarthy speaks from a powerful pulpit, nobody seems to have been converted. Intensified continuity is taken for granted in handbooks and film-school curricula. Daniel Arijon's *Grammar of the Film Language* (1976), a manual that professional directors sometimes consult in planning a scene, compiles many of the emerging staging and cutting schemas.[55] Later manuals incorporate instructions on sidewinding camera movements.[56] During a 1985 class at NYU, a professor advised a student to "capture the energy" of a pinball game with tracking shots: "Give the camera a life and energy as well."[57]

Films themselves sometimes comment on the style. We get parodic versions of it in the bombastic crane shot down to the chairman of the board in *Soapdish* (1991) or in the entirety of the short *George Lucas in Love* (1999). When characters discuss recent movies, prototypes of intensified continuity may appear on the agenda. The most celebrated example is the flamboyant long take that opens Altman's *The Player* (1992), during which characters argue about . . . flamboyant long takes. ("The pictures they make these days are all MTV. Cut-cut-cut-cut.") In *Swingers* (1994), the protagonists comment on the Copacabana shot in *GoodFellas*; later in the film a pastiche of that shot trails them through a kitchen and into a club. During the same scene, they praise the slow-motion shot of walking heist men in *Reservoir Dogs* (1992), and that shot is copied immediately, showing them strutting off to a party. To top things off, the men's conversation is filmed in arcing tracking shots around them sitting at a table, as in the diner opening of *Reservoir Dogs*. One character remarks, "Everybody steals from everybody. That's movies."

These passages from *Swingers* remind us that U.S. "independent" films

2.29. *Memento:* A wipe-by cut metamorphoses Sammy Jankis. . . .

2.30. . . . into Leonard Shelby, our memory-deprived hero, for a fraction of a second. Compare this to Figs. 2.13–2.14.

don't necessarily reject intensified continuity. In most respects, Allison Anders, Alan Rudolph, David Cronenberg, and their peers subscribe to the style. John Sayles's *Eight Men Out* (1988) is full of push-ins, spiraling camera moves, and close-up singles. In Julie Taymor's *Titus* (1999) intensified continuity achieves a thunderous weightiness. One manual for the independent filmmaker recommends creating a distinct style as a selling point, but the three choices that the author provides come from the intensified-continuity menu: use quick cuts (= nervousness), or a handheld camera circling the action (= chaos), or a floating camera homing steadily in on the actors (= lyricism).[58] Current conventions can create unreliable narration and enhance puzzle movies like *Memento* (2002; Figs. 2.29–2.30).

With regard to the techniques I've highlighted, the major distinguishing mark of off-Hollywood directors is greater average shot length. Hal Hartley and Whit Stillman work with ASLs of 8 to 12 seconds, while Billy Bob Thornton's *Sling Blade* (1996) has a remarkable ASL of 23.3 seconds. (Miramax distributed the film, so Harvey Weinstein evidently overlooked Thornton's fondness for static long shots.) Long takes aren't too surprising in the lower-budget sector. Apart from the indies' commitment to ensemble performances, directors may want to create scenes laden with a European gravitas. Interestingly, though, when an independent goes more mainstream, the cutting is likely to accelerate. Jim Jarmusch moved from the one-take scenes of *Stranger Than Paradise* (1984) to steadily shorter ASLs.[59] Thornton's second film, *All the Pretty Horses* (2000), is the polar opposite of *Sling Blade*, averaging 4.3 seconds per shot. Thornton has complained that his long-take final scene was dropped entirely: "They made me cut it out. . . . I didn't cover it, I did it in two shots and it lasted five minutes. These days, they want to cut everything like a rock video."[60]

These norms aren't restricted to North America. Werner Herzog (*Aguirre: The Wrath of God,* 1972), Rainer Werner Fassbinder (*Chinese Roulette,*

1976; *Veronika Voss*, 1982), and *cinéma du look* directors like Jean-Jacques Beineix (*Diva*, 1981) and Léos Carax (*Mauvais Sang*, 1986) elaborated on the intensified continuity devices emerging in Hollywood. The techniques can be found in Luc Besson's *Nikita* (1990), Jane Campion's *Portrait of a Lady* (1996), Tom Tykwer's *Run Lola Run* (1998), and several of Neil Jordan's films. More broadly, intensified continuity has become a touchstone for the popular cinema of other countries. The new style was a boon for marginal filmmaking nations; close-ups, fast cutting, sinuous handheld camera moves, long lenses on location, and scenes built out of singles were friendly to small budgets. In Hong Kong during the 1980s, John Woo and Tsui Hark reworked Western norms, sometimes to the point of outrageousness.[61] In 1999 a mainstream film from Thailand (*Nang Nak*), Korea (*Shiri; Tell Me Something*), Japan (*Monday*), or England (*Lock, Stock, and Two Smoking Barrels*) was likely to display all the marks of intensified continuity. It has become the baseline style for both international mass-market cinema and a sizable fraction of exportable "art cinema."

When Did the Sixties End?

Although the style didn't crystallize all at once, the 1960s mark a crucial transition. In British, European, and U.S. movies, devices of intensified continuity became much more salient, along with their canonized functions. In particular, Truffaut's *Shoot the Piano Player* (1960) and *Jules and Jim* (1962) showcased flashy technique. Not every critic was impressed, but many filmmakers and aspiring filmmakers were. A notable example is Tony Richardson, widely regarded as importing Truffaut's style in *The Loneliness of the Long-Distance Runner* (1962) and *Tom Jones* (1963). Richard Lester's high-profile films—the Beatles musicals *A Hard Day's Night* (1964) and *Help!* (1965), and the farce *A Funny Thing Happened on the Way to the Forum* (1966)—employed flagrantly artificial editing techniques. These eclectic movies spread a new menu before U.S. filmmakers, who began experimenting with fitting the devices to Hollywood genres.

Editors, particularly a few based in New York, discovered that swift cutting could suit dramas. Dede Allen became famous for her fast editing in *America America* (1963, 5.1 seconds ASL), *Mickey One* (1965, 3.8 seconds ASL), *Bonnie and Clyde* (1967, 3.8 seconds ASL), and *Alice's Restaurant* (1969, a remarkable 2.6 seconds ASL).[62] At the same time, Ralph Rosenblum developed "flash cutting" for *The Pawnbroker* (1965).[63] These bursts of three to six frame shots soon became a fashion, as in the glimpses of Mrs. Robinson's breasts in *The Graduate* (1967) and of Satan's face in *Rosemary's Baby* (1968). Jump cuts started to appear as well (e.g., *The President's An-*

2.31. A long lens allows the wide screen to crop faces tightly, a device that became common in the 1960s (e.g., *Camelot*).

2.32. *A Man and a Woman* (1966): The long lens, with its loss of focus and resolution, used for shimmering lyricism.

alyst, 1967), along with "concentration cuts," which rapidly enlarge a subject along the lens axis (a Kurosawa favorite revamped in *Grand Prix*, 1966, and *You Only Live Twice*, 1967). More quietly, fast cutting was slipping into ordinary conversation scenes. *Bonnie and Clyde*, *The Dirty Dozen* (1967; 3.5 seconds ASL), and *The Wild Bunch* (1969; 3.2 seconds ASL) used dynamic cutting during explosive action, but they also presented dialogue in the clipped, one-shot-per-line manner of *Dragnet*.

As faster cutting became salient, as we might expect, so did tighter framing. Nonanamorphic 1:2.35 processes like Techniscope exploited big close-ups as well as aggressive deep focus (e.g., in Sergio Leone's *Dollars* trilogy, 1964–1966, and Sidney J. Furie's *The Appaloosa*, 1966). When Panavision became the favored anamorphic format (and eventually pushed the aspect ratio to 2.40: 1), it proved capable of very tight close-ups, either in wide-angle or telephoto. *Reflections in a Golden Eye* (1967) includes some startlingly close foregrounds, while *Camelot* (1967) offered lengthy shots of faces captured by the long lens, often cropped at brow or chin (Fig. 2.31). In the squarer 1.85 format, *Bonnie and Clyde* signaled the trend toward tight framing, from the opening shots of Bonnie Parker twisting restlessly on her bed. Dede Allen acknowledged that these close views favored rapid editing: "We were able to go in with angles and close-ups and only pull back when we wanted to show what Arthur [Penn] called 'the tapestry.' Arthur really wanted to give it all this energy. He kept saying, 'Look at the film again. Make it go faster.'"[64]

I've already suggested the interest of many 1960s directors in wide-angle imagery, but even more evident was the rapid adoption of the long lens. Telephoto imagery, seen occasionally in some British and French films from the early 1960s, dominated Claude Lelouche's *A Man and a Woman* (1966) and Bo Widerberg's *Elvira Madigan* (1967). The loss of resolution and the

2.33. The planimetric composition lines up planes parallel to one another and perpendicular to the lens axis. In *Targets* (1968) it creates a calendar-picture family portrait.

2.34. Mixing wide-angle and long lens in the same scene of *The Ipcress File* (1965): A wide-angle shot presents the antagonists seen through a phone booth . . .

2.35. . . . before we cut to a telephoto shot of the fight on the steps.

many defocused planes (Fig. 2.32) helped associate the look with lyrical romance. Late in the decade, the long-lens shot became all-purpose and all pervading. The telephoto became the lens of first resort in many Westerns (*The Wild Bunch*, 1969) and musicals (*Goodbye, Mr. Chips*, 1969). A 500mm lens followed a singer during one number in *Finian's Rainbow* (1970).[65] We also find the long lens used to provide the squared-off planimetric image that became a crucial visual scheme in the 1970s (Fig. 2.33). With the dissemination of the telephoto image, we also find early instances of wipe-by cuts. In *Darling* (1965), the device marks an ellipsis. The long lens watches from the street as a couple enters a luggage shop; a bus passes in the foreground; cut to another vehicle passing, revealing the couple leaving the shop.

In sum, by the late 1960s, directors were comfortable with a wide range of lens lengths, and several were using the two extremes quite boldly, sometimes mixing them in the same scene (Figs. 2.34–2.35). Wide-angle lenses were often reserved for shooting on the set, where light, blocking, and focus could be controlled precisely, while the long lens facilitated shooting on location.

Studio directors of the 1930s and 1940s were as likely to track out (from a detail or major character to the whole ensemble) as to track forward, but by the 1960s, the closing-in framing was becoming dominant. Of course the zoom lens enhanced this tendency, and we don't lack examples of marked zoom-ins at the period (*Nikki, Wild Dog of the North*, 1961; *Send Me No Flowers*, 1964). Major twists in the plot of *Seven Days in May* (1964) are signaled by ominous dollies up to faces. George's revelatory "act 3" monologue in *Who's Afraid of Virginia Woolf?* (1966) is treated in a slow push-in. *The Chase* (1966) supplies an interrupted push-in on one character during a shot/reverse-shot passage. Practitioners also began to recognize that an unexpected craning movement down and in could goose up the most ordinary scene (e.g., *The Biggest Bundle of Them All*, 1968).

The tactic of circling around an embracing couple can be traced back at least to *Vertigo* (1957) and *Hiroshima mon amour* (1959), but the arcing camera came into its own in the 1960s. We find arcing shot/reverse shots (*Town without Pity*, 1961), arcing around a single figure to isolate him or her (*The Hustler*, 1961; *Popi*, 1969), arcing to reveal new information in the foreground or background (*You Only Live Twice*; *Bonnie and Clyde*, both 1967), and, of course, arcing around people gathered at a table (*The Group*, 1966; *The St. Valentine's Day Massacre*, 1967). As early as *Judgment at Nuremberg* (1961), the pictorial premises of the device are already in place. The witnesses on the stand are pinned down by an orgy of spiraling and craning camera movements. In this respect Stanley Kramer's film looks, for better or worse, utterly contemporary.

And what of the handheld camera, constantly rediscovered and always declaring itself brand new? Since the 1920s, handheld shots were usually associated with violence, an optically subjective point of view, or news reportage, and these functions were locked in place during the 1960s. In *The Miracle Worker* (1962), Helen's refusal to sit properly at dinner leads to a pitched battle with her teacher, Annie, which Arthur Penn renders in bumpy handheld shots. An assault on a military base in *Dr. Strangelove or: How I Learned to Stop Worrying and Love the Bomb* (1964) is presented as convulsive handheld footage. *Seven Days in May* (1964) opens with a violent street demonstration, and the thrashing shots recall television coverage of Jack Ruby's shooting of Lee Harvey Oswald. Because of its usage in cinema verité documentary, the handheld camera could imbue intimate confrontations in *A Man and a Woman*, *Who's Afraid of Virginia Woolf?* and *Faces* (1968) with a spontaneous edge. Robert Rossen's *Lilith* (1964) uses handheld shots sporadically throughout, sometimes to give a documentary feel to an asylum's encounter groups, at other moments to render the sensation of riding horseback. Handheld shots could also simply suggest authentic locations (*The Al-*

phabet Murders, 1966; *No Way to Treat a Lady,* 1968). Filmmakers were coming to believe that virtually any scene could benefit from the handheld shot's immediacy, urgency, and (the inevitable word) energy.

Seen from a sympathetic angle, all these devices have an ancestry stretching back several decades. A late silent film like *Beggars of Life* (1928) looks much like today's films, with its rapid cutting, dialogue played in tight singles, easygoing camera movements. Kuleshov and Pudovkin, with their insistence on suppressing establishing shots in favor of facial close-ups, in effect promoted an early version of intensified continuity,[66] and today's wilder tracking and panning shots recall those of Abel Gance (*Napoléon,* 1927) and Marcel L'Herbier (*L'Argent,* 1928). When sound came in, bulky cameras and recording equipment discouraged fast cutting and flexible camera movements. The camera was difficult to move, even merely to change setups, so directors were inclined to capture a scene in longish takes. This habit remained in place for decades. In the 1960s, one could argue, popular filmmaking began to recover some of the fluidity and pace of silent movies.

Yet this wasn't the line of defense most contemporary observers adopted. Critics who seldom saw eye to eye on anything agreed that the look of movies was changing, and not for the better. Tony Richardson was a favorite whipping boy, and his *Tom Jones* (1963) aroused fury. John Simon complained of "the most frenetic assortment of bustle, hubbub, camera movement and feverish cutting."[67] "All the outdated nouvelle vague stunts in *Tom Jones*," Andrew Sarris noted, "only emphasize Richardson's pathetic inability to tell a story with his camera, to describe a place with the slightest degree of spatial unity, or to move from shot to shot without making a separate production out of each time lapse."[68] Dwight MacDonald called Richardson "analphabetic, unable to compose a scene clearly in front of the camera and so forced to overuse the close-up. . . . Overstressing is his directorial trademark."[69]

Another target was Sidney Lumet. Of his *The Fugitive Kind* (1960), MacDonald wrote: "Lumet's direction is meaninglessly over-intense; lights and shadows play over the close-up faces underlining lines that are themselves in bold capitals; every situation is given end-of-the-world treatment."[70] Before she had established her reputation as a scourge of Hollywood philistinism, Pauline Kael was allowed to observe the production of Lumet's *The Group,* and in the spring of 1966 she wrote a report. Although she liked much of the finished film, she objected to Lumet's overbearing technique:

> The director follows a script like a general carrying out a plan who shoots hoping to hit something: he moves the people or the camera around to get some "movement" and hammers some simple points

home. And you are cued to react, you're kept so busy reacting you may not even notice that there's nothing on the screen for your eye to linger on, no distances, no action in the background, no sense of life or landscape mingling with the foreground action. It's all in the foreground, put there for you to grasp at once.

She found that actors were unable to sustain a scene in a long take, because everyone assumed that the action would be saved in the editing:

> The scenes will be chopped up with reaction shots and close-ups to conceal the static camera setups and the faults in timing, in acting, in rhythm of performances. Fast editing can be done for aesthetic purposes, but too much of it *is* done these days to cover up bad staging and shooting, and the effect is jerky and confusing. But, as it calls so much attention to itself, it is often taken to be brilliant technique. Explaining something he wants done, Lumet will say, "It can be very exciting"— which means what will work, not what may relate to any larger conception but simply something that will be effective here and now, in itself.[71]

By today's standards, *The Group* looks bland, but at the time Lumet, like Richardson and Lester, seemed to have forgotten subtlety, restraint, and the demands of a unified film.[72]

Except for extravaganzas like *Tom Jones*, most 1960s films don't milk intensified continuity devices to the fullest. Ironically, it was Lumet who believed that the most vivid devices should be held in reserve. Discussing *Fail-Safe* (1964), he explains that he filmed from one side of a room to avoid certain angles: "Because I was going to need them later on." Why did he dwell on a certain fixed setup for so long? "You use the static camera so you can save movement for when it has something to say, for when it has some real need. There is a move at the end of the picture when Fonda is talking with the Soviet premiere and Larry Hagman is translating. And there are two counter-dollies in there that I think are absolutely marvelous. They've been set up by all of these static shots."[73] Like Sergei Eisenstein, who advocated mapping a progression of techniques across a film in harmony with its plot development, Lumet suggests that an unfolding visual design can accumulate power in tandem with the rise of the drama.[74] In explaining how he wanted to achieve increasing claustrophobia in the jury room of *12 Angry Men* (1957), Lumet described using a "lens plot" moving from 28mm to 40mm lenses to 100mm as the drama heightened.[75] Kael, MacDonald, and others would probably reply that choosing a portentous technique in the first place obliges the director to move from a yell to a shout to a screech. Whatever his ambitions, Lumet and his contemporaries set the menu for the next decades, when the one-off options of the 1960s became preferred defaults for every scene. Our movies are sixties movies, only more so.

Shooting for the Box and Other Compromises

What created this change in the taken-for-granted norms of mainstream moviemaking? We might be tempted to look to broad cultural developments. Why are movies cut faster now? Perhaps viewers trained on television, videogames, and the Internet can absorb rapidly cut movies more easily than earlier generations could. Yet in the 1920s, audiences were perfectly able to assimilate ASLs of 5 seconds or less. Moreover, what in the cultural sphere could explain the prevalence of extreme lens lengths or florid camera movements? We need finer-grained explanations for the rise of intensified continuity.

As often happens, we can find the most proximate and plausible causes in technological change, craft practices, and institutional circumstances. The history of style in the studio system is governed by these very forces. When Hollywood converted from silent pictures to talkies, tools, work routines, and visual resources had to be coordinated. Cameras became heavier, illumination sources changed from arc lamps to incandescent bulbs, and film stock was converted from orthochromatic to panchromatic. These and many other changes posed problems, and the solutions were achieved not simply by trial and error. Engineers, technical workers, and creative personnel were guided by a loose, but not vague, idea of how they wanted the films to look and sound. The new technology was inserted into a framework of work routines and visual style that had served Hollywood well since the late 1910s. Along the way, both the routines (along with the division of labor they demanded) and the style (including its range of choice) were modified, in a to-and-fro process that fairly soon settled into a new but not radically different standard of professional filmmaking.[76]

A demand on one front produces a change on another, and this affects yet another. In the early years of sound, the main purpose was simply to get the scene on film, so directors might conceivably have returned to the rich tableau cinema of the 1910s, where staging in the static frame achieved great finesse. But filmmakers did not want to abandon the editing resources that they had mastered in the 1920s, so they filmed early sound scenes with multiple cameras, armed with lenses of various focal lengths. Yet this created new difficulties. The cameras weren't easily shifted around the set, lighting had to be flat, and it was rare for a camera to penetrate the scene as it did in the silent era, placing itself between characters or at unusual angles.

The pressure was to master sound recording so that directors could return to single-camera filming. In other words, the stylistic template in place during silent cinema had to be recovered. It was, rather quickly, and the sound camera even permitted new refinements of it (such as elegant reframings). In this interplay between technology, craft preference, and institutional possibilities, problems pile up, to be solved in ways that produce new problems—and opportunities. Striving for one thing, the filmmaker discovers something else in the process, and improving that can become a new goal. Compromises are inevitable, so filmmakers must be alert to several ways of achieving their aims or even to reconsidering what their aims should be. This shifting teleology, the interplay of goals, constraints, problems, trade-offs, revised goals, and unexpected solutions is characteristic of stylistic change throughout film history.[77] The emergence of intensified continuity exemplifies this sort of interplay. Because of all the forces at work, we can't tell a straightforward linear tale; we'll have to chart several causal factors crisscrossing a range of practices.

Television offers an obvious starting point. By the mid-1960s, after studios licensed their libraries to TV stations and began selling network broadcast rights for recent releases, most filmmakers realized that their films would wind up on the small screen. Some could refuse to "shoot for the box," but when cable and videocassettes took off in the early 1980s, no one could deny that more viewers would see a film on TV than in a theater. Across the period we're examining, many filmmakers shaped their visual design toward what one critic called "televisionization."[78] Television, many filmmakers believed, required closer shots. Cinematographer Phil Méheux remarks: "It's a shame that most films rely so much on tight close-ups all the time, filling the screen with an actor's head like you might for television, when there is so much more that you can show. The style is really just a result of what producers want for video release."[79] The belief that television favors medium shots and close-ups has been a commonplace in industry discourse for decades.[80] "The size of the television screen is small," points out a standard television production manual in 1976. "To show things clearly, you must show them relatively large within the frame of the screen. In other words, you have to operate more with closeups (CU) and medium shots (MS) than with long shots (LS) and extreme long shots (XLS)."[81]

Wide-screen film was not well suited to the smaller, squarer television frame, and U.S. broadcasters were reluctant to letterbox films because the image degraded when fewer scan lines were devoted to it. The most common solution for converting wide-screen film to television versions was "panning and scanning." The sides of each shot would be lopped off, and

2.36. The off-center face in anamorphic wide screen, easy to reduce to a screen-filling 1.33 format (*Kiss the Girls,* 1997).

2.37. A full-frame image from *Hannah and Her Sisters* (1985). The surprising amount of head-room will be eliminated in theater projection.

sometimes the TV camera would artificially swivel across the original image. The practice of panning and scanning held on for decades and lingers in some DVD releases.

Faced with the prospect of wrecked compositions, filmmakers began "shooting and protecting." Thanks to masks fitted to viewfinders, or precise markings etched on the finders, cinematographers could see the television "safe action area" within the 1.85 wide-screen frame. But confining action to this zone eliminated 30 percent of the original picture area, making symmetrical two-shots and densely packed long shots more difficult to compose for theatrical presentation. The strictures of the safe area probably helped steer directors toward singles and over-the-shoulder framings—compositional schemes, as Steve Neale has pointed out, that could easily be cropped for full-frame television (Fig. 2.36).[82] Shooting and protecting became even more difficult with compositions sprawled across the 2.40 format, so anamorphic productions began to rely as heavily on singles as did work in the 1.85 frame. More compromises emerged in the 1980s. Some filmmakers chose to film "full frame," in a nearly square format from which 1.33 or 1.85 versions could be extracted (Fig. 2.37). Others opted for the Super-35mm format, which used larger picture area on the filmstrip to support both anamorphic 2.40 theatrical prints and 1.33 video transfers. In either case, composition became more indeterminate than it had been at any point in film history: home viewers often saw more sky and ground than theater audiences did.

Common opinion held that shooting for the box demanded more than close framings. Television, people argued, is usually watched in a distracting environment, so it needs to hold attention by a constantly changing visual display.[83] A 1968 manual recommends that a TV director should seek out "animated visuals": "Can you dolly in to contract and concentrate the interest? Dolly out to expand the field of interest? Pan from one part of the subject to another? Arc around it for a progressively changing view?"[84]

The main means for refreshing the image, of course, is cutting. TV cutting appears to have accelerated over the same years that film cutting did. Before the 1960s many filmed TV programs had ASLs of 10 seconds or more, but in the decades since then I can find no ASLs averaging more than 7.5 seconds. Most programs fall in the 5-to-7-second ASL range, and a few (1960s *Dragnet* episodes, *Moonlighting* during the 1980s) run between 3 and 5 seconds. (Of course, TV commercials tend to be cut even faster: ASLs of 1 to 2 seconds are common for 30-second spots.) Perhaps cutting rates accelerated independently in the two media, or perhaps a feedback loop developed. Rapid editing in influential early-1960s films may have provided a model for television (particularly commercials and shows like *The Monkees* and *Rowan & Martin's Laugh-In*), which in turn encouraged theatrical films to be cut faster.[85]

Film people often detested what they considered the television look; as early as 1964, one editor could insult another by saying his work "looks like TV cutting to me."[86] Directors found subtle variations when a film played on different platforms. Chris Petit noted that working on video made him cut too abruptly: "Viewed on a monitor the cut felt correct. But whenever it was projected on a film screen, it looked off-beat and hasty. The image now had a primacy it didn't have in its reduced form, which worked more by suggestion or by a flicker principle that became irritating when enlarged."[87] Meanwhile others noticed that media norms were blending. Joe Dante remarked in 1987:

> From a director's standpoint, movies and television have become almost interchangeable. There's really very little difference these days between the way you shoot for television and the way you do for movies. . . .
> With so many movies making their money on cable and videocassette instead of in the theaters, the visual language[s] of movies and TV are overlapping and developing hybrids.[88]

Television influenced the intensified style at other levels too. Film has long recruited directors from television, so we ought to expect stylistic carryovers of the sort that Kael deplored in *The Group*. TV commercials and music videos have become the sort of training ground that anthology drama and filmed dramatic series were in the 1960s and 1970s. Today many directors, cinematographers, and technicians shoot commercials between fea-

2.38. The video assist presents a small, marked-out shooting area (*Gattaca*, 1997).

tures.[89] Brett Ratner, who directed over seventy music videos, says that making a film is "the same. You use the same crew and the same equipment. It's just more."[90] Since the 1980s, flashy technique has made TV-proven directors attractive to film producers. "These guys," noted an agent, "are risky bets but they offer a higher stylistic yield."[91]

Just as important, many new technologies have in effect preformatted a theatrical film for television. Complex scenes are "previsualized" on video or digital software, and actors' auditions are videotaped.[92] The Steadicam's viewfinder is a video monitor. In the 1970s, film crews began to rely on the video assist, which allows the director and cinematographer to watch a shot as it is being taken and play it back for scrutiny.[93] The results often lack detail, provide inaccurate color rendering, and favor singles and roomy wide shots rather than precision staging (Fig. 2.38).[94]

Video-based editing, first on tape and laser disc and now on computer, also preshapes the image for television.[95] Walter Murch notes that editors must gauge how faces will look on a small monitor: "The determining factor for selecting a particular shot is frequently, 'Can you register the expression in the actor's eyes?' If you can't, you will tend to use the next closer shot, even though the wider shot may be more than adequate when seen on the big screen."[96] In sum, video-based production tools may have reinforced filmmakers' inclination to emphasize singles and closer views, which are more legible in video displays all along the line.[97]

Admittedly, in the studio era editors scrutinized the film on the tiny Moviola screen. But they based cutting decisions on notes taken during screenings in a projection room. Today, screening the rushes is still advisable because of the low resolution of video-editing displays. "The Avid hides fine details," notes one producer, "and shots that work on the video might look horrifying on film. Say hello to boom shadows, reflections of hapless crew members in mirrors, and focus problems that were minimal on the Avid."[98] Many directors and cinematographers never see raw footage projected on film. One 2003 feature finished principal photography only to discover something that video dailies had hidden: nearly every shot was out of focus.[99]

As powerfully as television has shaped intensified continuity, it is probably only one of several influences. We shouldn't forget the example of prestigious filmmakers such as Welles and Hitchcock, whose works abound in the techniques that would coalesce into intensified continuity. Sergio Leone, while flaunting extreme lens lengths and soaring camera movements, also proved that tight close-ups could be striking in wide-screen formats. Sam Peckinpah and other 1960s directors showed that very fast editing was feasible, particularly if one alternated a few setups. During the 1970s Robert Altman introduced "creeping zooms," and he intercut them with an abruptness that anticipates the interrupted push-ins of today's movies.[100] Certain canonized films have probably had some influence too. The great set pieces of film history tend to consist of rapid-fire montages (the Odessa Steps sequence, the shower assault in *Psycho*) or virtuoso following shots (the party scene in *Rules of the Game*, 1939; the ball in *The Magnificent Ambersons*, 1942; the opening of *Touch of Evil*, 1958). And it's likely that the media's celebration of rapid cutting made filmmakers fear that static long takes were out of sync with the audience's taste. In 1990 Scorsese reflected ruefully, "I guess the main thing that's happened in the past ten years is that the scenes [shots] have to be quicker and shorter. *[GoodFellas]* is sort of my version of MTV . . . but even that's old-fashioned."[101]

Changing exhibition circumstances may have played a role as well. Ben Brewster and Lea Jacobs have suggested that in 1908–1917, as cinema moved from vaudeville houses to dedicated venues, screens got smaller; in order to seem correspondingly larger, actors were filmed from closer positions.[102] William Paul has argued that similar exhibition pressures in the 1920s inclined filmmakers to use more close-ups.[103] With the twinning and plexing of the 1970s, screens shrank once more, and perhaps filmmakers intuitively moved toward bigger faces, assuming as well that faster cutting would read adequately on smaller multiplex screens.

A great many aspects of intensified continuity can be traced to changes in production practices. Throughout the period we're surveying, producers tried to shorten filming schedules. The rising costs of production were usually cited as the rationale, but just as important in the 1980s and 1990s was the emerging multiplex phenomenon. A film had to hit its announced release date because the marketing campaign and exhibition venues had been coordinated around the all-important opening weekend, which could make or break the film in ancillary platforms. So there was pressure to work fast. One response to soaring budgets was to film more on location, which saved on set costs. As we've seen, long lenses helped in location shooting while also suggesting a documentary look.

Directors responded to compressed shooting schedules by shooting much more coverage, since producers insisted that there be many alternative takes available for postproduction adjustments. While directors can argue that a flashy tracking shot can complete several script pages efficiently, there are many pressures to multiply choices in the editing room. Coming to the United States to shoot *Cannery Row* (1981), Sven Nykvist claimed that the biggest difference he found between U.S. and European production was "the requirement for so many cover shots. . . . I believe that it comes from the fact that the producers usually have the final cut and they want to have all the material they can get in order to speed up the pace of the film or make other major changes that may be necessary."[104] Against producers' advice, Steven Soderbergh initially shot the auto-trunk scene in *Out of Sight* (1998) in a single take, but he learned his Kuleshovian lesson when the preview audience lost interest: "What I should have understood is that every time you cut away and came back, you bought so much, because the audience filled in the gap for you."[105]

Even independent filmmakers face a demand for coverage. On *Little Man Tate* (1991), Jodie Foster's producer requested more singles.[106] Christine Vachon, who produced many independent classics, asks directors to shoot both master shots and closer views. She agrees with her editor's complaint that "inexperienced directors are often drawn to shooting important dramatic scenes in a single continuous take—a 'macho' style that leaves no way of changing pacing or helping unsteady performances."[107] (For an older view of the gendering of style, compare Orson Welles: "A long-playing full shot is what always separates the men from the boys.")[108]

Coverage could be made more efficient by extending some older tactics. After the early talkie period (1929–1932), filmmakers usually worked with just one camera, retaking portions of the scene from different positions. So deeply entrenched was this practice that when Arthur Penn, accustomed to several cameras from live television work, demanded two cameras for dialogue scenes in *The Left-Handed Gun* (1958), his director of photography violently resisted.[109] Multiple-camera shooting was usually reserved for unrepeatable actions, such as fires, collapsing buildings, or vehicles plunging off cliffs.[110] In the 1960s, directors began to employ several cameras, and in the process they laid down some of today's common work routines. Penn and Richard Lester set two cameras side by side, one fitted with a wide-angle lens and the other with a long lens.[111] Starting with *Faces* (1968), Cassavetes employed one camera for master shots and primary action, reserving a B camera for what he called "accents," tight close-ups of actors or other areas of the scene.[112] In addition, perhaps inspired by Kurosawa,[113] Penn and Peckinpah began to shoot scenes of carnage with several cameras fitted with very long lenses. All these tactics would become standard practice in later decades.

In the 1970s, when location shooting and tight schedules required fast work, many directors began using multiple cameras to cover ordinary dialogue. The cruising scenes of *American Graffiti* (1973) were taken with two cameras, one showing both driver and passenger from straight on, the other favoring the driver.[114] Lumet used three cameras for *Dog Day Afternoon* (1975) because most of the lines were improvised. Expensive stars like Sean Connery were often shot with two cameras so they would not need as many retakes. "When you get someone like that earning big dollars by the day, there's a lot of pressure to finish scenes as quickly as possible. The second camera helped us do that."[115] Jor-El's monologue in *Superman: The Movie*, which Marlon Brando recited from cue cards, was recorded by no fewer than eleven cameras.[116] As producers demanded more coverage, extra cameras provided it, a situation that in turn made the editor more likely to assemble the scene out of singles taken from many angles.

Happily, a new generation of lighter cameras was more maneuverable in multicamera situations. During the 1980s, the B camera was frequently a Steadicam, roaming the set for coverage, and the fluidity of its movements around static actors may have made circling shots and push-ins strong candidates for inclusion in the final cut. By the time *Gladiator* (2000) was made, a dialogue might be filmed by as many as seven cameras, some of them Steadicams. "I was thinking," the director of photography explained, "'Someone has got to be getting something good.'"[117] The search for "something good" at each instant, from a wide range of angles, predisposed filmmakers to cut often.

The 1970s body-braced systems like Panaflex, Steadicam, and Panaglide were not originally designed to support B cameras. Their chief purpose was to smooth out handheld moves and to maneuver through spaces impossible for a dolly or crane to penetrate. Real locations or purpose-built sets could be traversed in an unprecedented fluid fashion, as was demonstrated in early Steadicam films like *Rocky* (1976), *Bound for Glory* (1977), and *The Shin-*

ing (1980).[118] Frame mobility was achieved by other new devices too. The Elemack "Spyder" dolly, introduced by an Italian company in 1962, and its successor, the Cricket, brought in a new generation of supple camera supports. These could glide the camera in any direction, thanks to sectioned rails that could snap together in various configurations. The Elemack had a small crane arm for intimate moves and, by 1980, included portable dolly tracks in circular sections.[119] The lightweight French Louma crane, adopted in the United States for *1941* and *Moonraker* (both 1979), set the camera on the end of an aluminum boom that could be extended fifteen feet in the air. It was controlled from a video monitor so that no operator would need to be carried. Later, airborne remote-controlled cameras such as Flying-Cam also made swooping high-angle shots easier.[120] Once these tools were in place, they clamored to be used: the compact cameras and flexible supports, designed to permit occasional fluidity, encouraged constant mobility.[121] The prowling camera had come into its own.

The demand for more coverage, the use of multiple cameras, the recruiting of the Steadicam: this is the sort of cascade of choices we should expect, with each phase influencing visual style. With more footage from various angles available, editors were tempted to cut more, assembling the best bits of several takes. This inclination meshed with new editing equipment and work procedures. Director John McTiernan has suggested that the rapid cutting seen in *The Wild Bunch* and other late-1960s films was encouraged by the arrival of Scotch-tape splicing. With glue-based splicing, the editor lost a frame on each side of the cut. The result was "a pressure against cutting when you weren't certain. . . . All of a sudden you could just slice it up, put a piece of Scotch tape over it, and try it."[122] In a similar way, faster cutting was encouraged by the process of editing on videotape in the early 1980s, which made it much easier to reorder shots. Editing on videotape was quickly superseded by digital systems like Avid, a Macintosh-based program introduced in 1988 and initially used for television production, and the PC-based Lightworks, which appeared three years later. In 1994 digital editing of features exploded, and within three years most features were cut on computer.[123] Along with their other advantages, Avid and Lightworks facilitated fast cutting, and they are a likely source of the rise in 2- and 3-second ASLs we find around 1993. Cutting very brief shots on celluloid is complicated and labor intensive. Trims of only a few frames can easily go astray, and if one decides to put them back one typically needs to request a new print of the footage. By cutting on computer, filmmakers can easily shave shots frame by frame, a process known as "frame-fucking."[124] Frame-fucking is one reason some action sequences don't read well on the big screen; after editing

The Rock's (1996) car chase on computer, Michael Bay saw it projected, decided that it went by too fast, and had to "de-cut" it.[125] "We see faster rhythms everywhere," remarks Steven Cohan, who edited one of the first digitally-cut features, *Lost in Yonkers* (1993), "which is at least partially due to the fact that we now have the tools to make that kind of editing easy."[126] McTiernan puts it more pointedly: "The [Avid] machine eliminated the last vestige of reluctance to cut, the cost of cutting."[127]

McTiernan's phrase reminds us that the new editing tools promised to save money in the assembly phase. Video-based editing systems could synchronize multiple-camera footage efficiently and lower lab costs, since there was no need to workprint all rushes.[128] At the same moment, the stream of footage into the editing bays became a flood. With demands for complete coverage and a belief that the movie could be made in the cutting room, directors were overshooting wildly. A 100-minute movie runs nine thousand feet, but to arrive at that the editor might hack through as much as six hundred thousand feet of material. Directors and producers began to subdivide editing labor. Rather than handle all the footage, the principal editor might supervise a team of several cutters, often making each responsible for one reel of the final cut. (This was called, with typical Hollywood delicacy, "gang-banging" the film.) The introduction of computerized editing systems allowed producers to demand even faster output. Now databases could track all the takes, and the physical act of splicing was not needed until the very last moment. Producers began to expect to see a rough cut in as little as a week. Editors complained that they were overworked and didn't have enough time to fine-tune the film.[129] Under these conditions, they evidently felt obliged to fall back on the default settings of the dominant style. "I'm concerned," remarked one director at the beginning of the trend, that "management will assume electronic equipment means editors should work faster. And faster means formula. Go to the master, two shot, close-up, close-up, and get out."[130] Likewise, assigning each editor a reel of a big project favored a neutral, standardized way of handling footage so that the completed film looked uniform throughout.

Intensified continuity can be traced in large part to changes in production demands (such as shooting on location, planning for the TV format, accelerating filming schedules), craft practices (particularly multiple-camera shooting), and technical tools (such as the Steadicam and digital editing). All were coordinated by a loose but shared urge to maintain some balance between new techniques and standard stylistic functions. The diverse production practices converged gradually, but many tools and craft routines seem to have been in place by the mid-1970s. A striking example is provided by *Rosebud* (1975). For his drama of international terrorism Otto Preminger deployed long lenses, both zooms and primes, and he relied on a version of video assist. His aerial shots were taken from a remote-controlled camera mounted on a helicopter. He shot dialogue scenes with two cameras, one of them a body-braced Panaflex. In postproduction, twelve editors were cutting the film simultaneously.[131] Preminger, once a devotee of the single-setup long take that so annoyed Harvey Weinstein, surrendered to the demands of a new time.

3. STYLE, PLAIN AND FANCY

We could trace the interactions among institutions, technology, tastes, and style in a lot more detail. We should also analyze changing sound and color practices, to discover whether these too fed into the style.[132] But let the foregoing stand as an outline of some major causal inputs. What concern me now are the functions of the new style. What sorts of cinematic texture does it yield? What aesthetic problems does it pose? What possibilities for innovation does it open up or close off?

Sampling the Menu

At the level of stylistic texture, we can trace out a spectrum of more or less aggressive uses of intensified continuity—stylistic registers, we might say. These options tend to cluster around certain genres, with the most high-pitched registers appearing in science-fiction, fantasy, and suspense movies. Geoff King has noted that big-budget action films tend to employ an aggressive approach to shooting and cutting. King calls this the "impact-aesthetic" because it seeks a visceral response.[133] He traces how editing and camera placement in *The Rock* (1996) create violent motion punching out of the screen or engulfing the viewer.[134] The power of such sequences has been enhanced by several of the devices we've already considered, such as close-ups, wide-angle lenses, rack focusing, the handheld camera, and free-ranging dolly movements. Spielberg is adept at blending these devices with thrusting movement to create forceful and witty action sequences. While the exciting tank combat in *Indiana Jones and the Last Crusade* (1989) displays his characteristic mix of long and short focal-length shots, it gives crammed depth compositions a rhythmic pulse, thanks not only to cutting but also to pans, tilts, and rack focusing (Figs. 2.39–2.40). Movement jumps from plane to plane, and some gags seem designed specifically for wide-angle and telephoto framings (Figs. 2.41–2.42).

This impact aesthetic illustrates once more the tendency of intensified continuity to revive and exaggerate devices that were occasional resources of earlier years. The classic studio films sometimes flung violent movement toward the camera, with low-angle shots showing locomotives, cattle, or stagecoaches hurtling over the viewer. These "pit shots" became a signature of second-unit director B. Reeves ("Breezy") Eason.[135] Anthony Mann, Robert Aldrich, Samuel Fuller, and other postwar directors took pleasure in staging aggressive action sequences. Even the more sedate Douglas Sirk provided a startling piece of to-camera violence (Figs. 2.43–2.44). The new screen formats of the early 1950s encouraged such funfair gimmicks, notably the thrill-ride

2.39. *Indiana Jones and the Last Crusade* (1989): Inside the runaway tank, a pistol drops into the foreground . . .

2.40. . . . and a smooth upward tilt and rack focus shows the jammed scene of action beyond.

2.41. *Indiana Jones and the Last Crusade:* The wide-angle lens allows the gag to fill the format.

2.42. *Indiana Jones and the Last Crusade:* The stacking effect of the long lens allows Jones to slay three Nazis with one bullet.

2.43. *Tarnished Angels* (1958): In an air circus a plane crashes . . .

2.44. . . . flinging a body suddenly to the camera.

views in *This Is Cinerama* (1953) and the in-your-lap bursts of 3-D films like *Hondo* (1953). More proximate sources of the impact aesthetic lie in the 1960s and early 1970s, when the chase sequences of *Bullitt* (1968), *The Italian Job* (1969), *Duel* (1971), *The French Connection*, and *The Seven-Ups* (1973) became set pieces admired by ambitious young filmmakers. (Cinematographer William Fraker claims that shooting automobile commercials taught him techniques that he was able to employ in the *Bullitt* chase in order "to allow the audience to experience the chase like they were in the cars.")[136] *Raiders of the Lost Ark* (1981), *Road Warrior* (aka *Mad Max II*, 1981), and *Termi-*

2.45. In *The Quick and the Dead*, outrageous wide-angle compositions stylize the round-robin gunfights.

nator (1984) pushed the envelope, with both long-lens and wide-angle shots employed to assault the viewer head-on. By the time *Highlander* (1986) was made, the visceral action style had become a delirious grandiloquence; at the climax, crane shots swoop around a duel, while swordsmen, neon signs, and floods of water are blasted out at the audience.

Action pictures don't have a monopoly on aggressive style, as is evident in suspense films like *Albino Alligator* (1997) and *Panic Room* (2002), with their sinuous tracking shots, abrupt close-ups, and fragmented cutting. Comedies will use fast cutting and extreme wide-angle lenses to add cartoonish exaggeration, as in *Dennis the Menace* (1993), *Monkeybone* (2001), and many films by Barry Sonnenfeld. Or a director may employ this register as part of a flamboyant personal style, regardless of genre. Oliver Stone brings the extremes of intensified continuity to musical biopic (*The Doors*, 1991), conspiracy thriller (*JFK*, 1991), satiric social commentary (*Natural Born Killers*, 1994), neo-noir (*U-Turn*, 1997), and sports drama (*Any Given Sunday*, 1999). Spike Lee does much the same, if less strenuously. The opening of *Summer of Sam* (1999) is a virtual anthology of intensified-continuity devices, displaying jumpy edits, a roaming camera, and a virtuoso following shot into a disco. Joel and Ethan Coen are likewise transgeneric in their application of the style, although they tend to use its extremes for grotesque farces like *Raising Arizona* (1987) and *The Hudsucker Proxy* (1994). Sam Raimi's Western *The Quick and the Dead* (1995; Fig. 2.45) plays its gunfights as outlandish exercises in the style.

At the other end of the spectrum we find a less florid approach. Most program pictures, prestige films, and ordinary comedies, dramas, and children's movies handle intensified continuity more modestly. Faster cutting, definitely.

Frequent close views, almost certainly. Long lenses for singles and for exterior landscapes, very likely. An occasional spiraling or craning shot for emphasis. Here, however, these devices rest quietly in a firm framework of standard continuity practices. Opening a scene with master shots, handling it through matched shot/reverse-shot coverage, going in for near views to underscore a point—persistently and pervasively, many directors pledge themselves to the tactics pursued by their predecessors from the 1920s to the 1960s. Such films offer strong evidence that the new style is best understood as a decorative and expressive elaboration of long-standing schemas.

Take *Two Weeks Notice* (2002), a contemporary equivalent of Doris Day comedies. Lucy Kelson is about to leave George Wade's company. As she interviews June Carter for her job, George comes in and quickly succumbs to June's flirtatiousness. Even though Lucy has resisted George's charms, this moment triggers her jealousy. As in traditional continuity, the scene provides orienting establishing shots (Figs. 2.46, 2.51) before supplying over-the-shoulder-shots and singles. The axis of action determines camera placement and actors' orientations and eyelines. The first axis joins June and Lucy at the desk (Figs. 2.47–2.48), then a new axis (a little awkwardly created with a nearly head-on shot of Lucy) bringing George into the office and triangulating among the three characters (Fig. 2.51–2.52). Gradually the shot scale increases as the drama develops. We get alternating medium shots as June praises Lucy as a legend at Harvard, but tighter shots on June, which allow us to gauge her calculating flattery (Fig. 2.49) and Lucy's reaction as June reads a corporate statement that Lucy has composed (Fig. 2.50). Once George has joined the conversation, the close singles show the growing rapport between him and June, as their eyelines lock Lucy out (Figs. 2.53–2.54). Lucy rises and leaves for her meeting, but they ignore her, and as she lingers at the door, June and George share the reverse angle, while she floats free in her single (Figs. 2.55–2.56). The dramatic action ends with an inversion: June was brought to Lucy's office, but Lucy is pushed out, leaving June in control of the boss. The scene closes with the obligatory dialogue hook to the next sequence—going to the Mets game—and the larger dangling cause establishing June as a rival to Lucy.

The scene obeys the classic precepts of Hollywood spatial construction: break the dramatic interaction into segments according to the dramatic curve, keep eyelines and posture coherent so that we always understand who is looking at whom. The result is a vanilla-flavored version of intensified continuity. There are no handheld shots or arcing tracks, no distorting wide angles. When Lucy strides around her desk, the camera pans smoothly to pick up George in the foreground, and there is a very brief,

2.46. *Two Weeks Notice:* An establishing shot supplies an orienting view of the scene's first phase—Lucy's interview with June.

2.47. Following a standard formula, one over-the-shoulder framing is matched . . .

2.48. . . . by a symmetrical one favoring Lucy.

2.49. The actors' faces take over in tighter singles, first of June, who praises George's social conscience . . .

2.50. . . . then of Lucy, who recalls that she authored the statement June quotes.

virtually unnoticeable reverse tracking shot as George enters. The scene's obedience to recent trends lies in its heavy use of singles (twenty-three of the forty-eight shots), its reliance on wide-angle lenses for establishing shots (Fig. 2.51) and rather long lenses for singles (Figs. 2.50, 2.53), and its average shot length, a typical 3.2 seconds. As is customary, the editing pace

2.51. A new establishing shot on the other side of the axis, partly motivated by a slight change in Lucy's eyeline, shows George's arrival.

2.52. George takes up a position at Lucy's desk for the scene's next phase.

2.53. As the conversation becomes more flirtatious, tighter singles than we've previously seen (Figs. 2.49–2.50) . . .

2.54. . . . signal the growing attraction between George and June.

2.55. After Lucy has left her desk and crossed to the doorway, forming a new axis of action, a two-shot shows the new bond between June and George . . .

2.56. . . . as Lucy gawks and then heads off to her meeting.

is achieved through rapid dialogue cutting and an abundance of reaction shots, often in the middle of lines.

In *Two Weeks Notice*, the straightforward technique throws all the weight onto the flow of the action. Another conversation, this one from *The Lord of the Rings: The Two Towers* (2002), adds more bells and whistles. Gandalf and the other Fellows of the Ring are urging King Théoden to face the Uruk-hai hordes directly, but he will decide to evacuate his people and make a stand at the fortress of Helm's Deep. Like the *Two Weeks Notice* passage, the scene consists of two phases. In the first, Éowyn, Gandalf, and Aragorn state the case for a direct fight, while Théoden listens, morose and troubled. In the scene's second stage, Théoden resists their advice, insisting that he will not risk open war. The scene ends with him about to announce his decision, which is articulated at the start of the next scene as his officers evacuate the city.

The staging is simple. In the first phase of the scene, Gandalf and Théoden are sitting on thrones, with Éowyn and the refugee children on our right. Aragorn, Legolas, and Gimli are eating at a table on our left. All three zones are fairly distant from one another, and the actors are remarkably stationary. The three Fellows remain at the table throughout the scene, and although Éowyn rises from and settles back to the table with the children, she doesn't walk anywhere. The second phase of the action, with Théoden taking charge of the decision, is marked by his abrupt rise from his throne and his commanding walk to the center of the three zones, answering objections from Gandalf and Aragorn.

Peter Jackson's staging and editing respect the conventions of classical continuity, although the scene's lone establishing shot is brief and comes halfway through the sequence (shot number 15). As in *Two Weeks Notice*, the drama is built out of intercutting the areas the characters occupy and linking them by eyelines and character orientation. At the start, Éowyn looks screen left at her uncle (Figs. 2.57–2.59), and the Fellows look screen left at her (Fig. 2.60). When Théoden takes the floor, the framing and cutting slightly reangle the axis of action as he turns to confront Gandalf, then Aragorn, then Gandalf again (Figs. 2.64–2.68). Théoden's challenge to Aragorn is underscored by reaction shots from the stolid Gimli, who eats, drinks, and belches, eyeing Aragorn (Fig. 2.69) along a secondary axis of action.[137]

This conventional scene layout is intensified through the devices we've been examining. The scene lasts only 98 seconds, but it consumes twenty-nine shots, yielding a 3.4-second ASL. At one point Éowyn is framed by a long lens, while a two-shot of her uncle and Gandalf is a shallow-focus wide-angle shot (Figs. 2.59, 2.61), so the binary extremes of the style are in place. Shot scales are also predictably close. As opposed to only three long shots, one extreme long shot (shot 15, the moving master), and just one *plan américain*, there are fourteen medium shots, nine medium close-ups, and two close-ups. Of the twenty-nine shots, twenty-two are simple singles or slightly modified singles (with one figure in focus in the foreground and distant figures lost in shadow or blur). And, in contrast to our *Two Weeks*

Notice scene, camera movement is almost incessant. The initial part of the scene, when all characters remain in their places, contains many push-ins or creeping zooms (nine out of the first twelve shots). In shot 13, Théoden strides to the center, captured in an abrupt pan, and thereafter the camera circles him in tight framings (Figs. 2.62–2.64). This fluid camerawork allows the axis of action to shift in the course of the conversation. During the last phase of the scene, there are several more push-ins and following shots as Gandalf confronts Théoden. The last shot tracks in to a tight close-up of Théoden as he ponders his decision (Figs. 2.71–2.72). In all, the camera moves in twenty-two of the scene's twenty-nine shots.

The primary purpose of the scene—to show Théoden standing firm in his refusal to confront the Uruk-hai—is fulfilled, but secondary aspects of the action aren't realized concretely. At this point Éowyn is falling in love with Aragorn, and Aragorn's questioning of Théoden's decision could be seen as rashness, thus shading his character a bit. A classical studio director, positioning his characters more compactly and giving them greater or lesser emphasis within a fuller frame, could evoke these subtexts more precisely. For example, if Éowyn were visible throughout the exchange between her uncle and her hero, the performer would have an opportunity to express her conflict between love and family loyalty. But glimpsed in an inexpressive cutaway, Éowyn's presence serves merely to break up the Théoden/Aragorn exchange and to allow Jackson to maneuver into a new axis of action. The scene's only pictorial inflection is thus the skeptical reaction of Gimli, given, as we'd expect, in close-ups.

Other dialogue scenes in *The Two Towers* display the same devices, deployed in much the same ways. Jackson and his colleagues, for all their obsession with details of castles, armor, and weaponry, have not devised distinctive visual strategies for individual scenes. In our sequence, the cuts and camera moves display no overarching pattern; the shots do not progress in a way contoured to the dramatic arc or emotional dynamic, except for the same sort of progression from medium close-ups to tight close-ups we found in the 1999 *Thomas Crown Affair* and in *Two Weeks Notice*. So, for instance, a slow, sustained track in to Théoden brooding on advice given from offscreen would have accumulated greater force than the compromise we get: three slices of this camera movement, interrupted by cutaways and two shots of Théoden and Gandalf from a striking but dramatically irrelevant angle. The result of cutting to every speaker for each line and fleeting reaction is a haphazard shot-snatching. Every shot is interrupted by another, as if to display a little of each angle of coverage; but no image can develop much power. Oddly, a strategy designed to amp up energy serves to dissipate it.

2.57. *The Two Towers:* After showing us the refugee children at the table eating, Jackson starts to build the space through eyelines. Éowyn looks off . . .

2.58. . . . at her uncle, Théoden, and at Gandalf at the head of the banquet hall.

2.59. A tighter single of Éowyn confirms the spatial relations before . . .

2.60. . . . a "partial master" establishes a third zone, that of Legolas, Aragorn, and Gimli, with the first two looking off at her.

2.61. A series of shots presents the two old men brooding . . .

2.62. . . . before Théoden strides forward to the center of the three zones that editing has marked out.

2.63. The camera arcs around him as he walks . . .

2.64. . . . picking up Gandalf . . .

2.65. . . . who challenges Théoden in a separate shot.

2.66. After a cutaway to Éowyn, Théoden replies . . .

2.67. . . . and turns back . . .

2.68. . . . to answer Aragorn's warning that they must stand and fight.

2.69. Théoden's stiff-backed reply is undercut by a belch from Gimli.

2.70. A cut to Gandalf, demanding the king's decision . . .

2.71. . . . is followed by Théoden's reaction . . .

2.72. . . . which is underscored by a push-in. The scene's tightest close-up comes at the very end.

A spurt of pictorial interest comes at the very end, when the push-in to Théoden yields the scene's most intimate view. In earlier instances, a cut has always interrupted the camera's trajectory, but now the track-in begins during the shot and ends before we cut away. Now, it might be argued, the scene's end coincides with a final stability of the image, holding on the old king's stricken expression. But is this rather standard effect worth all the choppy cutting that precedes it?

Intensified continuity often yields this catch-as-catch-can quality, but sometimes that very quality can have expressive value. Ron Howard's *The Paper* (1994) is an effort to revive the heedless drive of tabloid comedies like *Five Star Final* (1931) and *His Girl Friday* (1940). How to achieve this within today's dominant style? One scene, fairly early in the plot, reveals some possibilities. The protagonist, managing editor Henry Hackett, is juggling several problems. His wife, Marty, is in the late stages of pregnancy and yearns to return to her job at the newspaper office. Henry has that morning interviewed with the prestigious *Sentinel* and must decide this afternoon whether he will take the job. He is also trying to gather information on a double murder that his paper missed covering this morning. He has immediate deadlines as well: the 3:00 staff meeting, the deadline for the late edition of his paper, and his dinner date with Marty and her parents. The scene I'll examine takes place in his cramped office and rapidly brings together several plot lines. The staging, cutting, and framing squeeze into 4 minutes and 13 seconds a string of gags, bits of exposition, and premises for upcoming plot developments.

The first phase of the scene begins with Henry discovering his columnist, McDougal, sleeping on his office couch. Before Henry can assign him to check the backgrounds of the murdered men, McDougal reveals that he carries a pistol to protect himself against a city official he's been tormenting in print. (Naturally the official, and the pistol, become important at the film's climax.) Marty, distressed after a long lunch with an unhappy mother, bursts into the office pleading for Henry to take the *Sentinel* offer. So now Henry's request that McDougal investigate the banking backgrounds of the men interweaves with Marty's efforts to get Henry's attention. The scene shifts into a new phase as a reporter, Carmen, comes in to tell Henry that two teenagers were arrested for the murder. She begs for the chance to cover the story. McDougal says that the cops don't believe they have the killers, while Carmen asks Henry not to send the green photographer Robin to film the "perp walk" at 7:30 that night. (Needless to say, Robin does shoot it, as part of an intricate Henry scheme.) Immediately the squat and profane Wilder enters and accuses Carmen of poaching on his turf. This precipitates the final escalation. McDougal shouts that people should leave Marty alone with Henry. Carmen and Wilder pull Henry into a quarrel. Other staff burst into the office bent on their own missions. The senior editor yells from his office that people are late for the 3:00 meeting. Finally McDougal lugs in bundles of newspapers and silences the melee by firing a bullet into the stack. With a manic grin he spits out, "Let . . . Marty . . . talk . . . to her husband." After a moment of shock, the reporters disperse, muttering, and McDougal strolls out, assuring Henry he's on the case. Henry stares after them all, while Marty bursts out, *"God,* I miss this place!"

The cutting (ASL 3.8 seconds) is as rapid as it is in *Two Weeks Notice,* but the pace feels quicker, partly because of overlapping and simultaneous dialogue, a convention of newspaper movies. No less important, however, is Howard's more dynamic framing and staging, assisted by gentle Steadicam movement. The spatial layout is given by a shot that moves back with Henry as he hurries into his office, then pans to catch McDougal on the sofa. Thereafter, during the first phase an axis is established between McDougal and Henry (Figs. 2.73–2.74). As they talk, the panning camera catches Marty in the background, storming toward the office (Fig. 2.75) and demanding to talk to Henry. A cutaway to the senior editor shouting, "Three oh-seven!" (Fig. 2.76) covers a change of the axis connecting Marty and Henry when we return to the office. They play out their dialogue on that side of the axis (Figs. 2.77–2.78) before a new shot, breaking the axis (Fig. 2.79), shows Henry putting Marty on hold and stepping forward to question McDougal.

Howard has given his cast a good deal of physical activity—they stride, gesture, and indulge in bits of business—and he activates several zones of the office. McDougal crosses to the desk for some Pepto-Bismol as Marty starts pacing in the opposite direction, rebalancing the shot (Fig. 2.80). Then McDougal returns to his sofa, clearing the door to allow people to pile in (Fig. 2.81). Carmen is the first; a pan shot as she enters moves to Marty and Henry but allows McDougal to intervene from the depth of the frame (Figs. 2.82–2.84). Once Marty is settled into a chair, Henry becomes the central figure. He moves to his desk and becomes the pivot point of the action, usually with a constantly maintained axis (Figs. 2.85–2.86). Now the shots include more Steadicam push-ins and arcing movements. These are often, as in *The Two Towers,* interrupted by cuts, but here the choppy quality works better because several characters are talking at once, so a shot of a speaker pulls his or her lines out of the babble. At the height of confusion, with five characters hollering around the desk (Fig. 2.87), the sound of a gunshot off-screen motivates the cut to their reactions (Fig. 2.88) and a slow push-in to McDougal (Fig. 2.89). The scene ends by panning McDougal out of the office

2.73. *The Paper:* Henry arrives at his office, waking McDougal . . .

2.74. . . . and learning that he's carrying a pistol.

2.75. As McDougal explains, through the window we see Marty striding up to Henry's office.

2.76. A cutaway to the senior editor bellowing that a meeting is due to start . . .

2.77. . . . covers the shift to a new axis of action as over-the-shoulder shots show Henry . . .

2.78. . . . reacting to Marty's pleas to take the job at the *Sentinel.* This becomes a dangling cause that will be further developed in the following scene.

2.79. Another crossing of the line sets up a new arena for action; Henry will turn from Marty to ask McDougal about the Sonoma Bank.

2.80. McDougal trades places with Marty, fetching antacid from Henry's desk as Marty leaves to pace on the left side of the room.

2.81. As McDougal returns to his sofa, Carmen enters with an update.

2.82. The camera wheels to the left as she greets Marty . . .

2.83. . . . and it continues to move left to pick up Marty's reaction . . .

2.84. . . . before settling on a framing that allows McDougal to tell them, from the background, that the arrest of the two young men is camouflage.

2.85. In a single, Henry assumes command, assigning reporters to different angles on the story.

2.86. The chaos increases: Carmen and Wilder quarrel, and a disgruntled writer enters the fray.

2.87. As several characters speak at once a gunshot rips out . . .

2.88. . . . and a cut-in shows everyone going suddenly quiet.

2.89. The source of the sound is revealed: The camera pushes in to show that McDougal has fired into a stack of newspapers. He orders everyone to let Marty talk to Henry.

2.90. After the crowd clears, McDougal ambles out . . .

2.91. . . . and the camera follows him to pick up Marty in the foreground: "*God*, I miss this place!"

and picking up Marty's delighted reaction (Figs. 2.90–2.91), an inversion of the shot that introduced her (Fig. 2.75). Howard has given the scene energy, not through accelerated editing or flagrant camera movements but through the blocking and pace of the performances.

The *Paper* scene displays more nuanced and vivacious staging than we find in *Two Weeks Notice* or *The Two Towers*, and the jerky rhythms encouraged by intensified continuity suit the material. Even here, however, the style gravitates toward eclecticism. The problem goes beyond structuring a single scene cogently. If every sequence contains complex tracks, rapid cutting, tight views, and the rest, how can these flourishes be allocated across the entire film for maximum effect? One solution is to set up symmetries across parallel scenes. For *The End of the Affair* (1999), Neil Jordan sought to mark off flashbacks by having the camera circle the characters in one direction during scenes set in the past, and in the opposite direction in present-time episodes.[138]

A further step in this direction is to give the overall film a progression along a few dimensions. As we've seen, Lumet developed a "lens plot" for

12 Angry Men, systematically moving toward longer lenses and steeper angles as the action unrolled. Barry Salt calls this strategy an "expressive program," and he has remarked that it became particularly prominent in 1980s cinematography, when directors modified lighting or lenses across an entire film.[139] For *Ordinary People* (1980), the scenes in the psychiatrist's office were filmed with progressively longer lenses and framed in ever-tighter close-ups.[140] Ron Howard plotted *The Paper* along such a program. The film has camera movement throughout, but it starts with smooth dollies, segues into Steadicam movements, and climaxes with hand-held shots.[141]

Many of the filmmakers interested in mapping out a film's stylistic progression studied at the University of Southern California, where Bruce Block was an influential advocate of the practice. Interestingly, Block attributed this idea to Slavko Vorkapich, the former head of USC's film program, who purportedly took it from Eisenstein.[142] Whatever its source, the idea is now widespread, and most major films will be planned to execute an overall visual arc. *Requiem for a Dream* (2000) marked each of the script's three "acts" with a different color temperature: warm, hard light for the summer; colder tones for fall; and artificial fluorescent light and pushed film stock for winter.[143] Robert Zemeckis split *Cast Away* (2001) in two, reserving dynamic camera movement for the scenes up through the plane crash and then locking down the camera for the desert island aftermath, confining frame movement solely to ninety-degree pans or tilts.[144] As Martin Scorsese's *The Aviator* (2004) takes its story from the late 1920s through the 1940s, the imagery moves from Technicolor's early two-color palette to the richer three-color one.[145] The tacit model in such films may be the musical score, which shifts mood, tempo, and orchestration in operatic fashion across the movie.

The programmatic tendency came to prominence along with intensified continuity, and it seems likely that it offered a way for directors, faced with a plethora of technical options, to constrain their choices in a principled way. Significantly, however, most of the dimensions programmed have involved lens length, camera movement, lighting, color, and setting. Few directors have tried to "through-compose" techniques like cutting, shot scale, and staging.

Occasions for Innovation

Apart from devising a visual program, how might one innovate within the intensified-continuity style? No style is wholly standardized, and contrary to common belief, Hollywood cinema encourages variety, not sheer replication of formula. Studio-era filmmakers like Josef von Sternberg, Orson Welles, and Busby Berkeley explored many stylistic options, sometimes with a self-consciousness bordering on preciosity. Ang Lee has pointed out that a big-budget film like *Hulk* (2003) allowed him to experiment more than he had on his smaller pictures. Making a blockbuster provides "kind of an indulgence. . . . We shot excessively, we were able to use . . . big sets, use different film languages, putting shots together, weird lenses. . . . Actually, it gives you more freedom. In a smaller movie you cannot afford that kind of freedom in creating images."[146]

Novelty, however, has always been strongly controlled by aesthetic norms. Even Welles's baroque compositions in *Citizen Kane* (1941) were situated within classical cutting schemes. Similarly, today's new techniques are inserted into the stable system of representing space and time, and though they do gain a certain freshness, they are still tamed to well-established purposes. As we've seen, during one scene of *The Insider* (1999) Jeffrey Weigand breaks down from the pressure of informing on his tobacco company bosses, and he is filmed in increasingly stylized shots. At the climax, his hotel suite warps around him, and he sees himself, still in his armchair, in his backyard watching his daughters (see Fig. 1.21). The computer-image morphing of Weigand's hallucination produces an expressionistic image, but it is motivated in a traditional way: distorted imagery is permitted when it reveals a character's disturbed mind.

Classical studio filmmaking demanded innovation at the technical level, and it even encouraged occasional flagrant virtuosity, particularly in camera movements, color rendition, and set design. In the poststudio decades, some directors became identified with highly visible innovation. The most famous was Stanley Kubrick, who as a former photojournalist gave himself well-publicized pictorial challenges with each new project. He demanded front-projection special effects in *2001: A Space Odyssey* (1968) and a superfast lens for filming by candlelight in *Barry Lyndon* (1975). When Kubrick saw a demo reel of Steadicam footage, he figured out how the process worked, and when he began work on *The Shining* (1980) he asked for improvement in the video display.[147] In more recent years, Oliver Stone has staked his career on continuous technical innovation, from the novel crane shots in *The Doors* (1991) to the goulash of stocks and gauges in *JFK* (1991) and *Natural Born Killers* (1994). As directors learn of new technologies by making videos and television commercials, they try these out on features. Or the director may innovate through anachronism. Shooting *Alice Doesn't Live Here Anymore* (1975), Scorsese avoided big close-ups: "I wanted it to be very much in the old American style which is medium-shot, medium-shot, two-shot, wide shot."[148] As with story structure, novelty is driven by an acute consciousness of recasting or reviving tradition.

As 1990s plotting turned to unusual studio-era devices like multiple-pro-

2.92. *Confidence:* The long lens trained on an outdoor café creates a planimetric image.

2.93. In a variant of the "wipe-by" axial cut (Figs. 2.13–2.14), no one crosses in the master shot, but a blurry figure passes in the cut-in shot . . .

2.94. . . . revealing one of the thieves speaking.

tagonist stories, so 1990s film style sometimes pushed a rare technical device to a greater degree of prominence. We've already noted that the occasional to-camera thrust of classical chase scenes became a basis of "impact editing." Another clear example is the wipe-by cut. Our *Jaws* example (see Figs. 2.13–2.14) indicated that this was becoming a marked device in the 1970s, but in *Confidence* (2003), it is recast as a stylistic premise for entire scenes. The gang planning a heist meets several times in an outdoor café. Each time, director James Foley shoots the group from two sides: one perpendicular view from across the street, the other an opposite view from inside the café. Thus every cut either varies the view by exactly 180 degrees (cutting between street and interior views) or simply shifts directly along the lens axis (cutting into or back from a speaker). The very long lenses permit a lot of traffic and indeterminate figures to pass through the foreground. There are a few genuine wipe-by cuts in the sequence, but often a passing figure wipes away at the start of a shot, without any matching movement at the end of the previous shot (Figs. 2.92–2.94). These "half" wipe-by cuts yield a nervous tempo that Foley came to like. The "jumpy and elliptical" cutting was, he says, consistent with the hyped-up performers (their energy, to use the standard word).[149] The cuts also conformed to some transitional devices the filmmakers employed; several scenes are linked by abrupt in-camera wipes.[150]

This promotion of a one-off resource can be seen in Oliver Stone's con-

2.95. An interrupted quarrel in *Any Given Sunday:* The team manager makes a point . . .

2.96. . . . and Stone interpolates a shot from the practice session . . .

2.97. . . . before returning to the conversation, with the 180-degree line intact.

stant use of cutaways and brief flashbacks in *Any Given Sunday,* or the subliminal shots that preview the film's major moments at the start of De Palma's *Mission: Impossible* (1996). In *Magnolia* (1999), Paul Thomas Anderson makes the forward tracking shot, either following action or moving inexorably closer to a static actor, a dominant stylistic device, reinforcing it by an insistent score and by cuts that accentuate musical phrases. Stone's post-*JFK* films are probably the most disjunctive made in Hollywood—intercutting color and black-and-white, repeating shots, inserting an occasional long shot crossing the axis of action. As with Anderson, however, the soundtrack binds the shots together, with character dialogue serving as a kind of voice-over commentary on wide-ranging imagery. And the aberrations stand out as such, momentary deviations from a still-powerful cluster of norms to which Stone mostly adheres.

The central convention of classical spatial construction is the "180-degree line," or the axis of action. In a conversation scene, that line joins the primary participants in a dialogue. In an action scene, it delineates the primary direction of movement from place to place. If filmmakers abandoned or constantly violated the axis of action, wouldn't that be the ultimate innovation? And wouldn't it prove that they had left orthodox continuity behind? One sometimes hears that the line is gone now. Yet our examples from *Two Weeks Notice, The Two Towers,* and *The Paper* indicate that many film-

2.98. In the initial episode of the television drama *Homicide: Life on the Street* (1993), a cop interrogates a suspect . . .

2.99. . . . and the camera setups cross the axis of action. Spatial relations are kept clear by means of constant panning between the two characters.

2.100. *Hulk* (2003): As Betty pleads for mercy for Bruce Banner . . .

2.101. . . . the cutting jumps the line to a closer shot of her . . .

2.102. . . . and her father's reaction. The eyelines match here . . .

2.103. . . . and in this reverse shot.

2.104. But the next reaction shot flips the line again. The tactic seems designed to heighten the clash of father and daughter.

2.105. *8 Mile:* The protagonist faces his adversary on stage, and . . .

2.106. . . . a new angle crosses the axis.

2.107. *Man on Fire* (2004) strives for an edgy look, as when lines of dialogue pulse to the image surface, making the shot look like a layout in *Wired* magazine.

makers still organize their scenes around the axis of action. Now and then a cut breaks the line, usually to get the filmmaker out of an awkward staging problem (see Figs. 2.51, 2.79), but that happened in the studio era as well. Interestingly, filmmakers who flout other editing norms tend to preserve the axis of action, as when Stone embeds his sudden cutaways within the spatial unity of the principal scene (Figs. 2.95–2.97).

Still, the 1990s saw a slight tendency for the camera's viewpoint to hop back and forth across the 180-degree line during dialogue scenes. As usual with ragged technique, this approach was favored by filmmakers seeking a realistic, rough-edged look (Figs. 2.98–2.99). More elaborate recent variants derive from other technical choices favored by the intensified style. As more scenes were shot with two handheld cameras, directors created "200-plus-degree coverage." In this practice the A and B cameras favor one actor. Then the scene is repeated with the two cameras shooting the second player's lines and reactions. In both takes the cameras are placed on both sides of the axis linking the actors, so that shot/reverse-shot cuts may perceptibly jump the line (Figs. 2.100–2.104). Usually one camera provides a medium shot, while the other handles close-ups, but sometimes, as in the *Hulk* example, intercut shots can be quite similar in scale.[151]

Directors have long known that in stationary one-on-one dialogues, the axis of action provides redundant cues, and editors can occasionally break it without losing intelligibility. Some filmmakers, such as the 1920s Soviet montagists and the Japanese master Ozu Yasujiro, created alternative editing systems built out of the 180-degree norm.[152] In most contemporary American examples, the spatial relations are easy to grasp, and so disrespecting the axis isn't confusing. At the rap-competition climax of *8 Mile* (2002), the multiple cameras float freely around the two performers, yielding many line-crossing cuts (Figs. 2.105–2.106). But the cuts aren't disconcerting because the simple spatial layout—the hero and his adversary on stage turning to the crowd or to each other—has been clearly established, and the "incorrect" matches are embedded in stretches of normal continuity cutting. "It excites me," remarks a cinematographer, "when you can take a scene of two people sitting down and alter the language of it so it makes sense for the tone of the scene. Once we flip the line, you wonder where you are for a second. [In some cases] it's especially noticeable because we eventually cut back to the original perspective."[153] We may expect this sort of momentary axis breaking to become common, especially at moments of high tension.

Most of my examples of innovation have come from the last decade or so, and it may be that as I write, intensified continuity is itself intensifying. With this stylistic paradigm dominant for decades, it's not surprising that many filmmakers are pushing it further. The prominence of recherché stylists like Stone, Soderbergh, David Fincher, David O. Russell, and the Wachowski brothers is matched by a new self-consciousness in the work of more veteran directors. The jump cuts of Ridley Scott's *Matchstick Men* (2003) and the spatters of tiled framing in Joel Schumacher's *Phone Booth* (2003) and Lee's *Hulk* abandon the lush pictorialism that the directors had cultivated in earlier work. As directors compete to be novel, we may expect to see flamboyant variants of the style (Fig. 2.107)—intensifications of an intensified style. Perhaps the movies of the 2000s are the movies of the 1980s, only more so.

4. WHAT'S MISSING?

Despite all the historical changes and local variants we find in contemporary film style, we are still dealing with a version of classical filmmaking. An analysis of virtually any film from the period under consideration will confirm the simple truth with which I started: nearly all scenes in nearly all contemporary mass-market movies (and in most "independent" films) are staged, shot, and cut according to principles that crystallized in the 1910s and 1920s. Intensified continuity constitutes a selection and elaboration of options already on the classical filmmaking menu—some going back quite far. Building a scene out of tight rapidly cut singles was a strategy adopted by some B-filmmakers (e.g., James Tinling in *Mr. Moto's Gamble*, 1938; ASL 4.6 seconds) and a few A-list ones, like Sam Wood and Frank Borzage. Autonomous camera movement was likewise an option, although it was traditionally reserved for moments of high drama. The long lens had been used for close-ups since the 1920s, so by the 1960s it could be applied to other shot scales. In sum, the favored technical devices have changed, but the spatial *system* of classical Hollywood continuity remains intact.

Nonetheless, intensified continuity represents a significant shift within the history of moviemaking. The new technical devices, encouraging heavy stylization and self-conscious virtuosity, have changed our experience of following the story. Most obviously, the style aims to generate a keen moment-by-moment anticipation. Techniques that 1940s directors reserved for moments of shock and suspense are the stuff of normal scenes today. Close-ups and singles make the shots very legible. Rapid editing obliges the viewer to assemble many discrete pieces of information, and it sets a commanding pace: look away, and you might miss a key point. In the alternating close views, the racking focus, and the edgily drifting camera, the viewer is promised something significant, or at least new, at each instant. Television-friendly, the style tries to rivet the viewer to the screen.[154] Here is another reason to call it intensified continuity: even ordinary scenes are heightened to compel attention and to sharpen emotional resonance.

One result is an aesthetic of broad but forceful effects, often showing strain but sometimes summoning up considerable power. The schemas of intensified continuity can be handled in imaginative ways, as the films of Jonathan Demme, Spike Lee, David Lynch, John McTiernan, and Michael Mann illustrate. We have subdued versions (Nora Ephron, Ron Howard, Frank Darabont), more pumped-up ones (directors working in the Bruckheimer and Silver stables), and even parodically delirious ones (mid-career Sam Raimi, the Coen brothers). As if sensing the style's tendency to spin into sheer eclecticism, some directors have sought to apply it in a purified form. Todd Haynes's *Safe* (1995), for instance, heightens our sense of the artificiality of the style by injecting small doses of it into a texture that favors static long shots and slight, geometrical camera movements.

Action pictures ought to be excellent display cases for the style, riding as they do on self-professed energy, and a few are, notably those by James Cameron (*Terminator,* 1984; *Aliens,* 1986) and Katherine Bigelow (*Point Break,* 1991). Many, however, are staged, shot, and cut with a dismal lack of clarity and force. *Matrix: Revolutions* (2003) illustrates the problem. Immobile dialogue scenes that set declaiming characters face-to-face give way to hyperactive action sequences verging on visual chaos. For really elegant revelations of what intensified continuity can do, we must turn to Hong Kong cinema, and not only to scenes of violence; Hong Kong directors have long been committed to making even static scenes rhythmically powerful through cutting and figure movement.[155] In Johnnie To's *A Hero Never Dies* (1998), two hit men for rival gangs confront each other across a nightclub table. As a chanteuse croons the "Sukiyaki" tune, the bartender pours wine for each man. They begin a game. Each hurls a coin to shatter the other's wineglass, making the pitch more difficult at each round. Director To gives us tight, brief close-ups and a languidly arcing camera, but instead of using the devices haphazardly, as they were used by Jackson in the *Two Towers* sequence, he organizes them around the simple visual idea of man versus man. One glares, the other looks downward. As they take turns pitching coins, the sequence is built out of unusually symmetrical reverse shots, parallel movements of killers and camera, and cutting that reflects the mounting, preposterous triviality of the contest. Coins ricochet off the bar, tremble on the table's edge, plummet like lead weights to smash a glass on the floor. The result, timed to the measures of the song, is at once an ingenious tabletop action scene and a mesmerizing passage of mock-heroic cinema. As the song throbs to its end, the game reaches stalemate among shards of glass. The camera rises to supply our first full view of the scene, a "delayed master" that yields a satisfying coda: the two men relax at last, their postures hinting at their eventual alliance. Few Hollywood directors could have created the dynamically arousing fight scenes that fill 1980s Hong Kong films, and few American practitioners of intensified continuity could blend today's techniques into To's bold, precisely choreographed sequence.[156]

A Hero Never Dies relishes its cuts and camera movements, asking us to enjoy how they fall into expanding patterns of echo and reprise. In this respect it displays another tendency of intensified continuity: a push toward quite overt narration. Classical studio filmmaking was never wholly "transparent": figures in two-shots were usually slightly pivoted to the audience, and there were always stretches (montage sequences, beginnings and endings of scenes, beginnings and endings of films) acknowledging that the scene was addressing a spectator. Expansive camera movements and dynamic color schemes urged the viewer to enjoy self-conscious storytelling. Still, things have changed notably. Today gestures that earlier filmmakers would have considered flagrantly emphatic—arcing camera, big close-ups, and other flourishes—have become default values in ordinary scenes and minor movies. This swashbuckling style matches the overt play with narrative patterning that we find in contemporary films at all levels of ambition.

Again, it was in the 1960s that highly self-conscious narration became respectable. Godard, Truffaut, Fellini, and Bergman reveled in it. In the heyday of auteurism, Welles and Hitchcock, both flamboyant stylists, became model directors, at just the period Leone and Peckinpah were emerging. At the same time, genres that emphasize narrational gambits—thrillers, spy and mystery films, horror films—were earning greater attention. In *The Ipcress File* (1965), Sidney J. Furie filmed through telephone booths and hanging lampshades, prompting Michael Caine to call him a member of the "Look, Ma, I'm directing" school.[157] Similar stylistic gymnastics were on display in *Seconds* (1966) and *The Italian Job* (1969; see Fig. 2.7). In the supernatural thriller *Rosemary's Baby* (1968), Polanski reveled in ambivalent point-of-view shots (Figs. 2.108–2.113). Other 1960s tendencies, such as split-screen imagery, slow motion, and even the spiraling shot and the handheld camera, can be seen as signs of a willingness to make narration more obtrusive.

At the limit, a few directors have claimed that they want the viewer to recognize artifice. "I am constantly standing outside," claimed Brian De Palma in 1973, "and making people aware that they are always watching a film."[158] De Palma, who drops Bertolt Brecht's name, may have borrowed this notion from the version of Brecht's alienation-effect then starting to circulate in academic film studies. For De Palma, this process heightens the audience's appreciation of the director's shaping hand. For Altman, the reflexivity seems tied to satire: the opening of *The Player* serves "to remind the audience that this is a movie, that this is a movie about movies, and ultimately this becomes a movie about itself."[159]

But most filmmakers have wanted to have their cake and eat it, to flaunt style and yet somehow never throw the viewer out of gear with the fiction. A manual urging directors to create "eye candy" at every opportunity nonetheless insists that technique shouldn't call attention to itself. The author's prime example, a tightly composed moving master from *What Lies Beneath* (2000), is blocked to arouse suspense and then trigger surprise

2.108. *Rosemary's Baby:* A famous point-of-view cut shows Rosemary and others looking off at Mrs. Castevet making a phone call.

2.109. Polanski shoots the call so that Mrs. Castevet's face is just barely blocked by the door frame, causing, Polanski recalled, moviegoers to shift their head to try to see her.

2.110. The shot is prepared earlier in the film by a scene of Rosemary following her husband, Guy, to a ringing phone. As she leaves the shot . . .

2.111. . . . cut to Guy entering the bedroom.

2.112. He vanishes behind the doorway, answering the phone. The camera slowly slides rightward, as if representing Rosemary's effort to see him.

2.113. But Guy remains unseen as Rosemary steps into what we had taken for her optical point of view.

through a sudden shift from restricted to unrestricted narration.[160] The 1960s made us familiar with this sort of middling self-consciousness. The visual bravura of the 1990s suits the attitude projected by the plots of *Go* (1999), *Memento* (2002), and *Jackie Brown* (1997)—sly pieces of clockwork to be admired not for their realism but for their outlandish ingenuity.

Interestingly, a more outré technique usually doesn't prevent us from comprehending the story. Having become accustomed to a highly overt narration, we seem to have set the threshold for obtrusiveness higher. And like earlier audiences, we can appreciate displays of virtuosity—the legerdemain of wipe-by cuts, the soaring exhilaration of Flying-Cam shots. For such reasons, the new style suggests that we can't adequately describe the viewer's activity with spatial metaphors like "absorption" and "detachment." At any moment, stylistic tactics may announce themselves, even as viewers remain attentive to the action. Today's cinema would seem to ask its spectators to take a high degree of narrational self-consciousness for granted, to let a few familiar devices amplify each story point, to revel in displays of technique— all the while surrendering to the pull of a tale constructed on more or less traditional lines. It would not be the first time audiences would have been asked to enjoy overt play with form without sacrificing depth of emotional engagement. (Baroque music and rococo architecture come to mind, as do Ozu and Mizoguchi.) The triumph of intensified continuity reminds us that as styles change, so do viewing skills.

Still, every style excludes certain options, and intensified continuity has cut itself off from some rich resources of classical filmmaking. As the range of likely shot lengths has narrowed, mainstream directors have been discouraged from making a two-hour film out of fewer than five hundred shots. It's not that he or she can't use a long take—indeed, one or two seem de rigueur in every film—but a movie built primarily out of prolonged shots is very rare in today's Hollywood. (Significantly, *Unbreakable*'s long takes provided product differentiation for its publicity campaign.)[161]

Further, by concentrating on camerawork and editing, practitioners of intensified continuity have neglected ensemble staging. Two staging options have come to dominate current practice. There's what filmmakers call "walk and talk," with a Steadicam carrying us along as characters spit out exposition on the fly. When we find a long take in a recent film, it is likely to be a walk-and-talk shot. Alternatively, there's what filmmakers call "stand and deliver," where the actors settle into fairly fixed positions. Usually this layout is broken up into singles and over-the-shoulder angles, but we may get instead the floating-head treatment, with the characters fixed in place and the camera drifting around them. In either case, if the characters shift to another part of the setting, their movement isn't usually aiming at expressive effect; rather, it's a transition to another passage of stand and deliver. Interestingly, when a contemporary handbook discusses staging, it is conceived largely in terms of fixing actors into different patterns—a perpendicular row, a diagonal into depth, or in a circle—that remain static, to be cut up into closer shots.[162] Our scenes from *Two Weeks Notice* and *The Two Towers* exemplify stand and deliver (which often becomes sit and deliver).[163] It's likely that the prevalence of stand and deliver has encouraged 200-degree-plus cuts, as a way of injecting some variety. Breaking the axis in shot/reverse-shot cutting would be much more disorienting if the characters were constantly moving around the set.

Both stand and deliver and walk and talk were used in the studio years, of course, but so was complex blocking, as in Fritz Lang's and Otto Preminger's delicately changing two-shots or William Wyler's checkerboarding of figures in depth. Such blocking, however, has all but vanished from popular cinema. Having lowered set lighting levels to make cast and crew more comfortable, cinematographers commonly shoot at f2.8 or even f1.4, apertures that make deep staging virtually impossible.[164] Most filmmakers have come to prefer a shallow-focus look. (They find the deep space yielded by digital video a drawback.) For reasons such as these, today a shot's pictorial appeal doesn't spring from moment-by-moment changes in lateral or diagonal staging. Now it stems from the sort of detailing we find in the well-furnished worlds of special effects. The actors are swamped by decor and costumes, giving us lots of busy minutiae rather than a sustained blocking that articulates the development of the drama.

There are exceptions. A flagrant one is Peter Bogdanovich's anachronistic *At Long Last Love* (1975), with its insistent long shots and forty-second ASL (Fig. 2.114). Polanski's and Spielberg's early 1970s films show that they were trying to integrate fairly close framings (even in the anamorphic format) with staging in depth.[165] Perhaps under Spielberg's influence, other directors have occasionally tried out complex long takes that adhere to close views and fluid camera movement (Figs. 2.115–2.119). Still, these are modest efforts compared to the nimble staging that remained part of the director's craft in the waning studio years. Richard Brooks's *Cat on a Hot Tin Roof* (1958) is no masterpiece, but it does exemplify what every director was supposed to know. Figures are arrayed in flexible configurations with minimal camera movement (Fig. 2.120). Quite distant spaces, seen in slots and notches, channel the audience's attention (Fig. 2.121), and just one figure turning from the camera can carry a dramatic impact (Fig. 2.122). These strategies obliged Brooks to forego the tight close-ups and spiraling camera of today's cinema, but the payoff in nuance and visual variety was worth it.[166]

It seems almost certain that no contemporary Hollywood director could build scenes in this fashion. Today, with each shot usually making only one point, we lose what Charles Barr, in his fundamental essay on CinemaScope, calls *graded* emphasis within the shot—balancing primary items with other

2.114. Several scenes in *At Long Last Love* are played out in full shots reminiscent of 1930s screwball comedies.

2.115. In a single-take scene of *Sneakers* (1992), government agents blackmail Martin Bishop into undertaking a black-op mission. First the friendlier one calms down his colleague.

2.116. After some byplay around the dossier on the table, the men move to the desk and show Bishop a fax indicating the invention he is to steal.

2.117. Coming to the foreground, Bishop refuses, but the friendlier agent approaches to coax him.

2.118. After Bishop steps back and the unfriendly agent moves across the foreground, Bishop and the other agent settle down at the table. Abruptly the unfriendly one comes into the foreground, starting to box Bishop in.

2.119. When he refuses again, the agents rise and threaten to expose his crimes and send him to prison. As the camera closes in on him, the agents' arms lean into the shot. Offscreen one of them demands, "Don't say no."

2.120. At the climax of *Cat on a Hot Tin Roof,* conflicts play out among clusters of characters spread across the shot. A composition like this is virtually unthinkable in today's Hollywood.

2.121. *Cat on a Hot Tin Roof:* Packing players into layers of space and apertures, a common technique of cinema since the 1910s, creates a spectrum of dramatic nuances within the shot.

2.122. *Cat on a Hot Tin Roof:* Even the simple device of turning characters from the camera, and from each other, becomes dramatically charged when the distant shot is sustained.

2.123. In *Memories of Murder* (South Korea, 2003) Bong Joon-ho stages several scenes in long takes (this one is 74 seconds), allowing us to scan the shot for characters' reactions.

information that has its own, if lesser, gravity.[167] Even Woody Allen, despite his avoidance of close-ups and his very long takes (an ASL of 22 seconds for *Manhattan,* 1979; 35.5 seconds for *Mighty Aphrodite,* 1995), doesn't pursue this option, for his staging tends to be simple.[168] "In the old days," a Hollywood agent remarked to me, "directors moved their actors. Now they move the camera." Today it is Asian directors like Hou Hsiao-hsien and Edward Yang who are most assiduously exploring the resources of intricate choreography within the fixed frame, and even genre pictures may throw up some delicate long-shot staging (Fig. 2.123).[169]

With the loss of ensemble staging comes a greater constraint on actors' performances. The contemporary stress on close-ups is not that of the Russian montage filmmakers, who filled their films with hands, feet, and props in dynamic relation to the actors. In intensified continuity, the face is privileged, especially the mouth and eyes. If hands are seen, they are typically brought close to the head, to be in that crucial medium shot or close-up. Eyes have always been central to Hollywood cinema, but usually their information was supplemented by cues emanating from the body.[170] Cecil B. De Mille demanded that actors be given bits of physical business; planning *Union Pacific* (1939), he asked his screenwriters at the start of every session, "What does [Brian] Donlevy do with his hands?"[171] Studio performers could express emotion through posture, stance, carriage, the angle of the chin, and the angle of the arms. (Recall how James Cagney's cocked elbows raise his hands a little above his waist, as if readying themselves to punch.) Actors knew how to rise from chairs without using their hands to leverage themselves, to pour steadily for many seconds, to give away nervousness by letting a finger twitch. Physiques (beefed up, seminude) are now more frankly exposed than ever, but they seldom acquire grace or emotional significance. In popular cinema it's again the Hong Kong filmmakers who have best integrated intensified continuity with a respect for the kinetic expressiveness of human bodies.[172]

Most of today's films—those that escape notice by dwelling in the valleys—obey the tenets of intensified continuity. They are all, in this sense, like *Two Weeks Notice*. The more flamboyant instances of today's style remain classical in their assumptions about how dramatic space will be mapped out for our comprehension. Still, compared to productions of the studio era, they are not quite as redundant, they are more willing to create gaps and inconsistencies, and they strive to make the viewer appreciate their cunning artifice. As puzzle films, time-scrambling plots, and network narratives draw us into a game of story comprehension, the style asks us to become connoisseurs of pictorial contrivance.

We might draw a parallel between the most outré instances of intensified continuity and Mannerism in Italian painting of the sixteenth century. In both situations, artists were acutely aware that they were expected to innovate, but they worked in the shadow of towering predecessors. How to paint the human body after Leonardo, Raphael, and Michelangelo? How to tell a story authoritatively after Ford, Hawks, Hitchcock, and Welles? One option is to strain for novelty, to aim at bold strokes and tours de force, to replace calm with agitation—energy, we call it—and proportion with wildness. To read art historians describing Mannerism is to hear echoes of qualities I've invoked in post-1960 American cinema: "Jaded sensibilities demanded a more powerful impact" (Wölfflin, 1888). "Mannerism exists when forms that originally had a precise meaning and expressive value are taken over and carried to extremes, so that they appear affected, artificial, empty, degenerate" (Weisbach, 1910). "A completely self-conscious style, which bases its forms not so much on the particular object as on the art of the preceding epoch" (Hauser, 1957). "The idea that complexity, prolixity, and unreasonable caprice are beautiful, that virtuosity is something to be cultivated, and that art should be demonstrably artificial. . . . A consciously 'stylish style'" (Shearman, 1967). And Wölfflin again: "It wants to carry us away with the force of its impact, immediate and overwhelming. It gives us not a generally enhanced vitality, but excitement, ecstasy, intoxication."[173] This last sentence is not a bad description of a music video, and it reminds us that to a considerable degree the Brett Ratners, who see no difference between a video clip and a feature film, have come to replace the W. S. Van Dykes of the classical era, who "didn't get too artistic, they just told the story."[174]

The substantive analogy between Mannerism and intensified continuity could be explored further, but it probably shouldn't be taken too strictly. My main concern is a more general lesson. We don't have to posit a "postclassical" cinema, or a moment when spectacle overwhelms narrative, even if we now treat style as itself spectacular. Intensified continuity in its mildest, most common registers obeys classical precepts. In its wilder reaches, it presents a boisterousness in tune with the edgier examples of innovative narrative. Screenwriters' self-conscious reworkings of tradition find their counterpart in an audacious style that parades virtuosity while remaining within the ambit of a stable system. Now almost fifty years old, intensified continuity has already lasted as long as studio-era continuity did. It is, simply, the visual language of commercial cinema. Although it will often sink into gratuitous display, we should be glad whenever any filmmaker deploys it with freshness and felicity.

A Hollywood Timeline, 1960–2004

Bradley Schauer and David Bordwell

What follows is a chronology of some major changes in the business and technology of Hollywood moviemaking. We've also included a year-by-year account of attendance, Academy Award winners, box-office returns, and top-earning films in the U.S. market (which by imperial Hollywood tradition includes Canada).

The information comes from a variety of sources, chiefly *The Film Daily Year Book* (1961 onward), *The Motion Picture Almanac* (1961 onward), *The Encyclopedia of Exhibition* (National Association of Theatre Owners, various years), and the following reference works: Joel W. Finler, *The Hollywood Story*, 3d ed. (London: Wallflower, 2003); Susan Sackett, *The Hollywood Reporter Book of Box Office Hits*, rev. ed. (New York: Billboard, 1996); Christopher Sterling and Timothy Haight, *The Mass Media: Aspen Institute Guide to Communication Industry Trends* (New York: Praeger, 1978); and Harold Vogel, *Entertainment Industry Economics: A Guide for Financial Analysis*, 5th ed. (Cambridge, MA.: Cambridge University Press, 2001). Also useful was the website Box Office Mojo, www.boxofficemojo.com. Information on technological innovations was gathered from a wide range of books, articles, and Internet sources.

With regard to the number of films released in the United States each year, we supply two figures. One pertains to the films released by the members of the Motion Picture Association of America (MPAA). For the period we're covering, those companies were Buena Vista (Disney), Columbia (later Sony), Warner Bros., Universal, 20th Century Fox, Paramount, and MGM (for a time including United Artists). These companies, known as the "majors," also released films produced by "minimajors" like Orion, New Line, Miramax, and DreamWorks. The majors also currently release titles produced by their in-house divisions Screen Gems and TriStar (Sony), Fox

Searchlight, Focus Features (Universal), Sony Pictures Classics, Warner Independent, and Paramount Classics. In early decades of the period, the sum of MPAA features includes reissues, typically twenty to thirty a year.

In any year, the greater share of theatrical income flows to the MPAA releases, but these constitute a half or less of all features released to U.S. theaters. Most of the remainder are independently distributed American productions. Each year a few of these find financial success, and many more are artistically important. We have therefore listed the total number of feature releases, which includes non-MPAA movies. But the reader should remember that of these, several will be imported films and exploitation or special-interest titles.

The amounts earned by the five top films are based on estimates made by the companies, the trade press, the exhibitors, or the MPAA. There is currently no way to confirm these statistics, and so the amounts earned by U.S. films will probably never be known with great accuracy. For ease of reading we have rounded the figures to the nearest one hundred thousand dollars.

In reporting income from theatrical screenings, the film industry distinguishes between *grosses* and *rentals*. Grosses are the total receipts taken in at the box office. Rentals are the monies sent on to the distributor, after the exhibitor has deducted operating costs (the "house nut") and an agreed percentage of the gross. Typically the rentals are calculated on a sliding scale; for a film opening its run, the distributor might receive 90 percent of gross (minus the nut) in the film's first week, 80 percent in the second week, and so on. The longer a film stays in the theater, the larger the portion of ticket revenues returned to the exhibitor. If a major release fails spectacularly, the exhibitor and the distributor may renegotiate the percentage that should apply.

Before the early 1980s, the leading trade publication, *Variety*, listed films' rental income, not grosses, and most reference books followed suit. Then *Variety* and other sources began listing grosses instead of rentals. Most commentators hold that rentals average about half of grosses, and so in many cases the highest-renting picture would also be the highest-grossing picture. But there appears to be a considerable variation in the percentages of grosses returned to the distributor. For example, if a film was expected to draw a huge audience, the distribution firm might demand a bigger-than-normal share of receipts and a less steep sliding scale.

Because our purpose is to highlight the most popular films of each year, box-office grosses offer a rough measure. Unfortunately, we don't have access to figures on grosses for several top films before 1980, and in those instances we indicate the reported rental income instead, marked with an asterisk. We have striven to indicate relative ranking among titles when we know only rental income for some. Some popular films, notably Disney animated features and the *Star Wars* trilogy, enjoyed lucrative rereleases in later years, but their additional earnings aren't included in our figures. All grosses and rentals we list are those earned in the film's initial release (first and subsequent runs).

Needless to say, high-grossing or -renting films aren't inevitably profitable, since many such films incur big production and marketing costs. A top-grossing blockbuster may show less profit in its theatrical run than a low-budget movie that earns healthy box-office returns. Many blockbusters make a profit for their production companies only after receiving income from cable, home video, and other ancillaries. And, of course, overseas receipts can contribute mightily to the success of any film. Although offshore performance varies significantly film by film, in aggregate MPAA releases tend to earn about half their worldwide grosses overseas.

When sources conflicted, we followed what we believed to be the preponderance of plausible evidence. We welcome corrections and further information.

Year	Annual Data	Company Activities	Television, Video, and Internet	Moviemaking Technology
1960	*Major Statistics* Attendance: 1.39 billion Total releases: 248 MPAA releases: 184 Box office: $956 million Average ticket price: $0.69 Screens in the United States: 17,000 *Domestic Box Office Champs* 1. *Swiss Family Robinson* ($40.4 million) 2. *Psycho* ($32 million) 3. *Spartacus* ($11.1 million)* 4. *Exodus* ($8.3 million)* 5. *La Dolce Vita* ($8 million)* *Academy Award Winners* *The Apartment* (Picture, Director, Original Screenplay); *Elmer Gantry* (Adapted Screenplay)	For *Exodus* Otto Preminger credits Dalton Trumbo. This marks the first time a blacklisted screenwriter gets credit under his real name. In June the U.S. government loses its price-fixing lawsuit against Universal and Columbia. Barney Balaban announces that Paramount will downsize.	Screenwriters and actors go on strike for residuals from the sale of films to television. The strikes are settled in April and June. 54.7 million TV sets in operation, in 88 percent of U.S. homes.	Ilford introduces their HPS black-and-white stock. It is the fastest stock yet released, with an exposure index of 400. *Exodus* is the first major film to use Super Panavision 70, a nonanamorphic 65mm process.

Year	Annual Data	Company Activities	Television, Video, and Internet	Moviemaking Technology
1961	*Major Statistics* Attendance: 1.33 billion Total releases: 240 MPAA releases: 167 Box office: $955 million Average ticket price: $0.69 *Domestic Box Office Champs* 1. *101 Dalmatians* ($68.6 million) 2. *West Side Story* ($43.7 million) 3. *The Guns of Navarone* ($13 million)* 4. *El Cid* ($12 million)* 5. *The Absent-Minded Professor* ($11.4 million)* *Academy Award Winners* *West Side Story* (Picture, Director); *Judgment at Nuremberg* (Adapted Screenplay); *Splendor in the Grass* (Original Screenplay)	On December 1, Congress begins two days of hearings on runaway production. Fox, in the midst of its worst year since 1946, sells its 260-acre back lot for the Century City shopping and office complex.	"NBC Saturday Night at the Movies," the first prime-time series to show post-1948 films, premieres on September 23. *The Wonderful World of Disney* premieres on the ABC network.	

Year	Annual Data	Company Activities	Television, Video, and Internet	Moviemaking Technology
1962	*Major Statistics* Attendance: 1.29 billion Total releases: 237 MPAA releases: 162 Box office: $945 million Average ticket price: $0.70 *Domestic Box Office Champs* 1. *Lawrence of Arabia* ($37.5 million) 2. *The Longest Day* ($17.6 million)* 3. *In Search of the Castaways* ($10 million)* 4. *The Music Man* ($8.1 million)* *Academy Award Winners* *Lawrence of Arabia* (Picture, Director); *To Kill a Mockingbird* (Adapted Screenplay); *Divorce, Italian Style* (Original Screenplay)	In June Music Corporation of America acquires Universal-International-Decca. In July MCA leaves the agency business, purportedly eliminating conflicts of interest. In July Darryl Zanuck becomes president of 20th Century Fox, replacing Spyros Skouras, who becomes chairman of the board. In August Zanuck closes the studio for "retooling." In October Zanuck's son, Richard, becomes head of production.	On November 5, the Supreme Court rules that studios selling old films to TV in blocks violate anti-trust laws.	*The Wonderful World of the Brothers Grimm* is the first Cinerama fiction feature. *Mutiny on the Bounty* is the first film identified as being in Ultra Panavision 70, an anamorphic 70mm process creating an aspect ratio of 2.76:1. On earlier productions, the process was known as "MGM Camera 65."

Year	Annual Data	Company Activities	Television, Video, and Internet	Moviemaking Technology
1963	*Major Statistics* Attendance: 1.06 billion Total releases: 223 MPAA releases: 142 Box office: $942 million Average ticket price: $.85 *Domestic Box Office Champs* 1. *Cleopatra* ($57.8 million) 2. *How the West Was Won* ($20.9 million)* 3. *It's a Mad Mad Mad Mad World* ($46.3 million) 4. *Tom Jones* ($17.1 million)* 5. *Irma La Douce* ($11.9 million)* *Academy Award Winners* *Tom Jones* (Picture, Director, Adapted Screen-play); *How the West Was Won* (Original Screenplay)	United Artists sells its Santa Monica Blvd. lot, which becomes a shopping center. The Universal City theme park is launched. The first multiplex theater opens in Kansas City, Kansas.		In June Cinerama demonstrates a single-lens projector system to replace its three-lens array. *The Cardinal* becomes the first film in Pana-vision 70, a 35mm blowup process. Angenieux markets zoom lenses that can go from 25mm to 250mm, with a maximum aperture of f3.2.

Year	Annual Data	Company Activities	Television, Video, and Internet	Moviemaking Technology
1964	*Major Statistics* Attendance: 982 million Total releases: 242 MPAA releases: 144 Box office: $951 million Average ticket price: $0.93 *Domestic Box Office Champs* 1. *My Fair Lady* ($72 million) 2. *Goldfinger* ($51.1 million) 3. *Mary Poppins* ($31 million) 4. *The Carpetbaggers* ($15.5 million)* 5. *From Russia With Love* ($24.8 million) *Academy Award Winners* *My Fair Lady* (Picture, Director); *Becket* (Adapted Screenplay); *Father Goose* (Original Screenplay)	At Paramount, George Weltner takes over the presidency from Balaban, who retires. In July the Universal Studios tour opens. Warners closes its animation unit, home of Bugs and Daffy. Herbert Siegel's General Artists Corporation absorbs four other agencies.	Universal produces the first telefilm, *See How They Run*.	Robert Aldrich's *Four for Texas* is one of the first films to use the Tyler mount to create steady helicopter shots. *The Outrage* is the first Hollywood feature to use radio mikes, small microphones placed on the actor that transmit to a receiver connected to a recorder.

Year	Annual Data	Company Activities	Television, Video, and Internet	Moviemaking Technology
1965	*Major Statistics* Attendance: 1.03 billion Total releases: 279 MPAA releases: 167 Box office: $1.07 billion Average ticket price: $1.01 *Domestic Box Office Champs* 1. *The Sound of Music* ($158.7 million) 2. *Doctor Zhivago* ($111.7 million) 3. *Thunderball* ($63.6 million) 4. *Those Magnificent Men in Their Flying Machines* ($14 million)* 5. *That Darn Cat* ($12.6 million)* *Academy Award Winners* *The Sound of Music* (Picture, Director); *Dr. Zhivago* (Adapted Screenplay); *Darling* (Original Screenplay)	On January 1, Theater Owners of America merges with Allied States Association of Motion Picture Exhibitors to form the National Association of Theater Owners (NATO). In March Supreme Court decisions invalidate film-censorship laws in Maryland and New York. In March *The Pawnbroker*, which contains frontal nudity, is passed uncut by the PCA.		The Steenbeck flatbed editor is introduced in Germany. It does not find wide use in Hollywood until the seventies.

Year	Annual Data	Company Activities	Television, Video, and Internet	Moviemaking Technology
1966	*Major Statistics* Attendance: 975 million Total releases: 257 MPAA releases: 149 Box office: $1.1 billion Average ticket price: $1.09 *Domestic Box Office Champs* 1. *Hawaii* ($15.5 million)* 2. *The Bible* ($15 million)* 3. *Who's Afraid of Virginia Woolf?* ($14.5 million)* 4. *A Man for All Seasons* ($12.8 million)* 5. *Lt. Robinson Crusoe, USN* ($10.2 million)* *Academy Award Winners* *A Man for All Seasons* (Picture, Director, Adapted Screenplay); *A Man and a Woman* (Original Screenplay)	In April Jack Valenti replaces Eric Johnston as president of the MPAA. In September the production code is rewritten and liberalized. It recommends *Who's Afraid of Virginia Woolf*, which contains profanity, for mature audiences only. In October Paramount is bought by Gulf + Western. Charles Bluhdorn becomes president, replacing Koch. Robert Evans is named head of production. In November Jack Warner sells his stock in Warner Bros. to Seven Arts Productions. Lew Wasserman replaces Edward E. Muhl as head of Universal.	ABC pays $6 million for the rights to Fox's *Cleopatra*, making the film profitable at last. The high ratings for the broadcast of *The Bridge On the River Kwai* drive networks into a bidding war for movie premieres.	In June Bell Telephone Laboratories demonstrates computer-animated movies.

Year	Annual Data	Company Activities	Television, Video, and Internet	Moviemaking Technology
1967	*Major Statistics* Attendance: 927 million Total releases: 264 MPAA releases: 157 Box office: $1.1 billion Average ticket price: $1.20 *Domestic Box Office Champs* 1. *The Graduate* ($104.6 million) 2. *The Jungle Book* ($73.7 million) 3. *Guess Who's Coming to Dinner* ($56.7 million) 4. *Bonnie and Clyde* ($22.8 million)* 5. *The Dirty Dozen* ($20.4 million)* *Academy Award Winners* *In the Heat of the Night* (Picture, Adapted Screenplay); *The Graduate* (director); *Guess Who's Coming to Dinner* (Original Screenplay)	In April Transamerica buys United Artists. The American Film Institute is created in June, with Gregory Peck as its head. In December it announces the creation of an archive to house restored films. In July Jack Warner resigns as head of production at WB–Seven Arts, replaced by Kenneth Hyman. Bob Shaye founds New Line Cinema. Kinney Services announces the acquisition of Ashley Famous Agency.	CBS TV buys the Republic studio lot. Gulf + Western buys Desilu Studios.	Francis Ford Coppola's *You're a Big Boy Now* is the first major film to use the pushing technique, in which a film is intentionally overexposed during processing for aesthetic effect. Panavision introduces its first proprietary camera, the Panavision Silent Reflex. "Soft light" units, in which quartz-iodine lamps reflect light off the walls of a metal box before they strike a subject, are often used as fill lights (and as keys, in some cases). The Society of Motion Picture and Television Engineers introduces Time Code, a standard for synchronizing sound and image and for identifying each frame of film or videotape.

Year	Annual Data	Company Activities	Television, Video, and Internet	Moviemaking Technology
1968	*Major Statistics* Attendance: 979 million Total releases: 258 MPAA releases: 177 Box office: $1.3 billion Average ticket price: $1.31 *Domestic Box Office Champs* 1. *2001: A Space Odyssey* ($56.7 million) 2. *Funny Girl* ($52 million) 3. *The Odd Couple* ($44.5 million) 4. *Bullitt* ($19 million)* 5. *Romeo and Juliet* ($17.5 million)* *Academy Award Winners* *Oliver!* (Picture, Director); *The Lion in Winter* (Adapted Screenplay); *The Producers* (Original Screenplay)	In May Avco Corporation takes over Embassy Pictures, forming Avco-Embassy. In October the Justice Department forbids Westinghouse from merging with Universal. In October the MPAA abandons the Production Code, replacing it with a ratings system (G,M,R,X). Columbia is restructured as Columbia Pictures Industries, with Peter Guber as production head.		For *Hell in the Pacific* cinematographer Conrad Hall develops a process by which the film is desaturated through overexposing it and then correcting this overexposure during the printing stage. Eastman Kodak releases their 5254 stock, with an exposure index of 100, one stop faster than the 5251. Eastman Kodak introduces Color Reversal Intermediate stock, which allows the creation of a duplicate negative direct from the original negative without an interpositive. *2001: A Space Odyssey* contains the first use of front projection, among other innovations, including early motion control and a giant centrifuge that simulates weightlessness.

Year	Annual Data	Company Activities	Television, Video, and Internet	Moviemaking Technology
1969	*Major Statistics* Attendance: 912 million Total releases: 251 MPAA releases: 154 Box office: $1.4 billion Average ticket price: $1.42 *Domestic Box Office Champs* 1. *Butch Cassidy and the Sundance Kid* ($102.3 million) 2. *The Love Bug* ($51.3 million) 3. *Midnight Cowboy* ($44.8 million) 4. *Easy Rider* ($19.1 million)* 5. *Hello, Dolly!** ($15.2 million) *Academy Award Winners* *Midnight Cowboy* (Picture, Director, Adapted Screenplay); *Butch Cassidy and the Sundance Kid* (Original Screenplay)	In March Kinney National Service, headed by Steven J. Ross, merges with WB–Seven Arts. Ted Ashley is named head of production. In August Darryl F. Zanuck is elected chair and CEO of 20th Century Fox, while his son, Richard, becomes president. In October Kirk Kerkorian buys MGM. James Aubrey becomes the studio's third president in ten months.		Magna-Tech Electronics Co. wins an Academy Award for its electronic looping system. *The Rain People* becomes the first U.S. production to employ the Steenbeck flatbed editing machine.

Year	Annual Data	Company Activities	Television, Video, and Internet	Moviemaking Technology
1970	*Major Statistics* Attendance: 921 million Total releases: 306 MPAA releases: 153 Box office: $1.4 billion Average ticket price: $1.55 Screens in the United States: 13,750 *Domestic Box Office Champs* 1. *Love Story* ($106.4 million) 2. *Airport* ($100.5 million) 3. *M*A*S*H* ($36.7 million)* 4. *Patton* ($61.7 million) 5. *The Aristocats* ($26.5 million)* *Academy Award Winners* *Patton* (Picture, Director, Original Screenplay); *M*A*S*H* (Adapted Screenplay)	The Code and Ratings Administration raises the R and X age limits from sixteen to seventeen. Also, the M rating is changed to GP. In March the studios come to an antidiscriminatory equal-employment agreement with the Justice Department. In July Stanley Jaffe is promoted to president of Paramount, replacing Bluhdorn. An MGM studio auction is held on May 30. In September the studio sells one third of its Culver City lot. The studio also closes its U.K. studio, merging with EMI. In debt for $77.4 million, Fox cuts production. In December Richard Zanuck and executive David Brown are fired. Roger Corman forms New World Pictures.		The lightweight and economical Xenon arc light is used for exterior scenes. *The Landlord*, shot by Gordon Willis, is the first feature in which the film is underexposed during shooting but processed normally. *The Godfather*, also shot by Willis, will become another notable example of this technique. The Super-16 process is introduced. Super-16 film exposes to the edge of the perforations, where the soundtrack is usually contained. At Expo '70 in Osaka, IMAX is introduced. The rockumentary *Woodstock* becomes the first production to use the KEM flatbed editor, which employs two screens for comparing footage.

Year	Annual Data	Company Activities	Television, Video, and Internet	Moviemaking Technology
		Sidney Poitier, Paul Newman, and Barbra Streisand form First Artists Production Company.		
		Kinney renames itself Warner Communications Inc. Ted Ashley takes charge of production.		
		Universal, Paramount, and MGM-UA combine their overseas distribution units into Cinema International Corporation, renamed United International Pictures.		
1971	*Major Statistics* Attendance: 820.3 million Total releases: 313 MPAA releases: 143 Box office: $1.35 billion Average ticket price: $1.65 *Domestic Box Office Champs* 1. *Fiddler on the Roof* ($38.3 million)*	In January Herbert Solow is replaced by a "committee" as head of production at MGM. In March Richard Zanuck and David Brown join Warner Bros. as executives. In April Richard Nixon meets with industry leaders to discuss tax breaks. On December 10, Congress passes a tax bill that gives studios a 7 percent credit on domestic films.		*A Clockwork Orange* becomes the first film to use Dolby noise reduction (in postproduction), a technology adopted by the recording industry in 1965. Canon introduces a zoom lens with a 25–120mm. variable focal length that allows great magnification of small objects.

Year	Annual Data	Company Activities	Television, Video, and Internet	Moviemaking Technology
	2. *Billy Jack* ($32.5 million)* 3. *The French Connection* ($51.7 million) 4. *Summer of '42* ($20.5 million)* 5. *Diamonds are Forever* ($43.8 million) *Academy Award Winners* *The French Connection* (Picture, Director, Adapted Screenplay); *The Hospital* (Original Screenplay)	Robert Altman forms Lions Gate Films. At Paramount, Frank Yablans is hired, replacing Stanley Jaffe.		The Nagra SN sound recorder is released. It is small enough to be attached to an actor and is sometimes used in place of radio mikes, now in wide use. The Magnasync Moviola flatbed editor is released to compete with the Steenbeck.
1972	*Major Statistics* Attendance: 934.1 million Total releases: 312 MPAA releases: 145 Box office: $1.6 billion Average ticket price: $1.70 *Domestic Box Office Champs* 1. *The Godfather* ($133.7 million) 2. *The Poseidon Adventure* ($84.6 million)	CARA changes the GP rating to PG. In July Steven J. Ross becomes chairman of the board and CEO of Warner Communications. John Calley becomes president. In August Zanuck and Brown, free from Warners, begin producing films for Universal. Ned Tanen is appointed production head.	In April the government brings an antitrust suit against TV networks for producing films, to the mystification of the film industry. Home Box Office, a cable channel showcasing uncut versions of recently released films, is launched.	Arnold & Richter releases prototypes of the Arriflex 35BL camera, which can be effectively used on a cameraman's shoulder.

Year	Annual Data	Company Activities	Television, Video, and Internet	Moviemaking Technology
	3. *What's Up, Doc?* ($28 million)* 4. *Deliverance* ($22.6 million)* 5. *Jeremiah Johnson* ($21.9 million)* *Academy Award Winners* *The Godfather* (Picture, Adapted Screenplay); *Cabaret* (Director), *The Candidate* (Original Screenplay)	Directors Company, led by Peter Bogdanovich, Francis Ford Coppola, and William Friedkin, launches at Paramount. It will fold quickly. Midnight screenings of cult and offbeat movies become popular in urban and college-town theaters. The release of *Deep Throat* brings hardcore pornography to mainstream theaters.		
1973	*Major Statistics* Attendance: 864.6 million Total releases: 267 MPAA releases: 132 Box office: $1.52 billion Average ticket price: $1.77 *Domestic Box Office Champs* 1. *The Exorcist* ($193 million) 2. *The Sting* ($156 million)	On March 6, the Writers Guild strikes the Association of Motion Pictures and Television Producers in a jurisdictional dispute involving writer-directors. The strike is settled on June 21. In June Lew Wasserman becomes chairman of board of MCA, replacing Jules Stein.		Panavision introduces the small, light Panaflex, which allows filmmakers to shoot in conditions previously impossible with a standard 35mm camera. *The Sugarland Express* is the first film to use the camera. Using quadraphonic technology, Dolby's matrix system puts four channels on two optical tracks for *Tommy.*

Year	Annual Data	Company Activities	Television, Video, and Internet	Moviemaking Technology
	3. *American Graffiti* ($115 million) 4. *Papillon* ($53.3 million) 5. *The Way We Were* ($45 million) *Academy Award Winners* *The Sting* (Picture, Director, Original Screenplay); *The Exorcist* (Adapted Screenplay)	In June the Supreme Court decides that offensiveness is decided by community standards, which allows theaters to disregard the ratings system. R-rated films now outnumber films in every other category, a trend that will persist nearly every year thereafter. In September, after its worst annual loss, Columbia appoints the management team of David Begelman and Alan Hirschfield. In September MGM ceases distribution, which will now be handled through United Artists. James Aubrey is fired in October, replaced by Frank E. Rosenfelt. Kirk Kerkorian takes over as CEO. 20th Century Fox begins to shift openings from Wednesdays to Fridays to cut advertising costs and to minimize the effect of bad reviews.		

Year	Annual Data	Company Activities	Television, Video, and Internet	Moviemaking Technology
1974	*Major Statistics* Attendance: 1.01 billion Total releases: 268 MPAA releases: 129 Box office: $1.9 billion Average ticket price: $1.87 *Domestic Box Office Champs* 1. *The Towering Inferno* ($116 million) 2. *Blazing Saddles* ($119.5 million) 3. *Young Frankenstein* ($86.3 million) 4. *Earthquake* ($79.7 million) 5. *The Trial of Billy Jack* ($31.1 million)* *Academy Award Winners* *The Godfather Part II* (Picture, Director, Adapted Screenplay); *Chinatown* (Original Screenplay)	In March Michael Medavoy is named production head of United Artists. In June president Joseph Levine leaves Avco Embassy Pictures, replaced by William E. Chaikin. In September Barry Diller becomes chairman and CEO of Paramount, replacing Frank Yablans. Stanfill brings in Alan Ladd Jr. to head 20th Century Fox. *The Towering Inferno* is the first co-production by two major studios, Fox and Warner Bros. Exhibitor Relations is founded. The company pools information about grosses and release schedules.		*Earthquake* is the first movie in Sensurround, which uses a bass rumble to vibrate the theater. It also introduces a new camera-shaking device that wins a Technical Academy Award. Eastman Kodak introduces their 5247 stock, which is initially rejected by American cameramen because the dye hues had been changed from previous stocks. Kodak later releases "5247 Series 600," correcting the discrepancy. After discovering the reddening of 1950s and 1960s prints, Eastman Kodak releases the 5383 print stock, which is more resistant to fading. The Osram HMI metal halide arc light becomes popular for location shooting, although its frequency must be closely regulated by a special generator in order to prevent flicker. Dolby multitrack magnetic sound begins to be used for several films, including *The Little Prince*.

Year	Annual Data	Company Activities	Television, Video, and Internet	Moviemaking Technology
1975	*Major Statistics* Attendance: 1.0 billion Total releases: 215 MPAA releases: 97 Box office: $2.12 billion Average ticket price: $2.05 *Domestic Box Office Champs* 1. *Jaws* ($260 million) 2. *The Rocky Horror Picture Show* ($112.9 million) 3. *One Flew Over the Cuckoo's Nest* ($109 million) 4. *Dog Day Afternoon* ($50 million) 5. *Shampoo* ($49.4 million) *Academy Award Winners* *One Flew Over the Cuckoo's Nest* (Picture, Director, Adapted Screenplay); *Dog Day Afternoon* (Original Screenplay)	In January Creative Artists Agency is created by agents, including Michael Ovitz and Ron Meyer. In April Robert Evans leaves Paramount to do independent production. He is replaced by Richard Sylbert, who hires Don Simpson. In October Stanley Jaffe becomes production head at Columbia. At Warners, Ted Ashley and Jon Calley retire, leaving Frank Wells to run the studio. First convocation of ShoWest, the major trade show. Here the MPAA companies preview upcoming releases for exhibitors.	HBO begins satellite transmission to its cable TV network. In May Sony demonstrates the Betamax videocassette format. *Opening Soon at a Theater Near You,* a weekly movie-review program featuring Gene Siskel and Roger Ebert, begins broadcasting on public television. Siskel and Ebert will become the best-known critics in the United States. Saturation TV advertising for *Jaws* sets the standard for future film marketing campaigns.	Angenieux develops a lens with a 25–625mm zoom for the extreme zooms in *Barry Lyndon.* Kubrick uses adapted NASA 35mm and 50mm lenses, pushing the film one stop to 200 ASA so that he can shoot in candlelight. *Lisztomania* is the first feature released with a Dolby Stereo optical track. George Lucas's Industrial Light + Magic (ILM) is established to develop *Star Wars* effects. Technicolor ceases making prints in its celebrated dye-transfer process.

Year	Annual Data	Company Activities	Television, Video, and Internet	Moviemaking Technology
1976	*Major Statistics* Attendance: 957.1 million Total releases: 206 MPAA releases: 108 Box office: $2.04 billion Average ticket price: $2.13 *Domestic Box Office Champs* 1. *Rocky* ($117.2 million) 2. *A Star Is Born* ($37.1 million)* 3. *All the President's Men* ($70.6 million) 4. *King Kong* ($52.6 million) 5. *Silver Streak* ($51.1 million) *Academy Award Winners* *Rocky* (Picture, Director); *Network* (Adapted Screenplay); *All the President's Men* (Original Screenplay)	In August Alan Ladd Jr. becomes president of production at Fox, as Dennis Stanfill becomes president. On September 10, Columbia president David Begelman cashes a check on which he has forged the name of actor Cliff Robertson. In October Barry Diller hires ABC's Michael Eisner as Paramount's head of production. Carolco is founded as a low-budget production and sales company. Eventually it will finance some of the biggest blockbusters of the period. At Universal Ned Tanen is promoted to president under Lew Wasserman. Warners buys Atari for $26 million. Congress eliminates the tax shelter in film production.	HBO wins its challenge against the FCC's protection of broadcast television. The first VCRs are shipped for retail in the United States. On August 3, Paramount and Sony announce they will use Sony's Betamax technology to release movies on tape. MCA and Disney sue Sony, alleging that VCRs will be used to infringe on their copyright by taping films off the air.	The Steadicam is introduced by Garrett Brown.

Year	Annual Data	Company Activities	Television, Video, and Internet	Moviemaking Technology
		EDI, a firm that contacts theaters to learn daily receipts, is formed. It becomes the principal source of box-office information.		
1977	*Major Statistics* Attendance: 1.1 billion Total releases: 186 MPAA releases: 78 Box office: $2.38 billion Average ticket price: $2.23 *Domestic Box Office Champs* 1. *Star Wars* ($202.6 million) 2. *Smokey and the Bandit* ($126.8 million) 3. *Close Encounters of the Third Kind* ($116.4 million) 4. *Saturday Night Fever* ($94.2 million) 5. *The Goodbye Girl* ($41.8 million)*	In March MGM promotes Sherry Lansing to vice president for creative affairs. Because of a forgery scandal, Columbia's David Begelman is placed on leave. His return in December evokes much criticism. Roy Disney Jr. resigns his vice presidency but stays on the Disney board. Ron Miller is named head of production. CARA becomes the Classification and Ratings Administration and no longer examines scripts before production. MPAA establishes the Office of Film Security to combat piracy.	In August Fox releases fifty films to Sony for video distribution. Matsushita introduces the VHS format. The first computer-assisted editing systems are used for commercials and syndicated TV.	In March Dolby Labs announces that optical tracks in Dolby Stereo are now financially practical. The first wide release in Dolby Stereo is *Star Wars*.

Year	Annual Data	Company Activities	Television, Video, and Internet	Moviemaking Technology
	Academy Award Winners *Annie Hall* (Picture, Director, Original Screenplay); *Julia* (Adapted Screenplay)	The National Research Group, a firm devoted to test-marketing films before and after they are made, is founded.		
1978	*Major Statistics* Attendance: 1.13 billion Total releases: 191 MPAA releases: 91 Box office: $2.6 billion Average ticket price: $2.34 *Domestic Box Office Champs* 1. *Grease* ($160 million) 2. *Superman* ($134.2 million) 3. *National Lampoon's Animal House* ($120 million) 4. *Every Which Way But Loose* ($85.2 million) 5. *Jaws 2* ($77.7 million)	On January 3, Arthur Krim, Robert Benjamin, and Michael Medavoy, among others, resign from United Artists and form Orion Pictures. The new company is a joint venture with Warner Bros. In February David Begelman resigns from Columbia. He later pleads guilty to grand theft. President Alan Hirschfield, fired in July, is replaced by Daniel Melnick, who lasts five months before resigning. The first United States Film Festival is held in Salt Lake City; later it becomes Sundance Film Festival.	In December MCA launches the Disco Vision/Magnavox optical video disc. It fails to solve technical problems, and MCA sells out in 1981.	The Louma Crane, which puts the camera at the end of a boom controlled by motors, allowing it to shoot in hard-to-reach areas, is used for the first time in the United States. George Lucas founds Lucasfilm Computer Development Division (later Pixar) to develop digital applications for filmmaking.

Year	Annual Data	Company Activities	Television, Video, and Internet	Moviemaking Technology
	Academy Award Winners The Deer Hunter (Picture, Director); Midnight Express (Adapted Screenplay); Coming Home (Original Screenplay)	Superman's intense merchandising and cross-promotion campaign sets the pattern for future blockbusters.		
1979	Major Statistics Attendance: 1.12 billion Total releases: 214 MPAA releases: 93 Box office: $2.8 billion Average ticket price: $2.51 Domestic Box Office Champs 1. Kramer vs. Kramer ($106.3 million) 2. Rocky II ($85.1 million) 3. Star Trek: The Motion Picture ($82.3 million) 4. Alien ($79 million) 5. The Jerk ($73.7 million)	In March Michael Ovitz is named president of CAA. In April Cineplex Odeon opens an eighteen-screen multiplex in Toronto, the largest theater unit at that time. In July American International Pictures merges with Filmways. Sam Arkoff resigns in December. David Begelman replaces Shepherd at MGM, which resumes distribution in December. Cannon Pictures is taken over by Menachem Golan and Yoram Globus. Animator Don Bluth and associates resign from Disney.	Viacom enters cable through Nickelodeon. In June Warner announces the formation of its new videotape division.	Apocalypse Now employs split-surround sound field, with five discrete tracks.

Year	Annual Data	Company Activities	Television, Video, and Internet	Moviemaking Technology
	Academy Award Winners *Kramer vs. Kramer* (Picture, Director, Adapted Screenplay); *Breaking Away* (Original Screenplay)	Alan Ladd Jr. leaves Fox to form his own production company. Miramax is founded.		
1980	*Major Statistics* Attendance: 1.02 billion Total releases: 235 MPAA releases: 102 Box office: $2.75 billion Average ticket price: $2.69 Screens in the United States: 17,372 *Domestic Box Office Champs* 1. *The Empire Strikes Back* ($209.4 million) 2. *9 to 5* ($103.3 million) 3. *Stir Crazy* ($101.3 million) 4. *Airplane!* ($83.5 million) 5. *Any Which Way You Can* ($70.7 million)	At Fox Sherry Lansing becomes the first female president of production at a studio. In March Polygram announces the creation of Polygram Pictures, with Peter Guber as chair. The Screen Actors Guild strikes from July 21 to October 5. CBS's Robert Daley replaces Ted Ashley as chair and CEO of Warners. Robert Redford establishes the Sundance Institute to encourage independent filmmaking.	The start of video "colorization" of classic black-and-white films destined for tape rental and cable transmission. The trend fades quickly. Pioneer introduces the laserdisc format, with optically encoded video and digital sound. The format never breaks out of the high-end market, and by 1999 it is eclipsed by the DVD.	Fuji introduces A250, which has an exposure index of 250. Eastman Kodak follows in 1982 with its own EI 250 stock, 5293. This marks the first time color stock is as fast as black-and-white stock. Some special effects in *Flash Gordon* are generated on an electronic optical printer. The Chimera company, whose Chimera Lightbanks convert hard light to soft light more effectively than standard diffusion does, is founded.

Year	Annual Data	Company Activities	Television, Video, and Internet	Moviemaking Technology
	Academy Award Winners			
	Ordinary People (Picture, Director, Adapted Screenplay); *Melvin and Howard* (Original Screenplay)			
1981	*Major Statistics* Attendance: 1.067 billion Total releases: 240 MPAA releases: 112 Box office: $2.97 billion Average ticket price: $2.78 *Domestic Box Office Champs* 1. *Raiders of the Lost Ark* ($209.6 million) 2. *On Golden Pond* ($119.3 million) 3. *Superman II* ($108.2 million) 4. *Arthur* ($95.5 million) 5. *Stripes* ($85.3 million)	The Writers Guild strikes on April 12 until July 11. Oil magnate Martin Davis buys 20th Century Fox for $722 million. Stanfill resigns. On July 28, Kirk Kerkorian buys United Artists from Transamerica, forming MGM/ United Artists. David Begelman moves from MGM to United Artists. The film division reopens in October under Freddie Fields. In March the first American Film Market is held. It will become the major U.S. marketplace for foreign and independent films. Orion sets up a classics division.	On August 1, MTV begins broadcasting. *Entertainment Tonight*, the major TV program publicizing upcoming releases, begins its run.	*The Howling* contains Rick Baker's "change-o-head" technique, in which masks are manipulated with rods to simulate organic transformation.

Year	Annual Data	Company Activities	Television, Video, and Internet	Moviemaking Technology
	Academy Award Winners *Chariots of Fire* (Picture, Original Screenplay); *Reds* (Director); *On Golden Pond* (Adapted Screenplay)			
1982	*Major Statistics* Attendance: 1.175 billion Total releases: 428 MPAA releases: 103 Box office: $3.45 billion Average ticket price: $2.94 *Domestic Box Office Champs* 1. *E.T. The Extra-Terrestrial* ($359.2 million) 2. *Tootsie* ($177.2 million) 3. *An Officer and a Gentleman* ($129.8 million) 4. *Rocky III* ($125 million) 5. *Porky's* ($105.5 million)	In June Jeffrey Katzenberg becomes the new production head at Paramount. In June David Begelman is ousted from United Artists. In June CBS/Fox Video is formed. In June Columbia is bought by Coca-Cola. Guy Mc-Elwaine leaves International Creative Management to become president. TriStar Pictures is formed by Columbia, HBO, and CBS. In December Lansing resigns as president of Fox. She goes into independent production.		*Star Trek II: The Wrath of Khan* contains the first completely computer-generated sequence in history, courtesy of ILM. A short boom in 3-D, with *Jaws 3D, Friday the 13th Part 3*, and so on. *Tron* contains several lengthy sequences in which actors interact with computer-generated back-grounds. Reissue of Disney's *Fantasia* has rere-corded score using new Dolby multichannel system. Video assist, which transmits what the film camera sees to a TV monitor on the set, is by now standard equipment for high-budget films.

Year	Annual Data	Company Activities	Television, Video, and Internet	Moviemaking Technology
	Academy Award Winners *Gandhi* (Picture, Director, Original Screenplay); *Missing* (Adapted Screenplay)	Ned Tanen leaves Universal, replaced by Frank Price. Fox and Universal establish classics divisions.		
1983	*Major Statistics* Attendance: 1.197 billion Total releases: 495 MPAA releases: 106 Box office: $3.78 billion Average ticket price: $3.15 *Domestic Box Office Champs* 1. *Return of the Jedi* ($252.6 million) 2. *Terms of Endearment* ($108.5 million) 3. *Flashdance* ($92.9 million) 4. *Trading Places* ($90.4 million) 5. *WarGames* ($79.6 million)	Martin Davis becomes the new head of Gulf + Western upon the death of Charles Bluhdorn. In January Frank Mancuso is named the new president of Paramount Pictures.	John Landis (*Animal House*) directs Michael Jackson's long-form music video *Thriller*, which airs on MTV. Increasingly feature-film directors will sign music videos. Warners abandons its involvement in video games after Atari goes bust. Paramount prices VHS copies of *Airplane!* at under $30, aiming at consumer purchase. Success of the strategy shows the viability of the "sell-through" market, to become crucial to video revenues.	Eastman Kodak introduces its 7/5294 stock, with an EI of 320. Fuji releases its Fujicolor AX to compete. Its colors are more desaturated than Kodak's, but the stock is slightly less expensive.

Year	Annual Data	Company Activities	Television, Video, and Internet	Moviemaking Technology
	Academy Award Winners			
	Terms of Endearment (Picture, Director, Adapted Screenplay); *Tender Mercies* (Original Screenplay)			
1984	*Major Statistics* Attendance: 1.2 billion	In September a new management team, led by CEO Michael Eisner, Jeffrey Katzen- berg, and Frank G. Wells, takes over at Disney. In Feb- ruary Touchstone Pictures is established.	On January 17, the U.S. Supreme Court decides in favor of Sony in the video- tape copyright dispute.	Lucasfilm premieres EditDroid and SoundDroid at the National Association of Broadcasters conference. Moving- image data are stored on laser discs.
	Total releases: 536			
	MPAA releases: 116		In January, during the Super Bowl broadcast, Apple runs its "1984" commer- cial for the Macin- tosh. Directed by Ridley Scott (*Alien, Blade Runner*) it is seen in nearly half of all U.S. households and eventually plays for months in movie theaters.	
	Box office: $4.16 billion			The Nettmann Cam- Remote system, a motorized remote camera control, is introduced.
	Average ticket price: $3.36	In June the PG-13 rating is introduced.		
	Domestic Box Office Champs			The space battles in *The Last Starfighter* are entirely computer generated. This represents the largest amount of CGI in a film to this point.
	1. *Beverly Hills Cop* ($234.8 million)	In September Barry Diller be- comes the new chairman and CEO of Fox. Lawrence Gordon becomes production chief.		
	2. *Ghostbusters* ($229.2 million)			
	3. *Indiana Jones and the Temple of Doom* ($179.9 million)			*Greystoke: The Legend of Tarzan, Lord of the Apes* is the first thea- trical feature in Super- 35mm.
	4. *Gremlins* ($148.2 million)	Steven Spielberg forms Amblin with Kathleen Kennedy and Frank Marshall.		
	5. *The Karate Kid* ($90.8 million)			

Year	Annual Data	Company Activities	Television, Video, and Internet	Moviemaking Technology
	Academy Award Winners *Amadeus* (Picture, Director, Adapted Screenplay); *Places in the Heart* (Original Screenplay)	Cineplex Odeon opens its first luxury multiplex in the United States, a fourteen-screen theater in Los Angeles. Frank Mancuso becomes the new studio head at Paramount, with Ned Tanen as the head of the film division. Creative Artists Agency helps launch TriStar with *The Natural*.		
1985	*Major Statistics* Attendance: 1.056 billion Total releases: 470 MPAA releases: 105 Box office: $3.75 billion Average ticket price: $3.55 *Domestic Box Office Champs* 1. *Back to the Future* ($210.6 million) 2. *Rambo: First Blood Part II* ($150.4 million)	In March Alan Ladd Jr. replaces Frank Yablans as president and CEO of MGM/United Artists. In September Martin Davis sells 20th Century Fox to media mogul Rupert Murdoch for $325 million. Barry Diller is named production chief. In September Columbia buys Embassy Pictures and sells it to Dino DeLaurentiis.		*Young Sherlock Holmes* contains the first entirely computer-generated character in film history.

Year	Annual Data	Company Activities	Television, Video, and Internet	Moviemaking Technology
	3. *Rocky IV* ($127.9 million) 4. *The Color Purple* ($94.2 million) 5. *Out of Africa* ($87.1 million) *Academy Award Winners* *Out of Africa* (Picture, Director, Adapted Screenplay); *Witness* (Original Screenplay)	The 1948 divorcement decree is reversed, allowing the vertical integration of film studios. Viacom buys MTV from Warners. NBC exec Jeff Sagansky is named production head of TriStar, as CBS sells its share in the company. The Sundance Institute assumes control of the U.S. Film Festival, eventually renamed the Sundance Film Festival.		
1986	*Major Statistics* Attendance: 1.017 billion Total releases: 451 MPAA releases: 102 Box office: $3.78 billion Average ticket price: $3.71 *Domestic Box Office Champs* 1. *Top Gun* ($176.8 million)	In March Ted Turner buys MGM/United Artists for $1.5 billion. He then sells it back to Kerkorian, keeping the film and TV library. Major studios begin buying theater chains, with TriStar buying Loew's, Universal buying a stake in Cineplex-Odeon, and Gulf + Western buying the Mann chain.		Kodak introduces its 5295 stock, with an ISO of 400. It is made primarily for use with a blue screen. 3-D IMAX is introduced.

Year	Annual Data	Company Activities	Television, Video, and Internet	Moviemaking Technology
	2. *Crocodile Dundee* ($174.8 million) 3. *Platoon* ($138.5 million) 4. *The Karate Kid, Part II* ($115.1 million) 5. *Star Trek IV: The Voyage Home* ($109.7 million) *Academy Award Winners* *Platoon* (Picture, Director); *A Room with a View* (Adapted Screenplay); *Hannah and Her Sisters* (Original Screenplay)	At Columbia David Puttnam is appointed chairman. Leonard Goldberg comes from TV to become president of Fox. Steve Jobs, exiled from Apple, buys Lucas's controlling interest in Pixar.		
1987	*Major Statistics* Attendance: 1.09 billion Total releases: 509 MPAA releases: 86 Box office: $4.25 billion Average ticket price: $3.91	In April Guy Mc-Elwaine resigns as CEO of Columbia; in September David Puttnam is fired. In October Dawn Steel is named president. Orion takes fourth place in rentals for the year, as it expands into TV and larger films.	With VHS video-cassette format at 95 percent of market, Sony abandons the Betamax format.	*Robocop* and *Innerspace* are the first films to be released with Dolby SR, an advance on Dolby's original noise-reduction recording system. The easily maneuverable, color-corrected, flicker-free fluorescent Kino Flo lights are invented by DP Robby Mueller for *Barfly*. They quickly come into wide use in the industry.

Year	Annual Data	Company Activities	Television, Video, and Internet	Moviemaking Technology
	Domestic Box Office Champs 1. *Three Men and a Baby* ($167.8 million) 2. *Fatal Attraction* ($156.7 million) 3. *Beverly Hills Cop II* ($153.7 million) 4. *Good Morning Vietnam* ($123.9 million) 5. *Moonstruck* ($80.6 million) *Academy Award Winners* *The Last Emperor* (Picture, Director, Adapted Screenplay); *Moonstruck* (Original Screenplay)	Sumner Redstone takes control of Viacom, owner of MTV, Nickelodeon, Showtime, and other cable networks.		Lucas founds Skywalker Sound, a state-of-the-art postproduction facility.
1988	*Major Statistics* Attendance: 1.08 billion Total releases: 510 MPAA releases: 110 Box office: $4.46 billion Average ticket price: $4.11	The Writers Guild goes on strike from March 7 to August 7, triggering a demand for spec scripts. In September President Reagan signs the Film Preservation Act. De Laurentiis Entertainment folds.		*Who Framed Roger Rabbit* integrates animated characters into live action. *Willow* contains the first use of 2-D digital morphing, as a character changes into a variety of animals. Arriflex introduces a custom-made video assist for its standard camera.

Year	Annual Data	Company Activities	Television, Video, and Internet	Moviemaking Technology
	Domestic Box Office Champs			Avid digital editing system is introduced.
	1. *Rain Man* ($172.8 million)			
	2. *Who Framed Roger Rabbit* ($156.5 million)			
	3. *Coming to America* ($128.2 million)			
	4. *Big* ($115 million)			
	5. *Twins* ($112 million)			
	Academy Award Winners			
	Rain Man (Picture, Director, Original Screenplay); *The Accidental Tourist* (Adapted Screenplay)			
1989	*Major Statistics* Attendance: 1.26 billion	On March 4 Time and Warner announce the formation of Time Warner.	Tim Berners-Lee develops basic elements of the World Wide Web.	*The Abyss* contains the first 3-D computer-generated figure.
	Total releases: 501	In March Columbia and TriStar merge.		Eastman Kodak introduces their EXR stocks, which use T-grains, silver halide crystals shaped like plates. This allows for greater sensitivity to light with less emulsion coating.
	MPAA releases: 109			
	Box office: $5.03 billion	In April Gulf + Western changes its name to Paramount Communications. It tries to buy Time Inc.,		
	Average ticket price: $3.99			

Year	Annual Data	Company Activities	Television, Video, and Internet	Moviemaking Technology
	Domestic Box Office Champs 1. *Batman* ($251.2 million) 2. *Indiana Jones and the Last Crusade* ($197.2 million) 3. *Lethal Weapon 2* ($147.3 million) 4. *Look Who's Talking* ($140.1 million) 5. *Honey, I Shrunk the Kids* ($130.7 million) *Academy Award Winners* *Driving Miss Daisy* (Picture); *Born on the Fourth of July* (Director); *Field of Dreams* (Adapted Screenplay); *Dead Poets Society* (Original Screenplay)	which instead merges with Warner Communications. In August Joe Roth becomes the new chairman at Fox. In September Sony buys Columbia from Coca-Cola for $3.4 billion. Peter Guber and Jon Peters are named co-chairmen. Disney forms Hollywood Pictures. Mike Ovitz founds the Artists Management Group. It will be merged with another firm in 2002, when Ovitz departs.		HMI lights appear in 18 kW form, which makes them as bright as the old Brute arcs, but much lighter and using less power. ILM's VistaGlide, a computer-controlled dolly, is used in *Back to the Future Part II*. Panavision introduces its Primo line of lenses, which become the industry standard. SpaceCam, a remote-camera system that can mount on various parts of helicopters, is introduced.
1990	*Major Statistics* Attendance: 1.19 billion Total releases: 410 MPAA releases: 98	In February Michael Medavoy leaves Orion to become chairman of TriStar Pictures.	Time Warner receives the rights to the United Artists video library.	The six-channel Cinema Digital Sound System, using an optical bar code, premieres in *Dick Tracy* and *Days of Thunder*, but a series of malfunctions during screenings lead it to be surpassed by competing processes.

Year	Annual Data	Company Activities	Television, Video, and Internet	Moviemaking Technology
	Box office: $5.02 billion	Controversy over *Henry and June* allows the X-rating category to be replaced with NC-17.	In June ABC broadcasts its first episode of *Twin Peaks*, co-created by director David Lynch. The success of the series will lead other major filmmakers to try episodic television.	The Arriflex 535 camera is introduced, which has noise levels under 20dB and a built-in electronic time code. The electronic shutter can be changed while the camera is running, allowing for speed changes ("ramping") during a single shot.
	Average ticket price: $4.22			
	Screens in the United States: 23,814			
	Domestic Box Office Champs	In November, Pathé Communications buys MGM/United Artists from Kirk Kerkorian.		
	1. *Home Alone* ($285.7 million)			
	2. *Ghost* ($217.6 million)	Dawn Steel resigns as head of Columbia, to move to independent production. She is replaced by Jonathan Dolgen.		The Flying-Cam, a remote-controlled miniature helicopter designed to carry a video camera, is modified to carry a 35mm unit.
	3. *Dances with Wolves* ($184.2 million)			
	4. *Pretty Woman* ($178.5 million)			
	5. *Teenage Mutant Ninja Turtles* ($135.3 million)	New Line Cinema launches Fine Line Features, which will distribute art films.		
	Academy Award Winners	*Entertainment Weekly*, a Time-Warner magazine, begins publication.		
	Dances with Wolves (Picture, Director, Adapted Screenplay); *Ghost* (Original Screenplay)	In December Matsushita buys MCA/Universal for $6.1 billion.		
		Teenage Mutant Ninja Turtles, which New Line acquires for $3 million, grosses $135 million, becoming one of		

Year	Annual Data	Company Activities	Television, Video, and Internet	Moviemaking Technology
		the most profitable independent releases in history.		
1991	*Major Statistics* Attendance: 1.14 billion Total releases: 458 MPAA releases: 150 Box office: $4.8 billion Average ticket price: $4.21 *Domestic Box Office Champs* 1. *Terminator 2: Judgment Day* ($204.8 million) 2. *Robin Hood: Prince of Thieves* ($165.5 million) 3. *Beauty and the Beast* ($145.7 million) 4. *Hook* ($119.6 million) 5. *City Slickers* ($123.8 million)	In April Pathé owner Giancarlo Parretti, currently in prison, is forced by Credit Lyonnais Bank to relinquish control to Alan Ladd Jr. Columbia is renamed Sony Pictures Entertainment. Jon Peters resigns as co-chair and CEO in May. At Paramount Stanley Jaffe returns as president and COO, replacing Frank Mancuso. In May Brandon Tartikoff becomes chairman. In December Orion files for bankruptcy. Good Machine, an independent distribution company favoring niche films, is founded. United Talent Agency is founded out of two other agencies.	*Top Gun* becomes the first VHS title to ship more than one million units.	*Terminator 2's* "liquid metal" T-1000 displays new level of morphing technology and digital compositing. *JFK* is one of the first mainstream films to feature aggressive changes in film stock and format, mixing 35mm with 16mm and Super-8mm.

Year	Annual Data	Company Activities	Television, Video, and Internet	Moviemaking Technology
	Academy Award Winners *The Silence of the Lambs* (Picture, Director, Adapted Screenplay); *Thelma and Louise* (Original Screenplay)	Disney signs a three-feature contract with Pixar (raised to five after the success of *Toy Story*, 1995).		
1992	*Major Statistics* Attendance: 1.27 billion Total releases: 480 MPAA releases: 141 Box office: $4.87 billion Average ticket price: $4.15 *Domestic Box Office Champs* 1. *Aladdin* ($217.4 million) 2. *Home Alone 2: Lost in New York* ($173 million) 3. *Batman Returns* ($162.8 million) 4. *Lethal Weapon 3* ($144.7 million) 5. *A Few Good Men* ($141.3 million)	In February Barry Diller resigns from Fox. In May Credit Lyonnais Bank takes control of MGM/United Artists. In October Brandon Tartikoff resigns as chairman of Paramount Pictures. In November Sherry Lansing becomes production head at Paramount. Columbia launches Sony Pictures Classics with *Howards End*. Orion emerges from bankruptcy. In December Gerry Levin takes over as president of Time Warner upon the death of Steve Ross.	Turner Broadcasting System launches the Cartoon Network.	The Dolby Digital six-channel stereo sound system is launched with *Batman Returns* and quickly becomes an industry standard.

Year	Annual Data	Company Activities	Television, Video, and Internet	Moviemaking Technology
	Academy Award Winners			
	Unforgiven (Picture, Director); *A River Runs Through It* (Adapted Screenplay); *The Crying Game* (Original Screenplay)			
1993	*Major Statistics* Attendance: 1.24 billion Total releases: 462 MPAA releases: 156 Box office: $5.15 billion Average ticket price: $4.14 *Domestic Box Office Champs* 1. *Jurassic Park* ($357 million) 2. *Mrs. Doubtfire* ($219 million) 3. *The Fugitive* ($183. 8 million) 4. *The Firm* ($158.3 million) 5. *Sleepless in Seattle* ($126.6 million)	In March Blockbuster buys almost half of Spelling Entertainment Group. In April Disney buys Miramax. Credit Lyonnais Bank hires CAA as advisors about their MGM investment, a move not welcomed by other agencies. In July Credit Lyonnais replaces Alan Ladd Jr. with Frank Mancuso. In August John Calley is hired to head the restarted United Artists. In August Turner Broadcasting buys Castle Rock Entertainment and New Line Cinema.	On July 1, Sony, Matsushita, Philips, and seven other companies form the High Definition Digital VCR Consortium to set standards for high-definition broadcast.	*Jurassic Park* marks the first time that computer graphics have been used to represent a realistic creature. The film also introduces Digital Theater Systems (DTS), a CD-ROM digital sound system. Sony introduces Digital Betacam. Its high quality quickly makes it the preferred broadcast format, and several theatrical films, notably *The Buena Vista Social Club* (1999), will be shot on it. Digital Domain is founded, soon becoming a major visual-effects house. *Snow White and the Seven Dwarfs* (1937) is the first feature film to be digitally restored frame by frame.

Year	Annual Data	Company Activities	Television, Video, and Internet	Moviemaking Technology
	Academy Award Winners *Schindler's List* (Picture, Director, Adapted Screenplay); *The Piano* (Original Screenplay)			Eastman introduces a polyester-based film stock for release prints.
1994	*Major Statistics* Attendance: 1.29 billion Total releases: 453 MPAA releases: 156 Box office: $5.4 billion Average ticket price: $4.08 *Domestic Box Office Champs* 1. *Forrest Gump* ($329.6 million) 2. *The Lion King* ($312.8 million) 3. *True Lies* ($146 million) 4. *The Santa Clause* ($144.8 million) 5. *The Flintstones* ($130.5 million)	In February Viacom buys Paramount, merging it with Blockbuster Entertainment Corporation. Stanley Jaffe leaves. Disney's Frank Wells is killed in a helicopter crash, and in August Jeffrey Katzenberg leaves the company. DreamWorks studio is announced on October 12 by its founders, Steven Spielberg, Jeffrey Katzenberg, and David Geffen. Disney buys Merchant-Ivory. Michael Medavoy is ousted as chair of TriStar, replaced by Mack Canton.	The Turner Classic Movies cable channel is launched. Independent Film Channel launched. Internet movie advertising begins, with *Stargate* hosting one of the first movie-dedicated sites. In September seven major media conglomerates form the Digital Video Disc Advisory Group. The aim is to set the standard for the DVD format, including copy protection and superior picture and sound. Soon the firms split into two camps favoring rival DVD formats.	*Forrest Gump* features the digital insertion of Tom Hanks into newsreel footage of JFK, among other historical figures. Digital editing of feature films takes off, thanks to an upsurge in computer storage space and software mimicking the twenty-four-frame rate of film.

Year	Annual Data	Company Activities	Television, Video, and Internet	Moviemaking Technology
	Academy Award Winners *Forrest Gump* (Picture, Director, Adapted Screenplay); *Pulp Fiction* (Original Screenplay)	Guber resigns as chair and CEO of Sony, which posts a $3.2 billion loss. Miramax begins to emphasize film production over distribution.		
1995	*Major Statistics* Attendance: 1.26 billion Total releases: 411 MPAA releases: 212 Box office: $5.5 billion Average ticket price: $4.35 *Domestic Box Office Champs* 1. *Toy Story* ($191.8 million) 2. *Batman Forever* ($184 million) 3. *Apollo 13* ($172 million) 4. *Pocahontas* ($141.5 million) 5. *Ace Ventura: When Nature Calls* ($108.4 million)	Carolco files for bankruptcy after the failure of *Cutthroat Island*. In July Seagram buys Universal/ MCA from Matsushita. Ron Meyer becomes president and CEO of MCA. The first megaplexes, theaters housing sixteen or more screens, start to appear. The Slamdance Film Festival begins.	Two new cable networks are introduced: Time Warner's Warner Bros. (WB) and Viacom's UPN. In July Disney buys ABC for $19 billion, creating the world's largest media company. Disney also buys out Silver Screen Partners, a film investment consortium. The Internet is privatized and opened to commercial use. Netscape, Amazon, and eBay come online. In December rival Digital Video Disc formats are reconciled.	*Toy Story*, the first completely CGI feature, is produced by Pixar and released through Disney.

Year	Annual Data	Company Activities	Television, Video, and Internet	Moviemaking Technology
	Academy Award Winners			
	Braveheart (Picture, Director); *Sense and Sensibility* (Adapted Screenplay); *The Usual Suspects* (Original Screenplay)			
1996	*Major Statistics* Attendance: 1.34 billion	Jeffrey Katzenberg sues Disney for payment, settling in July.	The Telecommunications Act is signed, deregulating the industry.	Kodak introduces its 5/7277 and 5/7279 color-negative Vision stocks.
	Total releases: 471 MPAA releases: 215	In July Kirk Kerkorian and Seven Network buy MGM from Credit Lyonnais Bank for $1.3 billion.	The Sundance Channel is launched. Harry Knowles starts his Ain't It Cool website, where industry secrets are leaked to eager fans. The site will eventually attract over a million hits a day.	Sony introduces DVCAM, a professional video camera using digital tape. About 80 percent of Hollywood films are now edited digitally on either Avid or Lightworks.
	Box office: $5.9 billion Average ticket price: $4.42			
	Domestic Box Office Champs 1. *Independence Day* ($306.1 million)	In November Alan Levine and Mark Canton are fired from Sony, as John Calley is named president. Amy Pascal is named president of Columbia Pictures.	Consumer rollout of DVDs delayed by disputes about copy protection technology.	*Hamlet,* directed by Kenneth Branagh, is the last feature film shot in 65mm for 70mm exhibition.
	2. *Twister* ($241.7 million)			
	3. *Mission: Impossible* ($180.9 million)	MCA is renamed Universal Studios.		
	4. *Jerry Maguire* ($153.9 million) 5. *Ransom* ($136.5 million)	In September Time Warner buys Turner Broadcasting System and New Line Cinema.		

Year	Annual Data	Company Activities	Television, Video, and Internet	Moviemaking Technology
	Academy Award Winners *The English Patient* (Picture, Director); *Sling Blade* (Adapted Screenplay); *Fargo* (Original Screenplay)	The Walt Disney company signs a global ten-year marketing agreement with McDonald's. The fast-food chain is given exclusive rights to promote Disney films.		
1997	*Major Statistics* Attendance: 1.39 billion Total releases: 510 MPAA releases: 215 Box office: $6.37 billion Average ticket price: $4.59 *Domestic Box Office Champs* 1. *Titanic* ($600.7 million) 2. *Men in Black* ($250.1 million) 3. *The Lost World: Jurassic Park* ($229 million) 4. *Liar Liar* ($181.4 million) 5. *Air Force One* ($172.6 million)	Kenneth Lerberger is named president of Columbia TriStar group. In May Universal buys October Films. In July MGM buys Orion Pictures, Goldwyn Entertainment, and Motion Picture Corporation of America. Lions Gate and Artisan Entertainment are founded. Good Machine establishes a first-look deal with Fox. Miramax makes $250 million, more than all other indies combined. It also founds Dimension Pictures, a genre specialty division.	In February DVD players go on sale in the United States, but no discs are released until March. *The Mask* becomes the first DVD to feature deleted scenes and director's commentary. Viacom sells USA Networks to Seagram's and increases its stake in Spelling Entertainment to 80 percent. Fox buys the International Family Channel cable network. Sony Pictures Entertainment buys controlling interest in Telemundo Group, a Spanish-language broadcaster.	

Year	Annual Data	Company Activities	Television, Video, and Internet	Moviemaking Technology
	Academy Award Winners *Titanic* (Picture, Director); *L.A. Confidential* (Adapted Screenplay); *Good Will Hunting* (Original Screenplay)		The FCC allocates TV spectrum space for digital broadcast and mandates that by 2006 all broadcasts must be fully digital.	
1998	*Major Statistics* Attendance: 1.48 billion Total releases: 509 MPAA releases: 221 Box office: $6.95 billion Average ticket price: $4.69 *Domestic Box Office Champs* 1. *Saving Private Ryan* ($216.1 million) 2. *Armageddon* ($201.5 million) 3. *There's Something About Mary* ($176.4 million) 4. *A Bug's Life* ($162.7 million) 5. *The Waterboy* ($161.4 million)	The Digital Millennium Copyright Act is passed, banning technology designed to bypass digital encryption. The Sonny Bono Copyright Term Extension Act delays the expiration of copyrighted material by up to ninety-five years. Seven Network sells its share of MGM/United Artists to Kerkorian for $389 million. In May Seagram/Universal buys Polygram. Lew Wasserman resigns from the Seagram/Universal board.	Atomfilm, iFilm, and other dot-com companies begin offering short films on the Internet. Netflix, an online DVD rental service, is founded.	The Danish Dogme 95 film *The Celebration* proves that a movie shot on digital video can find success as a theatrical release. It inspires a wave of independent films shot in digital video formats. *What Dreams May Come* shows elaborate possibilities of entire settings created in CGI.

Year	Annual Data	Company Activities	Television, Video, and Internet	Moviemaking Technology
	Academy Award Winners *Shakespeare in Love* (Picture, Original Screenplay); *Saving Private Ryan* (Director); *Gods and Monsters* (Adapted Screenplay)	Sony folds TriStar into Columbia Pictures and revives the Screen Gems brand to distribute mid-range titles.		
1999	*Major Statistics* Attendance: 1.47 billion Total releases: 461 MPAA releases: 221 Box office: $7.45 billion Average ticket price: $5.06 *Domestic Box Office Champs* 1. *Star Wars Episode One: The Phantom Menace* ($431 million) 2. *The Sixth Sense* ($293.5 million) 3. *Toy Story 2* ($245.7 million) 4. *Austin Powers 2: The Spy Who Shagged Me* ($205.4 million) 5. *The Matrix* ($171.4 million)	The number of screens in the United States hits an all-time high of 37,185. In September a wave of theater-chain bankruptcies begins (WestStar/Mann/Cinemania). At Disney Studios, chairman Joe Roth resigns, as the company launches the Go Network on the Internet. Frank Mancuso, chairman and CEO of MGM, is replaced; Kerkorian appoints Alex Yemenidjian. Universal enters a long-term equity relation with Working Title. It buys Gramercy Pictures and	*The Blair Witch Project* attracts audiences through a daring Internet campaign built around fictional documents and witch sightings. In March *Titanic* becomes the first DVD title to ship one million units. In September Viacom (parent of Paramount) buys CBS TV network. In October a fifteen-year-old Norwegian hacker disseminates DeCSS, a program that defeats DVD encryption. Charged with piracy, he will be acquitted by an Oslo court in 2003 and a U.S. court in 2004. Studios begin to offer DVD versions of "screeners" for Oscar voters.	Over 90 percent of *Star Wars Episode One: The Phantom Menace* contains CGI. The film also features the first fully integrated computer-animated character, the widely loathed Jar Jar Binks. *The Matrix* introduces "bullet-time," in which performers on wires are photographed by an array of still cameras positioned around them. In the finished effect, it appears as though time has stopped while the camera continues to move. Panavision introduces its Millennium camera, a lighter and quieter version of the Panaflex, with many built-in accessories.

Year	Annual Data	Company Activities	Television, Video, and Internet	Moviemaking Technology
	Academy Award Winners *American Beauty* (Picture, Director, Original Screenplay); *Cider House Rules* (Adapted Screenplay)	creates Universal Focus, a specialty-film division. At Warners Bob Daly and Terry Semel step down as co-chairs of Warner Bros. Gerry Levin and Steve Case open talks for a merger between AOL and Time Warner.	TiVo introduces the Personal Video Recorder, which allows programs and movies to be stored digitally. Later PVRs will allow copying from the hard drive to DVD.	Apple launches Final Cut Pro. It will soon become the preferred editing platform for low-budget digital cinema. The first commercial digital theatrical screening takes place in June when *Star Wars Episode One* premieres on four U.S. screens.
2000	*Major Statistics* Attendance: 1.49 billion Total releases: 478 MPAA releases: 191 Box office: $7.66 billion Average ticket price: $5.39 *Domestic Box Office Champs* 1. *Dr. Seuss' How the Grinch Stole Christmas* ($260 million) 2. *Cast Away* ($233.6 million) 3. *Mission: Impossible 2* ($215.4 million)	In January AOL begins the process of buying Time Warner; the sale is approved in December. Several theater chains, including Carmike, General Cinemas, Edwards, Silver, and United Artists, file for bankruptcy. In June the French water-treatment company Vivendi buys Seagram, absorbing MCA and Universal Pictures into Canal Plus.	In August *The Matrix* becomes the first DVD title to ship 3 million units.	*O Brother, Where Art Thou?* employs digital color grading in postproduction, changing the overall look of the film.

Year	Annual Data	Company Activities	Television, Video, and Internet	Moviemaking Technology
	4. *Gladiator* ($187.7 million) 5. *What Women Want* ($182.8 million) *Academy Award Winners* *Gladiator* (Picture); *Traffic* (Director, Adapted Screenplay); *Almost Famous* (Original Screenplay)			
2001	*Major Statistics* Attendance: 1.42 billion Total releases: 482 MPAA releases: 188 Box office: $8.4 billion Average ticket price: $5.65 *Domestic Box Office Champs* 1. *Harry Potter and the Sorcerer's Stone* ($317.5 million) 2. *The Lord of the Rings: Fellowship of the Ring* ($313.3 million)	Exhibition bankruptcies continue with CinemaStar, Loews, and Regal chains as the latest victims. Vivendi renames itself Vivendi Universal and merges Universal Pictures and Studio Canal. In major overseas markets, *Harry Potter and the Sorcerer's Stone* opens simultaneously with its U.S. premiere. This "day-and-date" release strategy will become a common means of thwarting video piracy.	Internet marketing campaign for *A. I.* creates a parallel universe around the film. The BMW website features five digital films exclusively available online, directed by major filmmakers (Ang Lee, Wong Kar-wai). Sundance Film Festival begins screening films made in digital video. In December *Pearl Harbor*'s first-day DVD sales of $67.5 million surpass its May opening-weekend box office ($59.1 million).	*Final Fantasy: The Spirits Within* is the first CGI feature with a realistic depiction of humans. *Ali* blends film footage with digital imagery from lipstick-sized video cameras.

Year	Annual Data	Company Activities	Television, Video, and Internet	Moviemaking Technology
	3. *Shrek* ($267.6 million) 4. *Monsters, Inc.* ($255.1 million) 5. *Rush Hour 2* ($226.1 million) *Academy Award Winners* *A Beautiful Mind* (Picture, Director, Adapted Screenplay); *Gosford Park* (Original Screenplay)	In December Steve Case dumps Gerry Levin as CEO of Time Warner. Two Sony executives are suspended for publishing enthusiastic but fictional critical quotes for *A Knight's Tale*.		
2002	*Major Statistics* Attendance: 1.63 billion Total releases: 467 MPAA releases: 220 Box office: $9.4 billion Average ticket price: $5.80 *Domestic Box Office Champs* 1. *Spider-Man* ($405.8 million) 2. *The Lord of the Rings: The Two Towers* ($339.5 million)	As theater bankruptcies slow, AMC buys General Cinema. In May Richard Parsons becomes CEO of AOL Time Warner. In the wake of falling share prices, Messier resigns from Universal on June 30. J. R. Fouton takes over to dispose of assets.	Most major manufacturers agree on future standards for high-definition DVD. Episodes of *Animatrix*, animated prequels to *The Matrix*, are posted on the Internet to publicize two sequels to be released in 2003. At end of year, global DVD sales and rentals are found to have exceeded theatrical box office.	*Star Wars Episode Two: Attack of the Clones* is the first feature shot on Sony High Definition video using the 24p system. Kodak introduces its Vision2 stocks along with the 5/7218. For *The Two Towers*, Andy Serkis's performance as Gollum, played out in real space with other actors, is motion-captured and then animated by computer. In postproduction for *The Two Towers*, footage is transmitted from New Zealand to London via broadband, and then stored on

Year	Annual Data	Company Activities	Television, Video, and Internet	Moviemaking Technology
	3. *Star Wars Episode Two: Attack of the Clones* ($310.6 million)			iPod hard drives for hand carrying to director Peter Jackson's hotel.
	4. *Harry Potter and the Chamber of Secrets* ($261.9 million)			
	5. *My Big Fat Greek Wedding* ($241.4 million)			
	Academy Award Winners			
	Chicago (Picture); *The Pianist* (Director, Adapted Screenplay); *Talk to Her* (Original Screenplay)			
2003	*Major Statistics* Attendance: 1.57 billion Total releases: 473 MPAA releases: 194 Box office: $9.49 billion Average ticket price: $6.03 *Domestic Box Office Champs* 1. *The Lord of the Rings: Return of the King* ($376.3 million)	In January Steve Case resigns as chairman of the board of AOL Time Warner, followed by Ted Turner. In the fall, AOL is dropped from the name of the corporation. In September Vivendi's entertainment interests are acquired by NBC, owned by General Electric. The new company is renamed NBC Universal.	In June, for the first time, more DVDs than VHS tapes are rented in the United States. In November first-week sales of *Finding Nemo* on DVD surpass the film's entire U.S. theatrical receipts. In December the Writers Guild announces demand for a larger share of DVD residuals. In 2004 the Guild backs down.	*Cold Mountain* becomes the first major studio production to be edited on Apple's Final Cut Pro.

Year	Annual Data	Company Activities	Television, Video, and Internet	Moviemaking Technology
	2. *Finding Nemo* ($339.7 million) 3. *Pirates of the Caribbean: Curse of the Black Pearl* ($305.4 million) 4. *The Matrix Reloaded* ($281.6 million) 5. *Bruce Almighty* ($242.3 million) *Academy Award Winners* *The Lord of the Rings: Return of the King* (Picture, Director, Adapted Screenplay); *Lost in Translation* (Original Screenplay)	In October John Calley leaves as chairman and CEO of Sony for independent production. Lions Gate buys Artisan Entertainment. Roy Disney resigns from the Disney board, citing disappointment with the company's direction. He calls for Eisner's resignation. Rentrak, an online service reporting box-office receipts to studios in real time, is launched. On November 7, *The Matrix Revolutions* opens on twenty thousand screens in dozens of countries. It is the widest release in history. The average cost of making and marketing a U.S. theatrical feature passes $100 million for the first time. Sequels yield over 26 percent of total domestic box office, a new high.		

Year	Annual Data	Company Activities	Television, Video, and Internet	Moviemaking Technology
2004	*Major Statistics* Attendance: 1.54 billion Total releases: 483 MPAA releases: 199 Box office: $9.54 billion Average ticket price: $6.19 *Domestic Box Office Champs* 1. *Shrek 2* ($436.7 million) 2. *Spider-Man 2* ($373.4 million) 3. *The Passion of the Christ* ($370.3 million) 4. *The Incredibles* ($261.4 million) 5. *Harry Potter and the Prisoner of Azkaban* ($249.4 million) *Academy Award Winners* *Million Dollar Baby* (Picture, Director); *Sideways* (Adapted Screenplay); *Eternal Sunshine of the Spotless Mind* (Original Screenplay)	The major distributors turn down *The Passion of the Christ*. Released by Newmarket in February, it earns over $600 million worldwide, becoming one of the most profitable movies in history. Disney refuses to distribute *Fahrenheit 9/11*. Released by a consortium of companies, the documentary grosses over $210 million worldwide. In a frenzy of international synergy, Sony releases eleven different soundtrack CDs for *Spider-Man 2*, each one featuring artists familiar in local territories. In September Michael Eisner announces he will depart as Disney CEO by 2006. In early 2005, Robert Iger is named to succeed him. After years of dismal market share, Paramount	Digital video exhibition proves slow to take off: by midyear, there are only 250 digital screens in the world, nearly half of them in Asia. In November, taking an action modeled on the music industry's tactics, the motion picture studios start to sue individuals downloading copyrighted films from P2P networks. The penalty is claimed to run as high as $150,000 per film. Home video rentals and purchases, driven by the DVD format, reach a record high of $24.1 billion.	Jonathan Caouette's *Tarnation*, made on Apple's iMovie out of Super-8mm, VHS, and digital-video footage at an initial cost of $218, wins festival acclaim and theatrical distribution. Apple launches Final Cut Pro HD for high-definition video. *Sky Captain and the World of Tomorrow* becomes the first film to create all its settings in digital postproduction. Performers played all scenes against blue- or green-screen backdrops. *The Polar Express* employs Performance Capture, a digital-video motion-capture system that turns actors into computer-animated characters.

Year	Annual Data	Company Activities	Television, Video, and Internet	Moviemaking Technology
		head Sherry Lansing announces she will depart in 2005. She is succeeded by Brad Grey.		
		Viacom divests itself of Blockbuster in the face of competition from online DVD rental services.		
		A consortium of investors led by Sony purchases MGM, principally to acquire the four-thousand-title library.		
		In November President Bush signs a tax bill allowing low-budget film costs to be written off in a single year. This gesture is seen as a boost to the independent film community.		

Notes

INTRODUCTION. BEYOND THE BLOCKBUSTER

Epigraph: Quoted in Howard Meibach and Paul Duran, eds., *Ask the Pros: Screenwriting: 101 Questions Answered by Hollywood Professionals* (Hollywood: Lone Eagle, 2004), 28.

1. The most comprehensive survey of Hollywood's history is Joel W. Finler, *The Hollywood Story* (London: Wallflower, 2003); readers should also seek out the original 1988 edition for its splendid production values. See also Tino Balio, ed., *Hollywood in the Age of Television* (New York: Unwin Hyman, 1990), and Barry R. Litman, *The Motion Picture Mega-Industry* (Boston: Allyn and Bacon, 1998). For sheer detail on this period, nothing matches two volumes of the Scribner's *History of the American Cinema* series: David A. Cook, *Lost Illusions, American Cinema in the Shadow of Watergate and Vietnam, 1970–1979* (Berkeley and Los Angeles: University of California Press, 2000) and Stephen Prince, *A New Pot of Gold: Hollywood under the Electronic Rainbow, 1980–1989* (Berkeley and Los Angeles: University of California Press, 2000). The period is put into the context of worldwide trends in Kristin Thompson and David Bordwell, *Film History: An Introduction*, 2d ed. (New York: McGraw-Hill, 2003), chaps. 22 and 27. See also Douglas Gomery, *The Hollywood Studio System: A History* (London: British Film Institute, 2005), which criticizes the standard story as sketched here. On the business strategies of the contemporary industry, see Janet Wasko, *How Hollywood Works* (London: Sage, 2003), and Edward Jay Epstein, *The Big Picture: The New Logic of Money and Power in Hollywood* (New York: Random House, 2005).

2. See Janet Staiger, "The Package-Unit System: Unit Management after 1955," in David Bordwell, Janet Staiger, and Kristin Thompson, *The Classical Hollywood Cinema: Film Style and Mode of Production to 1960* (New York: Columbia University Press, 1985), 330–37.

3. For a detailed account of how this was accomplished, see Douglas Gomery, "The Hollywood Film Industry: Theatrical Exhibition, Pay TV, and Home Video," in Benjamin M. Compaine and Douglas Gomery, *Who Owns the Me-*

dia? Competition and Concentration in the Mass Media Industries (Mahwah, NJ: Erlbaum, 2000), 359–435.

4. I draw my original box-office figures from http://boxofficemojo.com.

5. For a lively account of how the megapicture affected exhibition, see Dade Hayes and Jonathan Bing, *Open Wide: How Hollywood Box Office Became a National Obsession* (New York: Miramax, 2004).

6. See *US Entertainment Industry: 2004 MPA Market Statistics,* Motion Picture Association, available at www.mpaa.org, and "Industry Boosted by $21.2 Billion in Annual DVD Sales and Rentals," *DVD News* (January 6, 2005), available at www.dvdinformation.com.

7. A detailed review of these ideas is provided by Peter Krämer, "Post-Classical Hollywood," in *The Oxford Guide to Film Studies,* ed. John Hill and Pamela Church Gibson (Oxford: Oxford University Press, 1998), 289–309. Also relevant is Robert C. Allen, "Home Alone Together: Hollywood and the 'Family Film,'" in *Identifying Hollywood's Audiences: Cultural Identity and the Movies,* ed. Melvyn Stokes and Richard Maltby (London: British Film Institute, 1999), 109–31. See also Robert Blanchet, *Blockbuster: Äesthetik, Ökonomie und Geschichte des Postklassischen Hollywoodkinos* (Blockbuster: Aesthetics, Economics, and the History of the Postclassical Hollywood Cinema) (Marburg: Schüren, 2003).

8. Tom Schatz, "The New Hollywood," in *Film Theory Goes to the Movies,* ed. Jim Collins, Hilary Radner, and Ava Preacher Collins (London: Routledge, 1993), 23.

9. Wheeler Winston Dixon, "Twenty-Five Reasons Why It's All Over," in *The End of Cinema as We Know It: American Film in the Nineties,* ed. Jon Lewis (New York: New York University Press, 2001), 363.

10. Elizabeth Cowie, "Storytelling: Classical Hollywood Cinema and Classical Narrative," in *Contemporary Hollywood Cinema,* ed. Steve Neale and Murray Smith (London: Routledge, 1998), 188.

11. Schatz, "New Hollywood," 10.

12. Richard Maltby, "'Nobody Knows Everything': Post-Classical Historiographies and Consolidated Entertainment," in Neale and Smith, *Contemporary Hollywood Cinema,* 26.

13. James Schamus, "To the Rear of the Back End: The Economics of Independent Cinema," in Neale and Smith, *Contemporary Hollywood Cinema,* 94.

14. Justin Wyatt, *High Concept: Movies and Marketing in Hollywood* (Austin: University of Texas Press, 1994), 8, 25–55, 80.

15. Murray Smith, "Theses on the Philosophy of Hollywood History," in Neale and Smith, *Contemporary Hollywood Cinema,* 14.

16. Krämer, "Post-Classical Hollywood," 307.

17. Warren Buckland, "A Close Encounter with *Raiders of the Lost Ark:* Notes on Narrative Aspects of the New Hollywood Blockbuster," in Neale and Smith, *Contemporary Hollywood Cinema,* 166–77.

18. Geoff King, *Spectacular Narratives: Hollywood in the Age of the Blockbuster* (London: I. B. Tauris, 2000), 184.

19. Kristin Thompson, *Storytelling in the New Hollywood: Analyzing Classical Narrative Technique* (Cambridge, MA: Harvard University Press, 1999), 345–46.

20. Wyatt, *High Concept*, 13.

21. William C. Martell, *Secrets of Action Screenwriting: From "Popeye Points" to "Rug Pulls"* (Studio City, CA: First Strike Productions, 2000), 7.

22. Jonathan Bing, "Hollywood's High on Higher-Concepts," *Variety* (September 23–29, 2002): 15.

23. Wyatt, *High Concept*, 53–60. Wyatt also proposes that high-concept films center on rather thinly drawn characters, but that charge would apply to most of the films on my parallel list too.

24. For example, in 1998 Richard Maltby argued that both blockbusters and high concept had made narrative of little consequence: "High concept has little commercial investment in narrative except as a vehicle for the movie's other pleasures, and equally little commitment to a classical hierarchization of a narrative system over those of space and time" (Neale and Smith, *Contemporary Hollywood Cinema*, 39). In Maltby's *Hollywood Cinema: An Introduction*, 2d ed. (Oxford: Blackwell, 2003), however, "postclassical cinema" is characterized by a sense of allusion and playfulness (e.g., 291). The term *postclassical* is nowhere defined, does not appear in the book's extensive glossary, and receives only two (minor) index entries. In his introduction, Maltby grants that Thompson has shown the continuity of Hollywood's narrative tradition in recent years but that "other approaches, more concerned with economic or technological aspects of Hollywood's history, stress moments of change or discontinuity" (17). Exactly; technological and economic changes aren't what Thompson sets out to explain.

25. Noel Carroll, "The Future of Allusion: Hollywood in the Seventies (and Beyond)," in *Interpreting the Moving Image* (Cambridge: Cambridge University Press, 1998), 244, 261.

26. Thomas Elsaesser and Warren Buckland, *Studying Contemporary American Film: A Guide to Movie Analysis* (London: Arnold, 2002), 66, 229–30, 70.

27. Carroll, "Future of Allusion," 262–63.

28. Elsaesser and Buckland, *Studying Contemporary American Film*, 76. Elsaesser and Buckland may want the foot-binding motif to be confirmed by their claim that the man giving the advice is Asian American (49). This seems not to be the case. Incidentally, foot binding doesn't curl the victim's toes; it breaks the bones in her feet.

29. See Thierry Kuntzel, "The Film-Work 2," *Camera Obscura* 5 (1980): 52–59; several of the essays collected in *Shades of Noir*, ed. Joan Copjec (London: Verso, 1993); and Robert Ray, *The Avant-Garde Finds Andy Hardy* (Cambridge, MA: Harvard University Press, 1996).

30. See my *Making Meaning: Inference and Rhetoric in the Interpretation of Cinema* (Cambridge, MA: Harvard University Press, 1994), chap. 11.

31. Rankings and figures are taken from http://boxofficemojo.com.

32. John Ptak, quoted in Mike Goodridge, "Hollywood's Indie Matchmakers," *Screen International* (May 7–13, 2004): 25.

33. See Douglas Gomery, "The Hollywood Blockbuster: Industrial Analysis and Practice," in *Movie Blockbusters*, ed. Julian Stringer (London: Routledge, 2003), 72–83.

34. See Adam Minns, "Reason to Be Cheerful," *Screen International* (September 3, 2004): 8.

35. See Kristin Thompson, "The Formulation of the Classical Style, 1909–1928," in Bordwell, Staiger, and Thompson, *The Classical Hollywood Cinema*, 155–240. For distant antecedents, see N. J. Lowe, *The Classical Plot and the Invention of Western Narrative* (Cambridge: Cambridge University Press, 2000).

36. Claire Goll, "American Cinema (1920)," in *German Essays on Film*, ed. Richard W. McCormick and Alison Guenther-Pal (New York: Continuum, 2004), 51.

37. The best survey of Hollywood's penetration of overseas markets remains Kristin Thompson, *Exporting Entertainment: America in the World Film Market 1907–1934* (London: British Film Institute, 1985).

38. On the user-friendly aspects of the mainstream style, see Noël Carroll, "The Power of Movies," in *Theorizing the Moving Image* (Cambridge: Cambridge University Press, 1996), 78–93.

39. André Bazin, "On the *politique des auteurs*," in *Cahiers du Cinéma: The 1950s: Neo-Realism, Hollywood, New Wave*, ed. Jim Hillier (Cambridge, MA: Harvard University Press, 1985), 258.

40. Leonard Meyer, *Style and Music: Theory, History, and Ideology* (Philadelphia: University of Pennsylvania Press, 1989), 20.

41. See my *Figures Traced in Light: On Cinematic Staging* (Berkeley and Los Angeles: University of California Press, 2005), 258–59, and my foreword to *Moving Image Theory: Ecological Considerations*, ed. Joseph D. Anderson and Barbara Fisher Anderson (Carbondale: University of Southern Illinois Press, 2005), ix–xii.

42. E. H. Gombrich, *The Story of Art* (London: Phaidon, 1950), 265. See also Gombrich, "The Renaissance Conception of Artistic Progress," and "Mannerism: The Historiographic Background," in *Norm and Form: Studies in the Art of the Renaissance I* (London: Phaidon, 1966), 1–10 and 99–106.

43. Gombrich, *Story of Art*, 265–72, 278–83. See also S. J. Freedberg, *Painting in Italy 1500–1600*, 3d ed. (New York: Yale University Press, 1993), 175–77.

44. For an effort to find more exact parallels between contemporary Hollywood and Italian Mannerism, see Marc A. Le Sueur, "Film Criticism and the Mannerist Alternative, or Pauline and Stanley and Richard and Agnes," *Journal of Popular Film* 4, no. 4 (1975): 326–33.

45. Recent examples are Gary Winecke (*Tadpole*, 2002; *Thirteen Going on Thirty*, 2004); Mark Waters (*House of Yes*, 1997; *Freaky Friday*, 2003); Bart Freundlich (*The Myth of Fingerprints*, 1997; *Catch That Kid*, 2004); and Karyn Kusama (*Girlfight*, 2000; *Aeon Flux*, 2005).

PART I. A REAL STORY

Epigraph: Quoted in Peter Brunette and Gerald Peary, "James M. Cain: Tough Guy," in *Backstory: Interviews with Screenwriters of Hollywood's Golden Age,* ed. Patrick McGilligan (Berkeley and Los Angeles: University of California Press, 1986), 128.

1. Cameron Crowe, "The 'Jerry Maguire' Journal," *Rolling Stone,* nos. 750/751 (December 26, 1996–January 9, 1997): 137.

2. Cameron Crowe, *Conversations with Wilder* (New York: Knopf, 2001).

3. Crowe, "'Jerry Maguire' Journal," 142.

4. A noteworthy exception is Preston Sturges, who incorporated film history in a startlingly modern way into *Mad Wednesday* (aka *The Sin of Harold Diddlebock,* 1947).

5. Quoted in Jim Hiller, *The New Hollywood* (New York: Continuum, 1994), 47.

6. I borrow the term from Harold Bloom, but I don't mean to accept his Freudian theory of literary influence. I use the term to describe any situation in which an artist follows outstanding predecessors and must carve out her distinctive contribution. See Bloom, *The Anxiety of Influence,* 2d ed. (New York: Oxford University Press, 1997), xxv.

7. Quoted in Axel Madsen, *The New Hollywood: American Movies in the '70s* (New York: Crowell, 1975), 27.

8. Noël Carroll, "The Future of Allusion: Hollywood in the Seventies (and Beyond)," in *Interpreting the Moving Image* (Cambridge: Cambridge University Press, 1998), 250.

9. Carroll, *Interpreting the Moving Image,* 262–63.

10. "What a grand piece of historical luck it was," writes one of the few critics to applaud the rise of the blockbuster, "to be in your early teens when *Raiders of the Lost Ark* came out—when Spielberg and Lucas were in their prime and the very act of going to the movies seemed to come with its own brassily rousing John Williams score." See Tom Shone, *Blockbuster: How Hollywood Learned to Stop Worrying and Love the Summer* (New York: Free Press, 2004), 11.

11. William C. Martell, *Secrets of Action Screenwriting: From "Popeye Points" to "Rug Pulls"* (Studio City, CA: First Strike Productions, 2000), 143.

12. Syd Field, *Going to the Movies: A Personal Journey Through Four Decades of Modern Film* (New York: Dell, 2001), 205.

13. A burst of books appeared in 1913–1920, as the major studios were consolidating and seeking talent. Another cluster came out in the transitional years 1928–1930, advising would-be scenarists how to write for the talkies. After this, the market fell off. The studios now had their own stables of contract writers, and amateur submissions were discouraged. Two remarkable manuals, Eugene Vale's *Technique of Screenplay Writing* (New York: Crown, 1944) and Lewis Herman's *Practical Manual of Screen Playwriting* (New York: World, 1952), stood virtually alone in the market until the 1970s.

For histories of the writer in the studio system, see Richard Fine, *Hollywood and the Profession of Authorship, 1928–1940* (Ann Arbor: UMI Research Press, 1985); Tom Stempel, *Frame Work: A History of Screenwriting in the American Film*, 3d ed. (Syracuse: Syracuse University Press, 2000); and Ian Hamilton, *Writers in Hollywood, 1915–1951* (New York: Carroll and Graf, 1991). See also McGilligan, ed., *Backstory* and *Backstory 2: Interviews with Screenwriters of the 1940s and 1950s* (Berkeley and Los Angeles: University of California, 1991).

14. See Janet Staiger, "The Package-Unit System: Unit Management after 1955," in David Bordwell, Janet Staiger, and Kristin Thompson, *The Classical Hollywood Cinema: Film Style and Mode of Production to 1960* (New York: Columbia University Press, 1985), 330–37.

15. See Thom Taylor, *The Big Deal: Hollywood's Million-Dollar Spec Script Market* (New York: Morrow, 1999), 6–19; T. L. Katahn, *Reading for a Living: How to Be a Professional Story Analyst for Film and Television* (Los Angeles: Blue Arrow, 1990); Kathie Fong Yoneda, *The Script-Selling Game* (Los Angeles: Michael Wiese, 2002), 45–55, 87–100; and Robin U. Russin and William Missouri Downs, *Screenplay: Writing the Picture* (Los Angeles: Silman-James, 2003), 3–15.

16. Constance Nash and Virginia Oakley, *The Screenwriter's Handbook: Writing for the Movies* (New York: HarperCollins, 1974), 3, 20–21; Syd Field, *Screenplay: The Foundations of Screenwriting* (New York: Delta, 1979), 8–13.

17. For objections, see Frank Daniel, introduction, in David Howard and Edward Mabley, *The Tools of Screenwriting: A Writer's Guide to the Craft and Elements of a Screenplay* (New York: St. Martin's Press, 1993), xix–xx; Andrew Horton, *Writing the Character-Centered Screenplay* (Berkeley and Los Angeles: University of California Press, 1994), 14–18, 91–95; William Froug, *Zen and the Art of Screenwriting: Insights and Interviews* (Los Angeles: Silman-James, 1996), 15–16; and Alex Epstein, *Crafty Screenwriting: Writing Movies That Get Made* (New York: Holt, 2002), 59–61.

18. Lew Hunter, *Lew Hunter's Screenwriting 434* (New York: Perigee, 1993), 94–95; Robert McKee, *Story: Substance, Structure, Style, and the Principles of Screenwriting* (New York: HarperCollins, 1997), 223–24.

19. Hal Ackerman, *Write Screenplays that Sell the Ackerman Way* (Los Angeles: Tallfellow Press, 2003), 81–97.

20. Ackerman, *Write Screenplays*, 107. See also Linda J. Cowgill, *Secrets of Screenplay Structure* (Los Angeles: Lone Eagle, 1999), 29. Syd Field first discusses the midpoint in *The Screenwriter's Workbook* (New York: Dell, 1984), 121–45.

21. Linda Seger, *Making a Good Script Great* (New York: Dodd, Mead, 1987), 19; Russin and Downs, *Screenplay*, 99–100; and Ackerman, *Write Screenplays*, 192–93.

22. McKee, *Story*, 303.

23. Christopher Keane, *How to Write a Selling Screenplay* (New York: Broadway Books, 1998), 84.

24. Billy Mernit, *Writing the Romantic Comedy: From "Cute Meet" to "Joy-*

ous Defeat": How to Write Screenplays That Sell (New York: HarperCollins, 2001), 111–16.

25. Both the Nash/Oakley book and Field's manual thank the Sherwood Oaks Experimental College in Los Angeles. Neither book mentions the other. Field claims that he began formulating the three-act paradigm when he was teaching at Sherwood Oaks in the mid-1970s. See Field, *Going to the Movies*, 171–88. See also Todd Coleman, "Story Structure Gurus," *Written By* (June 1995), available online at http://atalentscout.com/article_gurus.html.

26. A three-part structure is sometimes mentioned in the earliest scenario manuals. In 1913 one manual indicates that the film should consist of "cause, crisis, and climactic effect" (J. Arthur Nelson, *The Photoplay: How to Write, How to Sell* [Los Angeles: Photoplay, 1913], 76). Victor Freeburg, in *The Art of Photoplay Making* (New York: Macmillan, 1918), suggests the terms "Premise, Complication, and Solution" (238). Francis Taylor Patterson goes further to recommend a reel-by-reel organization: the first reel constitutes the premise; reels two, three, and four make up the complication; and the fifth is devoted to the solution (*Cinema Craftsmanship: A Book for Photoplaywrights* [New York: Harcourt, Brace and Howe, 1920], 11).

Later handbooks are vague about how to divide up the film, although Herman's *Practical Manual of Screen Playwriting* mentions that an outline should contain three acts (20). Studio memos also occasionally invoke the concept. Marshall Deutelbaum has found that producer Hal Wallis wrote to director Michael Curtiz about *Casablanca:* "The Epsteins have agreed to deliver the film's 'second act' the following day." See "The Visual Design Program of *Casablanca*," *Post Script* 9, no. 3 (Summer 1980): 38. Darryl F. Zanuck used the term *last act* in correspondence about *Viva Zapata!* and *On the Waterfront;* see *Memo from Darryl F. Zanuck: The Golden Years at Twentieth Century–Fox*, ed. Rudy Behlmer (New York: Grove, 1993), 173, 226.

In contemporary interviews, some older screenwriters invoke the concept; see McGilligan, *Backstory*, 96, 169, 327. For example, Philip Dunne remarks that he had to create an episodic structure for *How Green Was My Valley* because he "had no way of making a solid dramatic first act, second act, third act" (*Backstory*, 158). See also comments by Paddy Chayefsky and Ernest Lehman in John Brady, *The Craft of the Screenwriter: Interviews with Six Celebrated Screenwriters* (New York: Simon & Schuster, 1981), 50–51, 202–204.

27. See William Froug, *The New Screenwriter Looks at the New Screenwriter* (Los Angeles: Silman-James, 1992), 58–59.

28. See the comments by producers and development staff collected in Skip Press, *Writer's Guide to Hollywood Producers, Directors, and Screenwriter's Agents 2002–2003* (Roseville, CA: Prima, 2001), 46–47, 52, 68–69, 91, and in *Ask the Pros: Screenwriting: 101 Questions Answered by Industry Professionals*, ed. Howard Meibach and Paul Duran (Hollywood, CA: Lone Eagle, 2004), 48, 96–97, 103.

29. Novelist Meg Wolitzer accepts the template as gospel in *Fitzgerald Did It: The Writer's Guide to Mastering the Screenplay* (New York: Penguin, 1999),

10–11. For a summary of how college teachers present the three-act idea, see the articles collected in *Journal of Film and Video* 36, no. 3 (Summer 1984), an issue devoted to screenwriting.

Many of the top-selling manuals, like Field's and McKee's, are translated into other languages. For French examples advocating the three-act format, see Francis Vanoye, *Scénario modèles, modèles de scénarios* (Model Screenplays, Models for Screenplays) (Paris: Natan, 1991), 89–96; Michel Chion, *Écrire un scénario* (Writing a Screenplay) (Paris: Cahiers du cinema/INA, 1995), 139–58. Chihiro Kameyama, "the Bruckheimer of Japan," says that his *Bayside Shakedown 2* (2003) was based on Hollywood films. "Another model was *Star Wars*, whose three-act structure is close to perfection" (quoted in Mark Schilling, "The Japanese Bruckheimer," *Screen International* [April 30, 2004]: 9). See also Rachid Naougmanov, "Building a Screenplay: A Five-Act Paradigm, or What Syd Field Didn't Tell You," in Andrew Horton, *Screenwriting for a Global Market: Selling Your Scripts from Hollywood to Hong Kong* (Berkeley and Los Angeles: University of California Press, 2004), 141–51.

30. See, for example, Vale, *Technique of Screenplay Writing*, 102–5.

31. Hunter, *Screenwriting 434*, 76.

32. Russin and Downs, *Screenplay*, 72.

33. Ken Dancyger and Jeff Rush, *Alternative Scriptwriting: Writing Beyond the Rules* (Boston: Focal, 1991), 106.

34. Quoted in Jurgen Wolff and Kerry Cox, *Top Secrets: Screenwriting* (Los Angeles: Lone Eagle, 1993), 134.

35. Seger, *Making a Good Script Great*, 149. See also Linda Seger, *Advanced Screenwriting: Raising Your Script to the Academy Award Level* (Beverly Hills: Silman-James, 2003), 161–85.

36. Cowgill, *Secrets*, 217.

37. "Character drawing may also add to the plot value of a story by arousing or sustaining suspense in the minds of the spectators. Will the character improve? Will the character degenerate?" (Patterson, *Cinema Craftsmanship*, 44).

38. A stimulating discussion of troubled heroes in postwar Hollywood can be found in Lawrence Alloway, *Violent America: The Movies 1946–1964* (New York: Museum of Modern Art, 1971), 37–39.

39. Lajos Egri, *The Art of Dramatic Writing: Its Basis in the Creative Interpretation of Human Motives* (New York: Simon & Schuster, 1960), 70.

40. For concise reviews of the theatrical sources of these concepts, see Sharon Karnicke, "Stanislavsky's System: Pathways for the Actor" and David Krasner, "Strasberg, Adler and Meisner," in *Twentieth Century Actor Training*, ed. Alison Hodge (New York: Routledge, 2000), 21–28, 131. Horton Foote maintains that Stanislavsky had an inescapable influence on modern theater and cinema; see Joseph A. Cincotti, "Horton Foote: The Trip from Wharton," in *Backstory 3: Interviews with Screenwriters of the 60s*, ed. Pat McGilligan (Berkeley and Los Angeles: University of California Press, 1997), 121. On "beats," see Cincotti, "Horton Foote," 120; Seger, *Making a Good Script Great*, 14–17; Seger, *Advanced Screenwriting*, 170–80; and Dancyger and Rush, *Alternative Screenwriting*, 117.

41. Field, *Screenplay,* n. p.

42. Quoted in Joseph Campbell, *The Hero's Journey: Joseph Campbell on His Life and Work,* ed. Phil Cousineau (Novato, CA: New World Library, 2003), 187.

43. According to one biographer, Lucas merely listened to extracts of *Hero* on tape. See John Baxter, *Mythmaker: The Life and Work of George Lucas* (New York: Spike, 1999), 164.

44. Quoted in Campbell, *The Hero's Journey,* 187.

45. See Phil Cousineau, "Preface to the Centennial Edition," in Campbell, *Hero's Journey,* xi. See also Seger, *Making a Good Script Great,* 93–103.

46. Christopher Vogler, *The Writer's Journey: Mythic Structure for Story-tellers and Screenwriters* (Los Angeles: Michael Wiese, 1992), 3–7.

47. Christopher Vogler, *The Writer's Journey: Mythic Structure for Writers,* 2d ed. (Los Angeles: Michael Wiese, 1998), xxi–xxiii; Russin and Downs, *Screenplay,* 94–96, 102; and Michael Chase Walker, *Power Screenwriting: The 12 Stages of Story Development* (Hollywood: Ifilm, 2002), 53–108.

48. Walker, *Power Screenwriting,* 76.

49. Robert J. Ray, *The Weekend Novelist* (New York: Dell, 1994).

50. Thompson, *Storytelling in the New Hollywood,* 29–35.

51. Thompson, *Storytelling in the New Hollywood,* 28.

52. Thompson, *Storytelling in the New Hollywood,* 28.

53. Lew Hunter, quoted in Skip Press, *Writer's Guide to Hollywood,* 128.

54. Thompson, *Storytelling in the New Hollywood,* 36–40.

55. Thompson claims that *The Godfather* has two Development sections (*Storytelling,* 30), but I'm inclined to think that the plot is even more complex. It presents two Complicating Actions (one leading up to Michael's volunteering to kill Sollozzo, the other leading up to Michael's escape to Sicily) and two Development sections (one leading up to the death of Apollonia, the other leading up to the death of Don Vito). Once Don Vito is gone, Michael becomes the head of the family, and the Climax shows him wreaking his revenge.

56. I'd argue that this final section of *In Cold Blood* isn't an epilogue, because many things remain unsettled, chiefly whether or not Perry can come to understand why he committed such a heinous crime. This second Climax also drives home the anti–capital punishment theme of the film.

57. We might ask further questions about Thompson's model. Is it arbitrary? That is, could we carve films just as informatively into five or fifty parts? I think not, because she lays down fairly clear criteria (character goals and their vicissitudes) for demarcating the major segments.

Having this schema in mind, do we project it irresistibly onto the film, thereby missing more pertinent divisions? If the analyst feels that we are squeezing or stretching to make things come out right for the timings, that might be the case, but so far I don't think that's a serious worry. Thompson readily admits that not all films fit the four-part scheme.

More seriously, how might we explain historically the emergence of the four-part model? Since Thompson finds the four-part template in the finished film, not in scripts, we have to believe that not only screenwriters but also editors, producers, and directors tacitly tend to organize a movie in 20- to 30-minute portions. How did this extraordinary and tacit consensus arise? In *Storytelling*, Thompson suggests that the rough equivalence of a film's parts follows a well-established practice in music, architecture, and other arts (43–44). Still, it's odd that few practitioners have acknowledged this framework. Akiva Goldsman (see below) suggests that the four-part structure can be seen as a refinement of the three-act model, which at least some practitioners have owned up to following. Interestingly, the influential teacher Frank Daniel proposed a layout of parts that supports Thompson's intuition about structural balance. He claimed that a screenplay consists of eight roughly equal segments, with two sequences allotted to act 1, four to act 2 (with a midpoint break), and two to act 3. Daniel's approach is explained by Paul Joseph Gulino in *Screenwriting: The Sequence Approach* (New York: Continuum, 2004).

58. Quoted in Karl Iglesias, *The 101 Habits of Highly Successful Screenwriters: Insider Secrets from Hollywood's Top Writers* (Avon, MA: Adams, 2001), 52. Since this chapter was written, two recently published manuals have advocated the four-part structure: Allen B. Ury, *Secrets of the Screen Trade: From Concept to Sale* (Los Angeles: Lone Eagle, 2005), 122–25; and Christina Hamlett, *Could It Be a Movie? How to Get Ideas Out of Your Head and Up on the Screen* (Los Angeles: Michael Wiese, 2005), 96–99.

59. Kenneth Burke, "The Psychology of Form," *Counter-Statement* (Chicago: University of Chicago Press, 1957), 31.

60. Field, *Screenplay*, 9.

61. See Bordwell, Staiger, and Thompson, *Classical Hollywood Cinema*, 12–18; Thompson, *Storytelling in the New Hollywood*, 10–21.

62. See Thompson, *Storytelling in the New Hollywood*, 19–20, and Bordwell, Staiger, and Thompson, *Classical Hollywood Cinema*, 33, 376. Thompson and I adapt the term from Lewis Herman, who talks about transitional "hooks" in *A Practical Manual of Screen Playwriting* (New York: Meridian, 1952), 144. Interestingly, one recent manual has turned the analytical concepts we proposed into screenwriting tools. See Gulino, *Screenwriting*, 5–9.

63. See Thompson, *Storytelling in the New Hollywood*, 16–17. See also Bordwell, Staiger, and Thompson, *Classical Hollywood Cinema*, 44–45.

64. Quoted in McGilligan, *Backstory 3*, 309.

65. Michael Hauge, *Writing Screenplays That Sell* (New York: HarperCollins, 1991), 98; Keane, *How to Write a Selling Screenplay*, 51; McKee, *Story*, 401.

66. Martell, *Secrets of Action Screenwriting*, 65–66.

67. See Bordwell, Staiger, and Thompson, *Classical Hollywood Cinema*, 63–69.

68. See Bordwell, Staiger, and Thompson, *Classical Hollywood Cinema*, 31–33; David Bordwell, *Narration in the Fiction Film* (Madison: University of Wisconsin Press, 1985), 156–204.

69. Kyle Cooper set the fashion with his credits for *Se7en* and *Donnie Brasco* (1997). See Andrea Codrington, *Kyle Cooper* (London: Laurence King, 2003).

70. See Bordwell, Staiger, and Thompson, *Classical Hollywood Cinema*, 29, 44, 73–74; Bordwell, *Narration in the Fiction Film*, 186–88.

71. On this connection, see the comments on script structure in Erich Leon Harris, *African-American Screenwriters Now: Conversations with Hollywood's Black Pack* (Los Angeles: Silman-James, 1996), 11–12, 95–96, 141, 183. The three-act structure in independent films is examined in J. J. Murphy's forthcoming study of the American independent screenplay.

72. André Bazin, "On the *politique des auteurs*," in *Cahiers du cinéma: The 1950s: Neo-Realism, Hollywood, New Wave*, ed. Jim Hillier (Cambridge, MA: Harvard University Press, 1985), 258.

73. For a comprehensive survey, see Kevin Heffernan, *Ghouls, Gimmicks, and Gold: Horror Films and the American Movie Business, 1953–1968* (Durham, NC: Duke University Press, 2004).

74. See Adam Minns, "Comic Giant Fights for International Supremacy," *Screen International* (June 25, 2004): 7, and Tom Russo, "Monster Ink," *Entertainment Weekly* (May 10, 2002): 38–45.

75. A good discussion of *Raiders'* sources can be found in Ian Freer, *The Complete Spielberg* (London: Virgin, 2001), 97.

76. Quoted in Tom Shone, *Blockbuster: How Hollywood Learned to Stop Worrying and Love the Summer* (New York: Free Press, 2004), 12.

77. This is not to say that a genre or style can be exhausted; I doubt it. I'm trying merely to describe a shared sense among artists that it's very hard to compete in well-covered areas. Indeed, probably one feature that defines a classic is that successors think that it forecloses certain options.

78. Quoted in Todd McCarthy, *Howard Hawks: The Grey Fox of Hollywood* (New York: Grove, 2000), 159.

79. See the interview with Ernest Lehman in Brady, *Craft of the Screenwriter*, 182.

80. See McKee, *Story*, 35; Brady, *Craft of the Screenwriter*, 285; and Russin and Downs, *Screenplay*, 162. Longer scenes still seem to be the rule in films adapted from plays, like *Glengarry Glen Ross* (1992).

81. Quoted in Paul M. Sammon, *Future Noir: The Making of Blade Runner* (New York: HarperCollins, 1996), 47.

82. Quoted in Claire Clouzot, "The Morning of the Magician: George Lucas and *Star Wars*," in *George Lucas: Interviews*, ed. T. Jefferson Kline (Oxford: University Press of Mississippi, 1999), 58.

83. See Olen J. Earnest, "*Star Wars*: A Case Study of Motion Picture Marketing," in *Current Research in Film: Audiences, Economics, and Law*, vol. 1, ed. Bruce A. Austin (Norwood, NJ: Ablex, 1985), 1–18.

84. Thomas Schatz pointed to this "intertextuality" as a feature of blockbusters aimed at youth audiences. See Schatz, "The New Hollywood," in *Film Theory Goes to the Movies*, ed. Jim Collins, Hilary Radner, and Ava Preacher Collins (London: Routledge, 1993), 33–34.

85. Quoted in Clouzot, "The Morning of the Magician," 58.

86. A massive multiplayer online game of *The Matrix*, launched in 2004, was designed to "carry on the franchise," says an executive at Warner Bros. Interactive. "What happens in *The Matrix Online* is considered canon for the property." (Noah Robischon, "Will Gamers Save *The Matrix?*" *Entertainment Weekly* [November 5, 2004]: 48). Henry Jenkins discusses the current interest in worldmaking in "Searching for the Origami Unicorn: The Matrix and Trans-Media Storytelling" (lecture, University of Wisconsin, Madison, February 28, 2004). See also Jenkins, "Trans-Media Storytelling," *Technology Review* (January 15, 2003), available at www/technologyreview.com.

87. Xan Brooks, "We Are All Nerds Now," *The Guardian*, December 12, 2003, available at http://film.guardian.co.uk/features/featurepages/0,4120,1104848,00 .html.

88. Quoted in Mary Kaye Schilling, "The Second Coming," *Entertainment Weekly* (April 16, 2004): 29.

89. See the Miramax official website: www.killbill.movies.go.com/Kill-Bill -Production-Notes.pdf and *"Kill Bill* Study Guide" at www.hkflix.com/coupons/ hkflix_03-10-10.

90. See Mike Goodridge, "Tarantino Plots Anime Prequel to *Kill Bill*," *Screen Daily* (April 5, 2004) at www.screendaily.com/story.asp?storyid=17053.

91. Thompson, *Storytelling in the New Hollywood*, 11.

92. Interestingly, this is not a clue that Lecter intentionally drops; it's another screenwriting touch for the discerning viewer.

93. Thompson, *Storytelling in the New Hollywood*, 110.

94. I try to show that the film adheres to classical conventions in *"Die Hard und die Rückkehr des klassischen Hollywood-Kinos"* (*Die Hard* and the Return of Classical Hollywood Cinema), in *Der schöne Schein der Künstlichkeit* (The Beautiful Illusion of Artifice), ed. Andreas Rost (Frankfurt: Verlag der Autoren, 1995), 151–201.

95. For a detailed discussion of *American Graffiti's* handling of the compilation soundtrack convention, see Jeff Smith, *The Sounds of Commerce: Marketing Popular Film Music* (New York: Columbia University Press, 1998), 172–85.

96. Ted Elliott, quoted in Jeff Goldsmith, "The Craft of Writing the Tentpole Movie," *Creative Screenwriting* 11, no. 3 (May–June 2004): 53; italics mine.

97. Cameron Crowe, "Leave 'Em Laughing," in *The First Time I Got Paid for It: Writers' Tales from the Hollywood Trenches*, ed. Peter Lefcourt and Laura J. Shapiro (New York: Public Affairs, 2000), 30–35.

98. The best of these is Linda Aronson, *Screenwriting Updated: New (and Conventional) Ways of Writing for the Screen* (Beverly Hills: Silman-James, 2000). Nonlinear plot structures are also discussed in Seger, *Advanced Screenwriting*, 1–36.

99. The *Simpsons* episodes I have in mind are "22 Short Films about Springfield" (airdate April 14, 1996), a network narrative, and "Trilogy of Terror" (airdate April 29, 2001), which recounts a day's events from Homer's point of view, then Lisa's, and finally from Bart's. *Lion King* 1½ retells *The Lion King*

by organizing the plot around Timon the meerkat. It starts by showing his fraught relationship with his mother and then presents his original meeting with Pumbaa the warthog. Their story line eventually catches up with the original's main action, which is usually just glimpsed or relegated to the background of scenes between the two, in the manner of *Rosencrantz and Guildenstern Are Dead.* The parody is framed within a theater situation: Timon and Pumbaa watch the film with us, sometimes fast-forwarding or freezing sequences.

100. Quoted in Rob Feld, "Q and A with Charlie Kaufman," in Charlie Kaufman, *Eternal Sunshine of the Spotless Mind* (New York: Newmarket, 2004), 141.

101. Andy Klein, "Everything You Wanted to Know about *Memento,*" http://dir.salon.com/ent/movies/feature/2001/06/28/memento_analysis, 4.

102. Quoted in Chuck Stephens, "Past Imperfect," *Filmmaker* 9, no. 2 (Winter 2001): 86.

103. Soderbergh's admiration crystallized in a book interweaving a diary of his film projects with interviews with Lester: *Getting Away with It, or: The Further Adventures of the Luckiest Bastard You Ever Saw* (London: Faber and Faber, 1999).

104. Thanks to Jonathan Frome for this anecdote.

105. Quoted in James Riordan, *Stone: The Controversies, Excesses, and Exploits of a Radical Filmmaker* (New York: Hyperion, 1995), 405.

106. For a sensitive discussion of narrative and sound-image juxtapositions in *JFK,* see Art Simon, *Dangerous Knowledge: The JFK Assassination in Art and Film* (Philadelphia: Temple University Press, 1996), 209–19.

107. See Bordwell, *Narration in the Fiction Film,* 205–28. Some examples of this strategy can be found in Kieślowski's *Blind Chance* (1981) and Varda's *Sans toit ni loi* (aka *Vagabond,* 1985).

108. For an account of the film's publicity campaign, see James Mottram, *The Making of "Memento"* (London: Faber and Faber, 2000), 67–77. Naturally, Mottram chronicles the phases of production and distribution in reverse order.

109. Barbara Klinger suggests that young people often lump enigma-based movies together with other films that reward multiple viewings, such as *Trainspotting, Apocalypse Now,* and *Airplane!* She offers a multidimensional definition of the puzzle film and convincingly argues that this "supergenre" plays the role of defending marginal tastes and gaining "subcultural capital" for its participants. See *Beyond the Multiplex: Cinema, New Technologies, and the Home* (Berkeley and Los Angeles: University of California Press, 2006). In this section, my definition of the puzzle film is narrower and doesn't include narrative strategies that might also invite repeated viewing. Spectators might, for instance, revisit richly articulated worlds to discover new details of the milieu, or they might rewatch a film for more traditional aesthetic reasons, such as observing subtle coherence or deepening their emotional engagement.

Of course, films have always been open to repeated consumption. In the days before video, I saw *A Hard Day's Night* at least six times in its initial release, and *Jaws* made a great deal of its money from recidivists. Until the 1980s, rereleases of successful films were a significant part of a studio's annual output. Cable and home video have made it more apparent that everybody finds *some* movies worth watching endlessly. In this respect, movies have become like favorite books or musical pieces, to be savored at the consumer's convenience.

110. There is, needless to say, nothing to prevent viewers from finding puzzles in any narrative stratagem. We can turn *The Sixth Sense* into a "deep" puzzle film by asking questions the narration delicately avoids (how does the protagonist buy food or talk to passersby?). But posing such questions exemplifies a basic human skill, inferential elaboration in fleshing out a schematic situation, and the results are in principle endless (vide conspiracy theories). No narrative, indeed no human action, can anticipate all possible questions that might be asked about it. By opening the door a little wider than usual, puzzle films may encourage spectators to go far beyond what they're given—farther than any storyteller can anticipate.

111. Parker Tyler, *Magic and Myth of the Movies* (London: Secker and Warburg, 1971), 121.

112. Dancyger and Rush, *Alternative Screenwriting*, 201–3.

113. Bordwell, Staiger, and Thompson, *Classical Hollywood Cinema*, 42–44, 181–83.

114. Herman, *A Practical Manual*, 66; Vale, *Technique of Screenplay Writing*, 64.

115. See Bordwell, Staiger, and Thompson, *Classical Hollywood Cinema*, 43. See also my essay, "Neo-Structuralist Narratology and the Functions of Filmic Storytelling," in *Narrative across Media: The Languages of Storytelling*, ed. Marie-Laure Ryan (Lincoln: University of Nebraska Press, 2004), 215–17.

116. Quoted in Jeff Dawson, *Quentin Tarantino: The Cinema of Cool* (New York: Applause, 1995), 69–70.

117. On these forking-path narratives, see my "Film Futures," *Substance*, no. 97 (2002): 88–104.

118. Thompson, *Storytelling in the New Hollywood*, 131–54.

119. Cowgill, *Secrets*, 159–65; Aronson, *Screenwriting Updated*, 129–36.

120. Murray Smith, "Parallel Lines," in *American Independent Cinema*, ed. Jim Hillier (London: British Film Institute, 2000), 155–60.

121. Kenneth Tynan, "Thornton Wilder," in *Profiles*, selected and edited by Kathleen Tynan and Ernie Eban (New York: Random House, 1995), 106.

122. Thompson, *Storytelling in the New Hollywood*, 45–47.

123. See Tom Schulman's comments on his script in Wolff and Cox, *Top Secrets*, 268.

124. Evan Smith, "Thread Structure: Rewriting the Hollywood Formula," *Journal of Film and Video* 51, nos. 3–4 (Fall/Winter 1999–2000): 88–89. See also Cowgill, *Secrets*, 124.

125. For a detailed analysis of *Hannah and Her Sisters*, see Thompson, *Storytelling in the New Hollywood*, 307–34.

126. See Cowgill, *Secrets*, 128.

127. William Froug calls this the "ark picture," depicting "a group of people all caught in the same difficult circumstances" in *Screenwriting Tricks of the*

Trade (Beverly Hills: Silman-James, 1993), 54–55. His examples include not only disaster films but also films like *Lifeboat* and *Aliens*.

128. Probably *Four Weddings and a Funeral* isn't best considered a multiple-protagonist film, since the romantic fortunes of Charles and Carrie form the armature of the action. Still, the saliency of the secondary characters gives it the flavor of an ensemble piece, as does the clever decision to show only plot nodes associated with weddings and funerals.

129. A counterpart outside Hollywood is Alejandro González Iñárritu's *Amores Perros* (2000), in which an opening car crash sends ripples through several lives. Interestingly, like *Three Strangers*, *Amores Perros* feels obliged to bring all three characters back at the Climax, cutting among them to create a narration-based convergence that resolves each story line.

130. Stephen Halliwell, *The Poetics of Aristotle: Translation and Commentary* (Chapel Hill: University of North Carolina Press, 1987), 63.

131. Henry James, *The Art of the Novel: Critical Prefaces* (New York: Scribner's, 1962), 5.

132. For a nontechnical overview, see Philip Ball, *Critical Mass: How One Thing Leads to Another* (New York: Farrar, Straus and Giroux, 2004), 352–401.

133. Daniel Clowes, *Fightball* no. 22 (October 2001).

134. In the DVD commentary, Richard Curtis remarks that he had hoped that all the subplots would be allotted three scenes, "ten good beginnings, ten good middles, and ten good ends" (*Love Actually* commentary track, chap. 5, 36:02). See also Richard Curtis, *Love Actually* (New York: St. Martin's Press, 2003), where he compares his movie to *Nashville* ("my favorite film," 2) and which contains an affiliation diagram typical of network narratives (6–7).

135. Quoted in Goldsmith, "Craft of Writing the Tentpole Movie," 53.

136. Halliwell, *Poetics of Aristotle*, 37.

137. Murray Smith, "Theses on the Philosophy of Hollywood History," in *Contemporary Hollywood Cinema*, ed. Steve Neale and Murray Smith (London: Routledge, 1998), 13.

138. Geoff King makes this point in *Spectacular Narratives: Hollywood in the Age of the Blockbuster* (London: I. B. Tauris, 2000), 105–9, 113–14. See also his *New Hollywood Cinema: An Introduction* (New York: Columbia University Press, 2002), 202–8, where he analyzes the causal coherence of *Die Hard with a Vengeance* (1995) using concepts of construction set out in Bordwell, Staiger, and Thompson, *Classical Hollywood Cinema*.

139. I discuss Hong Kong plotting and principles of unity in *Planet Hong Kong: Popular Cinema and the Art of Entertainment* (Cambridge, MA: Harvard University Press, 2000), 18–25, 178–98.

140. James Schamus, "To the Rear of the Back End: The Economics of Independent Cinema," in Neale and Smith, *Contemporary Hollywood Cinema*, 94.

141. Quoted in Martin Barker and Kate Brooks, *Judge Dredd: Its Friends, Fans and Foes* (Luton, Bedfordshire: University of Luton Press, 1998), 149–50.

142. Steven E. DeSouza, quoted in Wolff and Cox, *Top Secrets*, 68.

143. Jack Epps Jr. and Jim Cash quoted in Froug, *The New Screenwriter*, 325.

144. Steven E. DeSouza, quoted in Wolff and Cox, *Top Secrets*, 68.

145. A thoughtful history of how violent physical action was presented and censored is Stephen Prince's *Classical Film Violence: Designing and Regulating Brutality in Hollywood Cinema, 1930–1968* (Rutgers: Rutgers University Press, 2003).

146. For a useful account of this cycle, see Yannick Dahan, "Le film d'action," *Positif* no. 443 (January 1998): 70–74.

147. Rex Weiner, "Actioners Speak Louder than Words," *Variety* (October 16–22, 1995): 11.

148. On Hong Kong's move to Hollywood-style action pictures, see Bordwell, *Planet Hong Kong*, 208. Rick Richardson discusses the genre's success in Poland in "Auds Line Up for Domestic Action Pix," *Variety* (July 28–August 3, 1997): 35, 44.

149. The only other genre that contains so many explicit and detailed rules would seem to be romantic comedy, as revealed beat-by-beat in the excellent manual by Mernit, *Writing the Romantic Comedy*.

150. Martell, *Secrets of Action Screenwriting*.

151. Martell, *Secrets of Action Screenwriting*, 237. *Die Hard* is also taken as the canonical example in Neill D. Hicks, *Writing the Action-Adventure Film: The Moment of Truth* (Studio City, CA: Michael Wiese, 2001), xi.

152. For some viewers, the Climax, which traces the bomber's efforts to escape in a subway hijacking, feels somewhat tacked on, given the impressive arc of excitement during the bus sequences. I agree, and so does the screenwriter (DVD commentary for *Speed*, chap. 26, 90:10). Still, the filmmakers have tried to smooth the transition via recurring motifs and the overarching idea of speed. Plot coherence is often a compromise, and the finest-woven plots are those that take advantage of such trade-offs.

153. DeSouza, quoted in Wolff and Cox, *Top Secrets*, 67; Martell, *Secrets of Action Screenwriting*, 51–53; Field, *Selling a Screenplay*, 81–83.

154. Quoted in Wolff and Cox, *Top Secrets*, 69, 70.

PART II. A STYLISH STYLE

Epigraph: Andrew Sarris, *Confessions of a Cultist* (New York: Simon & Schuster, 1971), 447.

1. Harold F. Kress, quoted in Gabriella Oldham, *First Cut: Conversations with Film Editors* (Berkeley and Los Angeles: University of California Press, 1992), 86.

2. Quoted in Sean M. Smith, "Who Does Brett Ratner Think He Is," *Premiere* (November 2002): 101.

3. Quoted in Scott Macauley, "Tracking Shots," *FilmMaker* 12, no. 1 (Fall 2003): 88.

4. Principles of continuity filmmaking are surveyed in David Bordwell and Kristin Thompson, *Film Art: An Introduction*, 7th ed. (New York: McGraw-Hill, 2004), 310–33. See also Tom Kingdon's comprehensive and thoughtful manual,

Total Directing: Integrating Camera and Performance in Film and Television (Los Angeles: Silman-James, 2004).

5. With the popularization of 16mm and 8mm filming in the postwar years, manuals aimed at a general readership began to appear. These also served as textbooks for the growing number of college filmmaking courses. Some examples are Arthur L. Gaskill and David A. Englander, *How to Shoot a Movie Story: The Technique of Pictorial Continuity* (New York: Duell, Sloan & Pearce, 1947); Emil E. Brodbeck, *Handbook of Basic Motion-Picture Techniques* (New York: McGraw-Hill, 1950); Raymond Spottiswoode, *Film and Its Techniques* (Berkeley and Los Angeles: University of California Press, 1951); Don Livingston, *Film and the Director* (New York: Macmillan, 1953); Karel Reisz, *The Technique of Film Editing* (New York: Hastings House, 1958); Joseph V. Mascelli, *The Five C's of Cinematography: Motion Picture Filming Techniques Simplified* (Hollywood: Cine/Grafic, 1965); Richard L. Bare, *The Film Director: A Practical Guide to Motion Picture and Television Techniques* (New York: Macmillan, 1971); and Terence St. John Marner, *Directing Motion Pictures* (London: Tantivy, 1972).

6. Jeff Gordinier, "1999: The Year That Changed Movies," *Entertainment Weekly* (November 26, 1999): 40. Chris Hodenfield claims that in the 1930s "the average film might be composed of no more than 150 cuts of film" ("Is Hollywood Dying the Death of a Thousand Cuts?" *Premiere* [July 2002]: 45).

7. Robert Primes remarks in "ASC Message to Japan," *Widescreen Review* 4, no. 6 (November–December 1995), 22. See also John Hora, "Cinematographers Publicly Oppose HDTV Standard: The American Society of Cinematographers' Viewpoint," *Widescreen Review* 4, no. 6 (November–December 1995): 98. The figure 1,200 seems to hold a powerful appeal for filmmakers; George Miller recalls *Road Warrior* (1981) as having that number of shots (Rob Medich, "What Is the Perfect Chase?" *Premiere* [March 2003]: 28), but I count 1,499.

8. The concept of average shot length derives from Barry Salt, *Film Style and Technology: History and Analysis,* 2d ed. (London: Starword, 1992), 142–47. All ASLs here are based on watching the entire film and dividing its running length, given in seconds, by the number of shots. Both images and intertitles are counted as shots, but production credits are not.

My estimates of studio-era norms are taken from David Bordwell, Janet Staiger, and Kristin Thompson, *The Classical Hollywood Cinema: Film Style and Mode of Production to 1960* (New York: Columbia University Press, 1985), 60–63. Salt's results from the post-1960 period can be found in *Film Style and Technology,* 214–15, 236–40, and 249. Whereas Salt seeks to condense the average shot lengths of a period into a "Mean Average Shot Length," Bordwell et al. argue for thinking of ASLs as occupying a range of probable choice.

More generally, ASL is a helpful but fairly blunt instrument. Naturally a film with one 10-minute take and eight hundred short shots can have the same ASL as one with fewer but approximately equal shots. Other measures of central tendency, such as mode and median, would allow us to make finer distinctions.

9. The rest of this essay draws its evidence from a group of over eight hundred Anglophone films made or distributed by U.S. companies, from the years

1961–2004. For each decade before the 2000s, I chose at least 135 films, and each year was represented by at least twelve titles. The corpus was not the result of a random sample; strict random sampling is not feasible for examining a body of films, because vagaries of preservation and canons of taste do not give each film made an equal chance of being studied. (See Bordwell, Staiger, and Thompson, *Classical Hollywood Cinema*, 388–89.) I have tried to pick films from a wide range of genres and directors, from both influential examples and casual items that fate has thrown my way. The sample is based on theatrical releases and may not hold good for straight-to-video titles.

10. For a detailed discussion of Peckinpah's rapid cutting, see Bernard F. Dukore, *Sam Peckinpah's Feature Films* (Urbana: University of Illinois Press, 1999), 77–150.

11. Salt finds a shortening in Mean ASL from 11 seconds to about 7 seconds in the period from 1958 to 1975, and a lengthening to 8.4 seconds in the years 1976–1987, though he is more tentative about the latter results (*Film Style and Technology*, 265, 283, 296). My results roughly agree with his for the first period, but for the second I find little evidence of a tendency for shots to lengthen. I cannot explain the discrepancy fully, but two factors may be relevant.

First, Salt's decision to seek a single Mean ASL for a period, instead of a range of more and less likely options, may skew the result, because a few very long-take films, such as those of Woody Allen, can push the average up farther than a few very fast-cut films can push it down. If most films of the period come in at around 6 seconds, as Salt believes, a few films with 12-to-20-second ASLs will push the mean more places upward than several films with 2-to-4-second ASLs can depress it.

Second, in the only publication in which Salt has explained his viewing procedures, he indicates that counting the shots during the first thirty to forty minutes of a film yielded an adequate measure of ASL ("Statistical Style Analysis of Motion Pictures," *Film Quarterly* 28, no. 1 [Fall 1974]: 14–15). In my experience, this isn't a trustworthy assumption about contemporary films, since a great many of them are cut significantly faster in the final stretches. The first 55 minutes of *Jaws* (1975) yield an ASL of 8.8 seconds, but the film as a whole has an ASL of 6.5 seconds. Sampling 34 minutes into *M*A*S*H* (1970) yields an ASL of 9.7 seconds, but the overall ASL is 7.0 seconds. If we sampled only the first 35 minutes of *Body Snatchers* (1994), we'd find an ASL of 10.8 seconds, significantly high for the period, but the ASL of the entire film is 7.7 seconds. Many modern filmmakers seem deliberately to weight the first part with long takes in order to enhance a fast-cut Climax. Perhaps, then, some of Salt's figures on 1976–1987 films derive from the sampling of only opening portions.

12. Other examples from 2001 are *Driven*, *Replicant*, and *Lara Croft: Tomb Raider*; from 2002 *The Transporter*; from 2003 *Bad Boys II* and *Paycheck*; from 2004 *Torque*, *The Bourne Supremacy*, *Sky Captain and the World of Tomorrow*, and *The Incredibles*.

13. Roman Polanski forsook a 15-to-16-second rate in *Rosemary's Baby* (1969) and *Chinatown* (1974) for an ASL of 7.8 seconds in *The Ninth Gate*

(1999). Likewise, Mike Nichols's *Wolf* (1994) and *The Birdcage* (1996), with ASLs of around 7 seconds, mark a dramatic change from *The Graduate* (1967; 17.8 seconds ASL) and *Carnal Knowledge* (1971; 25.5 seconds ASL).

14. Mike Nichols in DVD commentary for *Catch-22*, chap. 2, 10:35–10:54.

15. Todd McCarthy, "Noisy 'Armageddon' Plays 'Con' Game," *Variety* (June 29–July 12, 1998): 38.

16. See Sidney Lumet, *Making Movies* (New York: Knopf, 1995), 84.

17. See John Alonzo, "Behind the Scenes of 'Chinatown,'" *American Cinematographer* 56, no. 5 (May 1975): 572. See also my *On the History of Film Style* (Cambridge, MA: Harvard University Press, 1997), 238–44.

18. Telephoto lenses are long-focus lenses that have optically telescoped the lens elements so that they are physically shorter than their stated focal length. Thus a prime lens of 500mm length is physically longer than a telephoto lens of equal focal length. See Paul Wheeler, *Practical Cinematography* (Oxford: Focal Press, 2000), 28.

19. For more on this trend, see Bordwell, *On the History of Film Style*, 246–53.

20. See Joseph V. Mascelli, "The Technique of Follow-Focus," *American Cinematographer* 38, no. 12 (December 1957): 788–89, 810–12.

21. Verna Field uses this term in Tony Macklin and Nik Pici, eds., *Voices from the Set: The Film Heritage Interviews* (Lanham, MD: Scarecrow, 2000), 243, where she discusses the shots in *Jaws* shown in Figs. 2.13–2.14.

22. John Belton, "The Bionic Eye: Zoom Esthetics," *Cineaste* 9, no. 1 (Winter 1980–81): 26.

23. For more discussion, see Bordwell, *On the History of Film Style*, 253–60.

24. Quoted in James Riordan, *Stone: The Controversies, Excesses, and Exploits of a Radical Filmmaker* (New York: Hyperion, 1995), 154.

25. Gil Bettman, *First Time Director: How to Make Your Breakthrough Movie* (Studio City, CA: Michael Wiese, 2003), 113.

26. Cinematographer Ed Lachman and director Todd Haynes used nothing longer than a 40mm lens on *Far from Heaven* in homage to the Sirk films that inspired them. See Jon Silberg, "A Scandal in Suburbia," *American Cinematographer* 83, no. 12 (December 2002): 62.

27. Rick Lyman, "Memory's Independent Streak: Watching Movies with Harvey Weinstein," *New York Times*, April 27, 2001.

28. Quoted in *Schrader on Schrader*, ed. Kevin Hackson (London: Faber, 1990), 205.

29. "I shoot in long takes because I was trained in the theater. And I'm impatient. I don't like to sit in an editing room for a year." Quoted in Theodore Gershuny, *Soon to Be a Major Motion Picture: The Anatomy of an All-Star Big Budget Multimillion-Dollar Disaster* (New York: Holt, Rinehart and Winston, 1980), 25.

30. Quoted in *Directing the Film: Film Directors on Their Art*, ed. Eric Sherman (Boston: Little, Brown, 1976), 128.

31. See Jon Boorstin, *Making Movies Work: Thinking Like a Filmmaker* (Los Angeles: Silman-James, 1990), 90–97.

32. Quoted in Lyman, "Memory's Independent Streak."

33. For an example, see my discussion of a scene in *Jerry Maguire* in *Figures Traced in Light: On Cinematic Staging* (Berkeley and Los Angeles: University of California Press, 2005), 23–28.

34. Paul Seydor, "Trims, Clips, and Selects: Notes from the Cutting Room," *The Perfect Vision*, no. 26 (September–October 1999): 27.

35. Throughout *Secrets of Screen Acting* (London: Routledge, 1994), Patrick Tucker assumes that film acting is facial. He advises actors on how to cheat their faces to the camera in tight shots, how to react in close-up, and how to speak in close-up (44–45, 55–57, 75). Blocking, he remarks, "is a way of getting the camera to see your face" (129). See also Steve Carlson, *Hitting Your Mark: What Every Actor Really Needs to Know on a Hollywood Set* (Studio City, CA: Michael Wiese, 1998), 23–47, 63–81.

36. Jay Holben, "Alter Ego," *American Cinematographer* 81, no. 1 (January 2000): 70.

37. "When you go to the wider shots it gets all mushy," says cinematographer Uta Briesewitz, quoted in Patricia Thomson, "Horror in Hi-Def," *American Cinematographer* 82, no. 4 (April 2001): 67.

38. Miguel Arteta, quoted in Holly Willis, "The Art and Craft of Shooting DV," *Independent Film & Video Monthly* (November 1999): 39.

39. Quoted in "Emotion Pictures: Quentin Tarantino Talks to Brian De Palma," in *Brian De Palma Interviews*, ed. Lawrence F. Knapp (Jackson: University Press of Mississippi, 2003), 148.

40. Quoted in Mike Figgis, ed., *Projections 10: Hollywood Film-makers on Film-making* (London: Faber and Faber, 1999), 108.

41. Several types of contemporary camera movements are discussed in Jeremy Vineyard, *Setting Up Your Shots: Great Camera Moves Every Filmmaker Should Know* (Studio City, CA: Michael Wiese, 2000), 35–50.

42. Nonetheless, the camera movements in *Obsession* look discreet by comparison with the extravagant arcs around the transgressing couple in *Body Double* (1984).

43. *Schrader on Schrader*, ed. Kevin Jackson (London: Faber and Faber, 1990), 211.

44. Quoted in Anthony Decurtis, "What the Streets Mean," in *Martin Scorsese Interviews*, ed. Peter Brunette (Jackson: University Press of Mississippi, 1999), 181.

45. Bettman, *First Time Director*, 55.

46. Newton Thomas Sigel combined creeping zooms and push-ins for *The Usual Suspects*, and thereby, in one writer's words, "added subtle energy to scenes despite cramped practical locations and short shooting schedules" (David E. Williams, "Unusual Suspects," *American Cinematographer* 81, no. 7 [July 2000]: 38). The prevalence of this belief is illustrated by the remark of another cinematographer, John Seale: "I dislike gratuitous camera movement. When the director tries to use the camera to create energy in a scene, it's normally a sign that something is wrong with the script or the performance" (quoted in *Screen-*

craft: Cinematography, ed. Peter Ettedgui [Crans-Près-Seligny: RotoVision, 1998], 139).

47. Quoted in Joseph McBride, *Steven Spielberg: A Biography* (Simon & Schuster, 1997), 218.

48. On the expressive and decorative functions of style, see my *Figures Traced in Light*, 34–35.

49. Thanks to editor Danny Goldberg for his helpful comments on these points.

50. *Star Wars Episode IV: A New Hope* (1977) has an ASL of 3.4 seconds, quite short for the 1970s. *Episode V: The Return of the Jedi* (1983) has an ASL of 3.5 seconds, and *Episode I: The Phantom Menace* (1999) has an ASL of 3.8 seconds. *Episode II: The Attack of the Clones* (2002) is even more rapidly cut, averaging 2.5 seconds per shot.

51. Richard T. Jameson, "Style vs. 'Style,'" *Film Comment* 16, no. 2 (March–April 1980): 9–14.

52. See Noël Carroll, "The Future of Allusion: Hollywood in the Seventies (and Beyond)," in *Interpreting the Moving Image* (Cambridge: Cambridge University Press, 1998), 261.

53. Todd McCarthy, "'Gladiator' Prevails," *Variety* (April 24–30, 2000): 27–32.

54. Todd McCarthy, "Spy Pic's Bourne to Be Wild," *Variety* (July 26–August 1, 2004): 61.

55. Arijon presumes, for instance, that the director will rely on tight close-ups; see his *Grammar of the Film Language* (London: Focal Press, 1976), 112.

56. See, for example, Steven D. Katz, *Film Directing Shot by Shot: Visualizing from Concept to Screen* (Studio City, CA: Michael Wiese, 1991), 300, 315.

57. Quoted in David Edelstein, "NYU Rushes the Tinsel League," *Village Voice*, December 3, 1985.

58. Gregory Goodell, *Independent Feature Film Production*, 2d ed. (New York: St. Martin's Press, 1998), 222–23.

59. The ASLs run: *Mystery Train* (1989), 23 seconds; *Night on Earth* (1991), 11.3 seconds; *Dead Man* (1995), 8.2 seconds; *Ghost Dog: The Way of the Samurai* (1999), 6.8 seconds.

60. Quoted in Michael Fleming, "Lone Star," *Fade In* 7, no. 3 (2003): 45. For more on the wrangles around *All the Pretty Horses*, see Peter Biskind, *Down and Dirty Pictures: Miramax, Sundance, and the Rise of Independent Film* (New York: Simon & Schuster, 2004), 419–23.

61. See David Bordwell, *Planet Hong Kong: Popular Cinema and the Art of Entertainment* (Cambridge, MA: Harvard University Press, 2000), 22–25, 162–68, 224–45.

62. "I think," remarks West Coast editor Verna Fields, "that Dede was probably one of the early people who was not afraid of film at all and were willing to go into quick cuts" (quoted in Macklin and Pici, *Voices from the Set*, 239). On Allen's influence on the "New York School" of editors, see Ric Gentry, "An Interview with Dede Allen," *Film Quarterly* 46, no. 1 (Fall 1992): 12–22.

63. On *The Pawnbroker*'s subliminal cuts, see the somewhat differing ac-

counts offered in Lumet, *Making Movies,* 158–61, and in Ralph Rosenblum and Robert Karen, *When the Shooting Stops . . . The Cutting Begins: A Film Editor's Story* (New York: Viking, 1979), 148–53.

64. Quoted in Gentry, "Interview with Dede Allen," 21. Allen remarks that her cutting eventually became influential. "Even the way commercials are cut, with all that acceleration, was something that *Bonnie and Clyde* helped to start" (22).

65. See Joseph Gelmis, *The Film Director as Superstar* (New York: Doubleday, 1970), 184.

66. Lev Kuleshov, "Art of the Cinema," in *Kuleshov on Film,* trans. and ed. Ronald Levaco (Berkeley and Los Angeles: University of California Press, 1974), 67–109; V. I. Pudovkin, *Film Technique and Film Acting,* trans. and ed. Ivor Montagu (New York: Grove Press, 1960), 87–109.

67. John Simon, *Private Screenings: Views of the Cinema of the Sixties* (New York: Berkley, 1971), 104.

68. Andrew Sarris, *Confessions of a Cultist: On the Cinema, 1955/1969* (New York: Simon & Schuster, 1971), 101.

69. Dwight MacDonald, *On Movies* (1969; repr., New York: Da Capo, 1989), 393.

70. MacDonald, *On Movies,* 147.

71. Pauline Kael, "The Making of *The Group,*" *Kiss Kiss Bang Bang* (Boston: Atlantic Little-Brown, 1968), 82, 84.

72. Ironically, Lumet would become a model of restraint in later years. Many scenes in *Prince of the City* (1981), *The Verdict* (1982), and *Q & A* (1990) rely on both long takes and distant, quite static shots.

73. Sidney Lumet, DVD commentary for *Fail-Safe,* chap. 14, 56:43–57:18.

74. I discuss Eisenstein's ideas of through-composed stylistic patterning in *The Cinema of Eisenstein* (Cambridge, MA: Harvard University Press, 1994), 156–60.

75. See Lumet, *Making Movies,* 81.

76. The rationale for this model of explanation is provided in Bordwell, Staiger, and Thompson, *The Classical Hollywood Cinema,* 3–11. The transition to sound is discussed on 298–308.

77. On this problem-solving model more generally, see my *On the History of Film Style,* 268–70; and *Figures Traced in Light,* 249–54.

78. Vincent Canby, "A Revolution Reshapes Movies," *New York Times,* January 7, 1990. See also Janet Wasko, *Hollywood in the Information Age* (Cambridge, England: Polity, 1994), 166–67.

79. Quoted in David Williams, "Reintroducing Bond . . . James Bond," *American Cinematographer* 76, no. 12 (December 1995): 39.

80. See the comments gathered in Jack Kuney, *Take One: Television Directors on Directing* (New York: Praeger, 1990), 12, 29, 45, 46, 119. See also Frederick Y. Smith, "Rambling Thoughts of a Film Editor," *American Cinemeditor* 25, no. 2 (Summer 1975): 18–19. Director Bill Duke, shooting *Knots Landing* and *Falcon Crest,* remarked, "On our shows, we always do close-ups of everything we do. . . . [The shows] have certain formats and they expect you to get

very close coverage of all the major principals." Quoted in Jim Hillier, *The New Hollywood* (New York: Continuum, 1994), 155.

Despite practitioners' conceptions of the two media, we probably shouldn't see modern film as simply replicating TV style. With respect to shot scale, for instance, there wasn't and isn't just one televisual norm for film to match. Talk and game shows use long shots, while sitcoms and soaps rely on medium shots and *plans américains*. Video games are characteristically framed in long shot. Instead of blending the broadcast movie into the programming flow, filmmakers may have sought to create a distinct look for theatrical film *as seen on the box*, marking it with intense close-ups and flamboyant camera moves seldom found on other TV fare. (Still later, it seems, shows like *The X-Files* tried to look like a 1990s film as seen on TV.)

81. Herbert Zettl, *Television Production Handbook,* 3d ed. (Belmont, CA: Wadsworth, 1976), 72.

82. Steve Neale, "Widescreen Composition in the Age of Television," in *Contemporary Hollywood Cinema,* ed. Steve Neale and Murray Smith (London: Routledge, 1998), 130–41.

83. "In television," remarks Sydney Pollack, "you are always fighting for the viewers' attention because they watch in a lighted room, more often than not, with more than one person and all sorts of distractions" (quoted in Robert J. Emery, *The Directors: Take One* [New York: TV Books, 1999], 87).

84. Colby Lewis, *The TV Director/Interpreter* (New York: Hastings House, 1968), 164.

85. According to a *Laugh-In* editor, sometimes there were ten or more cuts per minute in parts of an episode. See Arthur Schneider and George Schlatter, *Jump Cut! Memoirs of a Pioneer Television Editor* (Jefferson, NC: McFarland, 1997), 131. An in-depth study of television techniques of the period I'm considering can be found in John Caldwell, *Televisuality: Style, Crisis, and Authority in American Television* (Rutgers: Rutgers University Press, 1995).

86. Quoted in O'Steene, *Cut to the Chase,* 24.

87. Chris Petit, "Pictures by Numbers," *Film Comment* 37, no. 2 (March–April 2001): 40.

88. Quoted in Covece, "The Greening of TV," *American Film* 12, no. 6 (April 1987): 52.

89. For examples of how TV commercials and music videos have influenced film, see Maria Demopoulos, "Blink of an Eye: Filmmaking in the Age of Bullet Time," *Film Comment* 36, no. 3 (May–June 2000): 34–39, and Ken Dancyger, *The Technique of Film and Video Editing: History, Theory, and Practice,* 3d ed. (Boston: Focal Press, 2002), 184–213.

90. Quoted in Nicholas Jarecki, *Breaking In: How 20 Film Directors Got Their Start* (New York: Broadway, 2001), 252. Ratner also claims that producers became interested in recruiting music-video directors when MTV started attaching the directors' names to the videos around 1992 (250).

91. Quoted in John Brodie and Dan Cox, "New Pix a Vidiot's Delight," *Variety* (October 28–November 3, 1996): 85.

92. On this practice, see the remarks in Jeremy Kagan, ed., *Directors Close Up* (Boston: Focal Press, 2000), 50–52, 55–56, 59, 63, 66, 71–72, 76–77.

93. For a good study of the video assist, see Jean-Pierre Geuens, "Through the Looking Glass: From the Camera Obscura to Video Assist," *Film Quarterly* 49, no. 3 (Spring 1996): 16–26. See also the historical information in Michael Frediani, "On the Set with Video Assist," *The Operating Cameraman* 5, no. 2 (Fall 1995/1996): 56–69, and David Samuelson, "More about Video Assist," *The Operating Cameraman* 6, no. 1 (Spring/Summer 1996): 49–50.

94. Cinematographer Roger Deakins offers several comments on how composing shots on a video monitor yields less attention to detail in *Cinematography: Screencraft*, ed. Peter Ettedgui (Crans-Près-Céligny, Switzerland: Rotovision, 1998), 166.

95. For a concise history of editing on video, see Gary H. Anderson, *Video Editing and Post-Production: A Professional Guide*, 4th ed. (Boston: Focal Press, 1999), 2–9.

96. Walter Murch, *In the Blink of an Eye: A Perspective on Film Editing* (Los Angeles: Silman-James, 1995), 88.

97. Editor Paul Seydor notes that long shots and extreme long shots might not read well on home TV monitors, especially if they come at the end of a scene, where they could be mistaken for an establishing shot opening the next scene. Although Seydor prefers to retain such shots, he notes that many editors might not do so. See "Trims, Clips," 29.

98. Christine Vachon and David Edelstein, *Shooting to Kill: How an Independent Producer Blasts through the Barriers to Make Movies That Matter* (New York: Avon, 1998), 265. See also Roy Perkins and Martin Stollery, *British Film Editors: "The Heart of the Movie"* (London: British Film Institute, 2004), 154.

99. The film was Lodge Kerrigan's *In God's Hands*. See "Double Vision," *Screen International* (November 7, 2003): 9. Also see Bob Fisher, "The Case for Film Dailies," *American Cinematographer* 85, no. 4 (April 2004): 90–94.

100. See Paul Mazursky's comments in Figgis, *Projections 10*, 25.

101. Quoted in Brunette, ed., *Martin Scorsese Interviews*, 155.

102. Ben Brewster and Lea Jacobs, *Theatre to Cinema: Stage Pictorialism and the Early Feature Film* (Oxford: Oxford University Press, 1997), 164–68.

103. William Paul, "Screening Space: Architecture, Technology, and the Motion Picture Screen," *Michigan Quarterly Review* 35, no. 1 (Winter 1996): 145–49.

104. Sven Nykvist, "Photographing 'Cannery Row,'" *American Cinematographer* 62, no. 4 (April 1981): 377.

105. Ann Thompson, "Steven Soderbergh," *Premiere* 14, no. 4 (December 2000): 65.

106. Rachel Abramowitz, *Is That a Gun in Your Pocket? Women's Experience of Power in Hollywood* (New York: Random House, 2000), 361.

107. James Lyon, quoted in Vachon and Edelstein, *Shooting to Kill*, 263.

108. Orson Welles and Peter Bogdanovich, *This Is Orson Welles* (New York: HarperCollins, 1992), 201.

109. Gelmis, *Film Director as Superstar*, 215–16.

110. In the silent era William C. de Mille often used multiple cameras to preserve the continuity of performance. See Peter Milne, *Motion Picture Directing* (New York: Falk, 1922), 45–46.

111. Andrew Yule, *Richard Lester and the Beatles* (New York: Primus, 1995), 14; Steven Soderbergh, *Getting Away with It, or: The Further Adventures of the Luckiest Bastard You Ever Saw* (London: Faber and Faber, 1999), 211–12.

112. Ray Carney, *Cassavetes on Cassavetes* (London: Faber and Faber, 2001), 177, 395.

113. See Stephen Prince, *Savage Cinema: Sam Peckinpah and the Rise of Ultraviolent Movies* (Austin: University of Texas Press, 1998), 51–56.

114. Verna Fields, "Dialogue on Film," *American Cinemeditor* 26, no. 3 (Fall 1976): 18.

115. Anonymous, "The Five Films Nominated for 'Best Cinematography' of 1980," *American Cinematographer* 62, no. 5 (May 1981): 503.

116. David Michael Petrou, *The Making of Superman: The Movie* (New York: Warner Books, 1978), 61.

117. John Mathieson, quoted in Douglas Bankston, "Death or Glory," *American Cinematographer* 81, no. 5 (May 2000): 38.

118. See Jean-Pierre Geuens, "Visuality and Power: The Work of the Steadicam," *Film Quarterly* 47, no. 2 (Winter 1993–1994): 13–14. See also Serena Ferrara, *Steadicam: Techniques and Aesthetics* (Oxford: Focal Press, 2001); and "Le Steadicam a-t-il une âme?" (Does the Steadicam Have a Soul?) *Vertigo*, no. 23 (2004)

119. Advertisement for Samuelson supply house of London, *American Cinematographer* 61, no. 11 (November 1980): 1124.

120. For a survey of aerial cameras, see David Weiner, "Bird's-Eye View," *American Cinematographer* 81, no. 8 (August 2000), 92–107. On the Flying-Cam see Elina Shatkin, "View to a Kill," *ICG Magazine* 75, no. 5 (May 2004): 41–42.

121. For general reviews, see John Calhoun, "Putting the 'Move' in Movie," *American Cinematographer* 84, no. 10 (October 2003): 72–85; David W. Samuelson, "A Brief History of Camera Mobility," *American Cinematographer* 84, no. 10 (October 2003): 86–96.

122. Quoted in Thom Taylor, *The Big Deal: Hollywood's Million-Dollar Spec Script Market* (New York: Morrow, 1999), 289.

123. For detailed accounts of the development of digital editing at the period, see two essays in *Transitions: Voices on the Craft of Digital Editing*, ed. Alan McCann (Birmingham, England: Friends of ED DVision, 2002): Eric C. Andersen, "The Changing Face of Editing I," 107–21, and Patrick Gregston, "The Changing Face of Editing II," 130–49.

124. See Peter Bart, *The Gross: The Hits, the Flops—The Summer That Ate Hollywood* (New York: St. Martin's, 1999), 232; and David Kleiler Jr. and Robert Moses, *You Stand There: Making Music Video* (New York: Three Rivers Press, 1997), 168.

125. David Ansen and Ray Sawhill, "The New Jump Cut," *Newsweek* (September 2, 1996): 66.

126. Quoted in Thomas A. Ohanian and Michael E. Phillips, *Digital Filmmaking: The Changing Art and Craft of Making Motion Pictures* (Boston: Focal Press, 1996), 177.

127. Quoted in Taylor, *The Big Deal*, 288.

128. Bruce A. Rady, "Editing Feature Films Electronically," *American Cinematographer* 40, no. 1 (Spring 1990): 28.

129. Other aspects of new work processes are discussed by Rebecca Swender in her essay "The Revolution Will Be Digitized: Digital Technology and the Distribution of Labor in the Cutting Room" (Madison: University of Wisconsin, 2004); Matt Rothman, "Cutting Rooms Invaded by Cutting-Edge Tech," *Variety* (June 21–27, 1993): 9; see "Summer Pic Push Addles Editors," *Variety* (May 15–21, 1995): 12, 16, and Ted Johnson, "Summer Pix Race Pushes Editors to Post Haste," *Variety* (March 17–23, 1997): 9, 12. After working around the clock on high-pressure productions, some editors reported computer-related health problems. See Katharine Stalter, "Editors Getting Short End," *Variety* (December 4–10, 1995): 34, 66; Katharine Stalter, "Digital Danger Flagged," *Variety* (March 11–17, 1996): 39.

130. Leonard Nimoy, quoted in Denise Abbott, "Film Maker Leonard Nimoy: Trekking Through Post-Production," *American Cinemeditor* 38, no. 3 (Fall 1988): 15.

131. The production of *Rosebud* is documented in Gershuny, *Soon to Be a Major Motion Picture*, 37–39, 73, 220, 281, 322–23.

132. On contemporary sound practices, there are illuminating essays in two collections: *New Perspectives in Sound Studies*, ed. Dominique Nasta and Didier Huvell (Brussels: P.I.E.-Peter Lang, 2003), and *Soundscape: The School of Sound Lectures 1998–2001*, ed. Larry Sider, Diane Freeman, and Jerry Sider (London: Wallflower, 2003).

133. Geoff King, *New Hollywood Cinema: An Introduction* (New York: Columbia University Press, 2002), 246.

134. Geoff King, *Spectacular Narratives: Hollywood in the Age of the Blockbuster* (I. B. Tauris, 2000), 91–116.

135. On Eason's pit shots, see Ezra Goodman, *The Fifty-Year Decline and Fall of Hollywood* (New York: Simon & Schuster, 1961), 300–302. Another specialist in stunts and action sequences, Yakima Canutt, suggested, "To put punch into it, put it right in the audience's lap" (quoted in Louis McMahon, *Yakima Canutt: A Directors Guild of America Oral History* [Los Angeles: Directors Guild of America, typescript (1977?)], tape 5B, 31).

136. William A. Fraker, "Why We Light," *ICG Magazine* 74, no. 12 (December 2003): 74. See also Tico Romao, "Guns and Gas: Investigating the 1970s Car Chase Film," in *Action and Adventure Cinema*, ed. Yvonne Tasker (New York: Routledge, 2004), 134–39.

137. Jackson expresses his attention to spatial continuity at several points in the DVD commentary for the extended editions of *The Lord of the Rings*

films. In the *Two Towers* commentary track (chap. 15, 51:37–52:15), he tells of flopping shots to make the eyelines match properly.

138. See David Heuring, "Impeccable Images," *American Cinematographer* 81, no. 6 (June 2000): 92, 94.

139. Salt, *Film Style and Technology*, 288.

140. Anonymous, "Photographing 1980's Best Picture: *Ordinary People*," *American Cinematographer* 62, no. 6 (June 1981): 581.

141. John Seale, "The Newsroom Scene from *The Paper*," in "Let There Be Light," supplement to *International Photographer* 65, no. 10 (October 1994): 14.

142. Bruce Block, *The Visual Story: Seeing the Structure of Film, TV, and New Media* (Boston: Focal Press, 2001), xi. See also 173–229. I'm grateful to Patrick Keating for suggesting that I consider Block's influence on current filmmaking practice.

143. Stephen Pizzello, "Downward Spiral," *American Cinematographer* 81, no. 10 (October 2000): 52, 54.

144. Jay Holben, "Sole Survivor," *American Cinematographer* 82, no. 1 (January 2001): 40.

145. John Pavlus, "High Life," *American Cinematographer* 86, no. 1 (January 2005): 48–53.

146. Ang Lee, director commentary on *The Hulk* DVD, chap. 17, 74:16–75:00.

147. Vincent LoBrutto, *Stanley Kubrick: A Biography* (New York: Donald I. Fine, 1997), 409–10, 422–25.

148. Quoted in American Film Institute, "Dialogue on Film: Martin Scorsese," in Brunette, ed., *Martin Scorsese Interviews*, 47.

149. James Foley, DVD commentary for *Confidence*, chap. 4, 12:51–13:23.

150. Stephen Pizzello, "Con Artistry," *American Cinematographer* 84, no. 5 (May 2003): 94.

151. This system of shooting and cutting is discussed in several articles in *American Cinematographer* 85, no. 2 (February 2004). See especially Douglas Bankston, "On the Clock," 45–46; Christopher Probst, "Lighting the World," 75–76.

152. I discuss Ozu's spatial system in my *Ozu and the Poetics of Cinema* (Princeton: Princeton University Press, 1988), chaps. 5 and 6.

153. Matthew Libatique, quoted in Pizzello, "Downward Spiral," 51. He is discussing "flipping the line" in *Requiem for a Dream*.

154. Noël Carroll discusses how a constantly changing display maintains viewer attention in "The Power of Movies," *Theorizing the Moving Image* (Cambridge: Cambridge University Press, 1996), 80–86, and "Film, Attention, and Communication: A Naturalistic Account," *Engaging the Moving Image* (New Haven: Yale University Press, 2003), 25–40.

155. I discuss some differences between Hollywood and Hong Kong action sequences in "Aesthetics in Action: Kung Fu, Gunplay, and Cinematic Expressivity," in *At Full Speed: Hong Kong Cinema in a Borderless World*, ed. Esther C. M. Yau (Minneapolis: University of Minnesota Press, 2001), 73–93. See also my *Planet Hong Kong*, 19–25, 199–247.

156. Though Brian Helgeland manages quite well in *Payback* (1999). The crisp cutting and staccato choreography of the Chinese gang's attack on Porter suggest that Helgeland has studied classic Hong Kong movies.

157. Quoted in Michael Friedland, *Michael Caine* (London: Orion, 1999), 216.

158. Quoted in Richard Rubinstein, "The Making of *Sisters:* An Interview with Brian De Palma," in *Brian De Palma Interviews*, ed. Knapp, 9.

159. Quoted in Gavin Smith and Richard T. Jameson, "The Movie You Saw Is the Movie We're Going to Make," in *Robert Altman Interviews*, ed. David Sterritt (Jackson: University Press of Mississippi, 2000), 163.

160. Bettman, *First Time Director*, 55, 92–109.

161. Benjamin Svetkey reports that thirty scenes in *Unbreakable* consist of single shots. "That's an astounding thing to have in a film," remarks Bruce Willis ("Fractured Fairy Tale," *Entertainment Weekly* [1 December 2000]: 38). In the straight-to-video sector, *Running Time* (1997) was promoted by virtue of its telling its heist story in a single shot. (Actually, it hides its numerous cuts in the manner of *Rope*, 1948.)

162. See Steven D. Katz, *Film Directing: Shot by Shot: Visualizing from Concept to Screen* (Los Angeles: Michael Wiese, 1991), 173–93. Somewhat more dynamic are the exercises in his later book, *Film Directing: Cinematic Motion: A Workshop for Staging Scenes* (Los Angeles: Michael Wiese, 1992). Still, even these lessons tend to build scenes around passages of stand-and-deliver, connected by minimal shifts in the actors' positions around the set.

163. For further discussion of current Hollywood staging practices, see my *Figures Traced in Light*, chap. 1.

164. See Paul Malcolm, "Driving Light: Michael Katz, Gaffer," *LA Weekly* (11–17 May 2001): 43.

165. I discuss an example from *Jaws* in *On the History of Film Style*, 253–55.

166. For a subtle analysis of similar staging practices in another film of the period, see Joe McElhaney, "Medium Shot Gestures: Vincente Minnelli and *Some Came Running*," *16x9* (June 2004): 11, at www.16-9.dk/2003-06/side11_minnelli.htm.

167. Charles Barr, "CinemaScope: Before and After," *Film Quarterly* 16, no. 4 (Summer 1963): 18–19.

168. Allen explains that he seldom cuts within a scene because a sustained master is faster and cheaper to shoot, actors prefer it, and he doesn't have to worry about matching shots. See Douglas McGrath, "If You Knew Woody Like I Knew Woody," *New York Magazine* (October 17, 1994): 44.

169. I discuss the work of Hou, Yang, and other contemporaries in my *Figures Traced in Light*, chaps. 5 and 6.

170. See Janet Staiger, "The Eyes Are Really the Focus: Photoplay Acting and Film Form and Style," *Wide Angle* 6, no. 4 (1985): 14–23.

171. Quoted in Jesse L. Lasky Jr., *Whatever Happened to Hollywood?* (New York: Funk and Wagnalls, 1975), 171.

172. See Bordwell, *Planet Hong Kong*, 200–45.

173. Quotations from Heinrich Wölfflin, *Renaissance and Baroque*, trans.

Kathrin Simon (Ithaca: Cornell University Press, 1965), 73; from Werner Weisbach, in "Mannerism," *Encyclopedia of World Art*, vol. 9, ed. Luisa Becherucci (New York: McGraw-Hill, 1964), 447; from Arnold Hauser, *The Social History of Art*, vol. 2: *Renaissance, Mannerism, Baroque* (New York: Vintage, 1957), 100; from John Shearman, *Mannerism* (Harmondsworth: Penguin, 1967), 186; and from Wölfflin, *Renaissance and Baroque*, 38.

174. Kress, quoted in Oldham, *First Cut*, 86.

Index

Page numbers in *italic* refer to illustrations.

Text: 10/13 Aldus
Display: Aldus
Compositor: Integrated Composition Systems
Indexer: Barbara Roos
Printer and binder: Thomson-Shore, Inc.